CYCLING TO
XIAN
and other excursions

Text, photos & maps
Copyright © 1988 Michael Buckley
All rights reserved

All photos were taken by the author
except those on Leaf 13 (shots by
Scott Harrison and Rajan Gill)
Book designed by the author
Maps drawn by Jacki Ritchie

Published by CRAZYHORSE PRESS
PO Box 33962, Station D
Vancouver, BC V6J 4L7, Canada

Distributed in North America by
ITMB LTD, 736A Granville Street
Vancouver, BC V6Z 1G3, Canada
For phone-orders, call 604-6873320

Copies of this book may be obtained
through local bookstores, or ordered
direct from the distributor above

Typeset by The Typeworks, Vancouver
Printed and bound in Canada

ISBN 0-9693370-0 0

CYCLING TO XIAN –

being part of a journey overland from Shanghai through the Middle Kingdom to Kathmandu via Xian, Chengdu & Lhasa –

& other excursions . . .

excursion *ikskûr'shon,* *n* 1 a short journey or ramble for pleasure 2 a round trip on a train, ship, etc, at a reduced rate 3 deviation or digression [L *ex-*, out, *currere, cursum,* to run]

MICHAEL BUCKLEY

CONTENTS

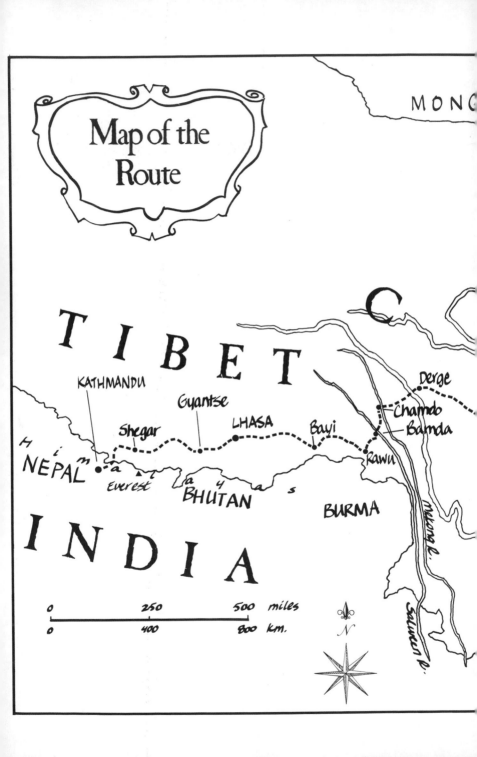

Map of the Route

MONG

TIBET

KATHMANDU

Gyantse

Derge

Shegar

LHASA

Bayi

Chamdo
Bamda

NEPAL

Rawu

Everest

BHUTAN

BURMA

INDIA

| 0 | 250 | 500 miles |
| 0 | 400 | 800 km. |

N

Mekong

Salween

OLIA
PEKING
Yellow R.
North China Plain
Yellow Sea
Huaibei
Kaifeng
Grand Canal
Luoyang
XIAN
Zhengzhou
Suzhou
Huashan
Bengbu
Nanjing
SHANGHAI
H
Yangtse R.
CHENGDU
I
N
A
TAIWAN
CANTON
HONG KONG
VIETNAM
South China Sea

PREFACE

Most of the travelogue that follows is taken from on-the-spot notes, written in the present tense; other material, taken from memory or research, is narrated in the past tense. Conversations with non-English speakers (in the presence of a bi-lingual translator) have been miraculously converted into fluent English for the benefit of the reader. Such passages appear in *italics*. On the other hand, second language speakers attempting English have had their efforts preserved so that their suffering may be shared. Likewise, the doomed attempts of the author to talk other languages have been included in the original.

Place-names in China have been rendered in the pinyin system of romanisation. Although this system has been adopted by modern cartographers, the spelling continues to fox English speakers. 'X', for instance, is pronounced 'Sh', so 'Xian' is pronounced 'Shee-Ahn', and 'Wuxi' is 'Wu-Shee'; 'Zh' sounds like 'J', so 'Suzhou' is pronounced 'Su-Joe', and 'Zhengzhou' is 'Jen-Joe'; 'Qi' is pronounced 'Chi', so 'Qingdao' becomes 'Ching-Dow'. For the Tibetan region, a simple phonetic rendering of place-names has been adopted.

The British system of miles, feet, inches, pounds and other abnormalities has been employed throughout. However, the Chinese, in addition to their own garbled traditional measures, follow the metric system: reference has been made to 'k-stones', which pop up along the highways and byways in China. These are 'kilometre stones'; the Chinese term for kilometre is 'gongli'.

In Japan, they drive on the left; in Russia it's on the right; in China they drive straight down the middle (give way to largest oncoming object). In Tibet they didn't drive at all – not until the 1950s anyway. They still don't – it's mostly the Chinese who do the driving. This is neither here nor there, but something that should be mentioned anyway . . .

走馬觀花

FLOWERS from HORSEBACK

上海

SHANGHAI MAIN STATION, 5.30 a.m., December '81, forty degrees Fahrenheit: the shambles of arrival. The train disgorges its load: passengers tumbling out of the carriages, running; puffs of smoke hissing out of nearby engines. Everything looks grey and dull – a combination of fog, smoke and pollution. I have arrived. The problem is how to get to the hotel. What hotel? I dig out a small notebook and flip the pages: *Jinjiang Hotel, dorm 6 yuan, long way from station, bus 41.* Other than that, the only thing I know is that Nixon stayed there when normalising US-Chinese relations. Obviously not in the dormitory.

I grab my backpack and move down through the ticket-barriers. A milling crowd propels me through an exit; an attendant takes my ticket and rips it in half. Outside, bewildered passengers are rapidly matched up with their next form of transport – be it a taxi, bus, or a motorised three-wheeler. It is freezing cold: passengers are wearing padded blue or green coats, and ear-flap headgear that makes them look like delegates to a Snoopy Convention. A confident cab-driver claims me: I put up no resistance. At this hour of the morning, I have absolutely no desire to take on the bus-system.

This taxi is different – is it Russian or something? No, it's a Shanghai Saloon – made in Shanghai. Looks like a vintage Mercedes. The radio is Soviet-made. I check the odometer: 310,000. I check that again: 310,000 *what*? Kilometres? *'Gongli?'* I ask the driver, pointing at the figures. *'Gongli',* he confirms. With that many kilometres, the taxi must've been on the road since... the 1950s.

There is a whirr of activity outside the cab, made all the more mysterious by the pale light of the rising sun filtering through the smog. The driver curses and hits the horn at one-minute intervals as walls of pedestrians spill over into the streets; billboards advertising Japanese products flash by; high-rise buildings; shoppers crowding into covered markets; shoppers emerging victorious with a fish or a cabbage; groups of older Chinese practising *taichi* in a park. And then the driver swings in a different direction – a new magic revealed – a different architectural presence – buildings of one or two storeys; the boulevards wider; the parks

11

more spacious; and we pass some cafés where the business of breakfast has steamed up the windows.

The driver changes tack again – plunges into small alleys thronged with cyclists on their way to work. There's a prim woman with immaculate white gloves, and a white teamug clipped to her rear rack; a man with a child mounted up the front of his bike, between his legs; a tricycle with massive spokes hauling a huge load of furniture; a legless rider using a rearrangement of sprockets to manipulate his three-wheel cycle with his hands.

The gates of the Jinjiang Hotel. A uniformed attendant opens the taxi-door. I pay the driver.

In the compound is a grand array of buildings centred on a lawn – oddly reminiscent of the Gothic design of a university quadrangle. The larger buildings, I quickly surmise, are bound to be expensive. Must find reception . . .

'The dormitories are aw-ful,' says the clerk at the reception desk. He has a large mole on his cheek with several long strands of hair coming out of it.

'Yes, I know that, but I still want a bed,' I tell him.

'You're not understand. Aw-ful. AW-FUL.' He waves his hand about the place.

'How awful?'

'Very aw-ful.'

My God, the dormitories must be absolutely dreadful. Rats, cockroaches, bed-lice – the works.

'Look, I know they're awful, but please, let me see first.' I've heard from other travellers that the hotels will try and talk western visitors into the most expensive rooms, thinking that anything else is below par.

The clerk shoots me an angry look, and throws up his hands.

'AW-FUL!' he shouts, 'AW-FUL!' He turns around after this theatrical outburst, sits down with his back to me, and starts reading a newspaper.

I sink down on a bench and ponder my fate. It is a long way to the next hotel, and in any case, the Jinjiang has, as far as I know, the only dormitory in Shanghai for foreigners. I haven't dared ask the prices of the regular Jinjiang rooms – most likely astronomical. A foreign businessmen in a suit walks through, swinging a briefcase. Then a long-haired westerner strides past. I intercept him.

'Um – excuse me – are you staying in the dormitory?'

'Sure am.'

'Is it full?'

'No – the men's dorm has three empty beds I think.'

'And, er, how *are* the beds?'

'What do you mean?'

'Are they in good shape?'

'Well, they've got legs and mattresses, and woollen blankets, and sheets – and pillows.'

'I can't seem to get the clerk to give me a bed.'

'Ah! You've been talking to Mr Awful?'

'Mr Awful?'

'Yes, that one over there. The one with the hairy mole. We call him Mr Awful because he's always saying the dorm's all full – can't pronounce it properly.'

'Oh, I see!'

'You'll have to wait till the other clerk gets back. You'll never get anything out of Mr Awful. Anyway, why don't you come and look at the dorm?'

George, who is from New York, takes me over to the men's dorm. I throw my pack on one of the vacant beds to claim it.

Reception either has no idea how many free beds there are in the dorm, or they don't care. Each day I go back and ask for a bed in the dorm, and each time, Mr Awful, who doesn't recognise me from one visit to the next, insists it is fully booked. I don't particularly care either – in the end I just give up. I have, after all, attempted to pay legitimately for the bed. If they aren't interested, then why bother them?

'Jinjiang Hotel, dorm 6 yuan, long way from station, bus 41.' That piece of the puzzle falls into place. I cast my mind back to the source of that information – to a hotel kitchen in Kyoto, a month ago . . . I'd flown in from the Canadian west coast, and Valder, the Dane, was coming east from Hong Kong – we collide at dinner-time. I sit entranced as he recounts details of his trip on the Trans-Mongolian Express to Peking, and his voyages through China to Hong Kong. China is wide open, he says, to the ordinary traveller – for the first time since the 1930s. Travellers can get visas under the table in Hong Kong.

I milk Valder for every scrap of information I can: 'The tomb of the 6000 warriors in Xian . . . don't miss that . . . the Jinjiang Hotel in Shanghai . . . in Peking, the Guanghua Hotel, bus number 9 from the station . . . the blackmarket is best in Guilin . . .' I take notes at random; I have some jigsaw pieces. The next day I'm off on the bullet-train to Tokyo – en route to Hong Kong.

Nine days later I'm on an express-train bound for Peking – soft-class compartment; poached eggs on toast being served by the conductor. Opposite me sits Marie, a pretty Parisian of Vietnamese extraction – we met while getting Chinese visas at a Hong Kong travel-agent. Both of us wearing blue silk jackets purchased in Hong Kong. The silk wadding on the interior, it is hoped, will keep out the cold of the Peking winter that we are about to stray into.

I'm in my element with the impromptu change of travel plans – this promises to be a real adventure. The whole scenario, shifting as it does with the backdrop of rice-paddies and factories, could not be further removed from reality. Waking up in this compartment – on the move through China – I have to wonder if I'm not still locked in last night's dream. And what am I escaping? Oh, the usual – work, phone-bills, credit card companies, the taxman, supermarkets, an impending divorce – hell, who cares? I've even managed to escape the English language – conversation with Marie proceeds only in French.

The conductor returns with our breakfast bills. He wants us to pay with our fancy Chinese tourist money, Foreign Exchange Certificates. This diplomatic lucre makes me very nervous – I've been in China two days and already I'm dealing on the blackmarket – between Foreign Exchange Certificates and People's Money. What are the penalties for this offence if caught? Is it legal for me to be in possession of People's Money? Well, whatever the drawbacks, the blackmarket has got us upgraded from an uncomfortable hard-class seat to a deluxe soft-class sleeper, and also worked wonders with the dining-car. I lap up my first impressions of China – the greed of the train-conductor; a baby-faced PLA soldier; hordes of bicyclists waiting at a train-crossing; a railway worker in her blue Wellington boots, lolling around a platform, looking decidedly punkish.

In Peking we get a cheap room at the Guanghua Hotel. There we find a human phrasebook in the person of Robert, a young Briton who is adept at Mandarin. He's been travelling around Taiwan and the People's Republic for two months, refining his language skills. Robert is the decoder – he can put things in perspective.

Blackmarket mysteries are unravelled. The heavy trading revolves around a downtown institution called the Friendship Store – where pampered foreigners can buy imported goods at duty-free prices, or Chinese-made goods that are in short supply. Purchases can only be made with Foreign Exchange Certificates. Since they are barred from entering the Friendship Store, local Chinese can only get access via contacts, and by somehow trading, at a premium, their dirty, rumpled People's Money (RMB) for crisp new FECs. I carry both currencies – in my left pocket, wads of RMB for smaller tabs such as bus-tickets and restaurants; in the right pocket, FECs – which must be used to pay for taxis and for hotel-bills. Sometimes, just for the shock-effect, I mix the currencies together when paying.

None of the Chinese can figure out serene-faced Marie. It's the hairstyle, the touch of Parisian fashion, the hint of make-up, and the fact that she doesn't speak Chinese. She eludes their pigeon-holing system. Is she from Vietnam, France, Hong Kong, South-West China – where is she from? They are unsure how to deal with her, as there is a different pricing system based on the kind of face they see – Chinese, Hong Kong Chinese, Overseas Chinese, or big-nosed foreigner. The big-nose, of course, is the highest-paying category – the bigger the nose, the higher the premium. Big-noses are expected to pay up to double the local Chinese price – and sometimes more than double. Marie, with her flat nose, learns how to turn the category game to her advantage. She is used to the game; in France she is still a 'foreigner', even though she grew up there. I had to admire her spirit.

Peking is a revelation. I am mesmerised by life down the tiny backalleys, by the sea of bicycles, by the long buses rammed full of people, by the traffic policemen swivelling like robots on podiums in the centre of sub-zero Peking. There is much to explore. There are little bakeries that serve steamed dumplings and bowls of hot water – half the clients just want to escape the bitter cold outside. There are scruffy department stores where knots of customers battle to get some item in short supply. At dawn, despite the freezing temperatures, there is a mass taichi turnout in the parks.

One evening, Robert takes us down the subway in order to get to a restaurant. The subway is part of an elaborate air-raid shelter system, constructed during the 1960s when China's relations with Russia soured. It is fast, efficient, clean and cheap. No crime, no graffiti. About 200 trains a day. It's only been open to foreigners for a few years – previously off-limits. The State has strange secrets: telephone numbers are classified (since the only Chinese with private phones are liable to be high up); Chinese newspapers are top secret. And the

15

subway does not appear on any tourist map. How is it then that if Peking is open, parts of it, like the subway, could previously be off-limits to foreigners? That's easy, says Robert – a xerox machine can be 'closed' if the State wants it closed. A mountain can be closed, even though the area around it is open. A whole area can be closed, but the railway-station in the middle of it can be open.

Nobody seems to know which places are open to foreigners. There is a list of 100 such places, but the information is not available. The authorities don't really have to worry about restricting the movements of foreigners – fear, confusion, inability to speak Chinese, and lack of information forestall attempts on the great unknown. Getting a train-ticket to a sanctioned tourist-spot is, in itself, a logistical nightmare. Even the sanctioned spots require a travel-permit; I go down to the Peking Public Security Bureau to get this document, as I'm planning to make a few stops on the way back to Hong Kong.

November 30th. It comes to a parting of the ways. Tomorrow Robert leaves for Europe on the Trans-Mongolian. He looks like a Russian already – full beard, fur-lined hat. He has been stocking up like a squirrel for the long journey ahead – knowing that the food will be bad on the train. We have struck up a firm friendship – I'm convinced we'll meet again one day. Marie is off to Paris in a few days to start a training-course as an airline hostess – so she will be flying all over the world next year, possibly even my way. And I have booked a ticket on the express-train to Shanghai – due to leave the day after next. We celebrate our new-found friendships with a big bottle of Chinese champagne purchased – where else? – from the Peking Friendship Store.

In Shanghai I have lost this camaraderie. There are other foreigners at the Jinjiang Hotel, but they don't share the same sense of adventure. It is cold in the mornings: those in the dorm sleep in late – sometimes till noon. I am out and about by 7 a.m., poking around the streets, left to my own devices. But I feel quite at home in the Jinjiang. The dorm is comfortable enough – it is carpeted, has lots of windows, is well heated. The bathroom is the kind you avoid at all costs – but there are much classier toilets in the main north building.

The Jinjiang Hotel is sited in what was formerly the French Concession of Shanghai – otherwise known as 'Frenchtown'. In the morning, from an 11th floor dining-room of the Jinjiang north building, there is an expansive view over this part of Shanghai. It is an incongruous breakfast setting for the handful of backpackers from the dormitories, this palatial dining-room – chandeliers, art deco fittings and lamps, wood panelling, stupendous views. Here they serve a fine western breakfast – eggs, toast and jam, delivered on vintage crockery and silverware. The backpacker's boast is that the meal can be had for no more than two yuan – the student price – whereas the Rolls Royce executive at the next table pays five times that. It is still too early for the restaurant staff to figure out where the backpackers fit in. They make no distinction between a foreigner in a suit and one in faded jeans – both, as far as they are concerned, are foreign, and thus millionaire VIPs. The staff are therefore astonished when a backpacker demands a cheap student rate for the food.

The Jinjiang is a mini-state type of hotel. The north block is 14 storeys high – once Cathay Mansions, a posh apartment-hotel. It was built in 1929 by Sir Victor Sassoon, who owned the choicest properties in Shanghai. It now contains deluxe suites used by visiting heads of state. To the south is a 5-storey addition to the Jinjiang complex, constructed in 1965. In the middle of the grounds is an 18-storey block, used by group-tours and formerly known as Grosvenor House, built in 1934. Forming the west wall are six three-storey blocks, also built around 1934 – it is in this section that the dorms are located, overlooking the street. Other parts of the west wing are used by the Chinese staff, and by some foreigners resident for short periods in Shanghai. A pamphlet on the hotel informs me that there are altogether 700 rooms in this labyrinth, with 1400 beds.

The visitor need never leave the confines of this fortress – everything is on the premises. There are half a dozen restaurants, a bar, post-office, telex office, shops, foodstore, bookstore and barbershop.

Opposite the west gates of the Jinjiang Hotel there is an even more extraordinary period-piece – the Jinjiang Club. It is a two-storey building with a sweeping driveway. I go to visit one evening: a foreign face is enough to gain entry. Inside is a wonderful museum of 1920s nightlife. Near the entrance there is a grand ballroom with a parquetry floor, a Steinway piano, and opulent lights, chandeliers and fittings; a billiard-room with overhanging lamps; a restaurant serving French cuisine; and an Olympic-sized heated pool – the original one – with a bar.

The swimming-pool is deserted – probably because a swimming licence must be produced to use it, and visiting foreigners don't have such a ridiculous thing. But, for the rest of it, it is very easy to visualise what the original function of the place was: to imagine the Saturday afternoon tea-dances in the ballroom, or the roof-garden dancing. The place once functioned as the Cercle Sportif Français, an exclusive club for sporting and social events in the 1920s and 30s. In 1949 it was closed down – rumoured to be Mao's private Shanghai residence – but in 1979 it reopened as a place for entertaining foreign businessmen. A six-lane bowling alley, a video-game room and a tennis-court were added by the Chinese, along with a financial information centre. Then a Dixieland band was dredged up – where from? – to provide music for the ballroom; and serenading violinists were appointed to the French restaurant. So much for the revolution: this confirms my impressions that the foreigners are once again returning to their old haunts, to the exclusion of the ordinary Chinese.

I come back to the Jinjiang Hotel area like a homing pigeon from my forays into Shanghai. This area is my haven – it has the uncanny feeling of a real neighbourhood. First there is the foreign enclave of the Jinjiang itself; and then there are other places nearby that I get to know. Just down the street is a café – open late – serving addictive French pastries; near this is an excellent dumpling place; around the corner a sweetshop and a dairy; out the gates of the Jinjiang and straight ahead is a quiet residential area.

Honk! Screech! Jingle! Ding-aling! Beep Beep! Hoot! Squawk! Bang! The policeman mounted in a crow's-nest high in the middle of the intersection tries to orchestrate the traffic. He has a microphone, directed at wayward pedestrians, and he works the lights. Trouble is, this is much more than an intersection – it is a kind of roundabout with a variety of exits, and the police-post is stuck in the middle. The task is futile – bicyclists pay little heed to the red lights operated from the pillbox (one explanation offered is that during the Cultural Revolution cyclists were told to stop on green lights and proceed on red – the revolutionary colour red was synonymous with going *forward!*). The traffic lights sway on wires, suspended above the streets. There they join a thick spider-web of trolley-lines, power-lines, and laundry on bamboo poles.

On terra firma, there are old men with red 'Serve the People' armbands – they are helping out with the traffic in their retirement. They have more success with traffic offenders – I watch one nimbly hurdle a railing to catch a jaywalker. He gives the jaywalker a firm talking-to; the policemen have the power to fine cyclists, or even confiscate their bikes – but rarely do. If the intersection sees 20,000 cyclists in an hour during peak-period, the traffic police have their hands full just directing the traffic – there is no time to deal with offenders.

In the thick of the fray is the most insane collection of things on two, three and four wheels imaginable: furniture removalists, with a whole couch on the rear of a tricycle carrier; a farmer with a gaggle of geese tied upside-down over the back wheel of his bike; a night-soil collector with two huge wooden caskets balanced on the sides of his bike; a tricycle carrier stacked with 400 pounds of rice; a rider coated in grey dust, pedalling a load of charcoal briquettes . . .

Chinese law makes it an offence for a motorised vehicle not to warn a cyclist of an impending approach. The result is a battery of weapons to announce the right of way. Buses have microphones, megaphones, bells, buzzers and hooters; taxi-drivers might as well have a permanent siren installed; truck-drivers have a selection of horns – a tweeter for mild annoyances, a klaxon for greater annoyances, and an earsplitting airhorn for when the driver gets *really* annoyed. The traffic policemen have megaphones, microphones, telephones and flashing lights. Tricycle carriers and bicyclists work in phalanxes – safety in numbers – creating a gamelan orchestra of tinkling bells. Pedestrians have no early warning systems, and just rely on their fast legs.

This is what I am doing – relying on my fast legs. I have given up on the buses. Even though it is four miles from Shanghai's waterfront – the Bund – back to the Jinjiang, I prefer to walk the distance. It takes over an hour, but I can have my peace of mind. The queues for the buses are long: when the bus arrives, the boarding-parties rush forward – shoving and pushing. Most of the trolley-buses are of the 'concertina' design: they are composed of two bus-bodies, joined together with a rubber section, much like long train-cars. This way, dead buses can be recycled, and more passengers can be crammed into one run with one driver. The bus takes off from the stop with its pile of crushed humanity: nobody can move; nobody can get out; nobody can see where they're going; there is a suffocating jumble of arms, legs and torsos.

At the next stop, another frantic wave of commuters ambushes the bus – and there is yet another attempt on the Guinness Book of Records. The bus lurches forward again; the driver screams through his microphone at some cyclists in his way. The cyclists scream back obscenities – cyclists hate bus-drivers with a fierce passion – a feeling that is mutual. Finally, half the population of Shanghai unloads from the bus – it has reached its terminus, and the dishevelled passengers rearrange their clothing and check to see if pickpockets have been at their trade.

There has to be an easier way to get around, I reason. Taxis are an alternative – but they're expensive, hard to get hold of, and inconvenient for random stops. They can only be obtained from the larger hotels, or places like the railway station. There is a smaller, cheaper three-wheel taxi: this motorised chariot is great for recharging the batteries if feeling depressed – the drivers are madmen who scare the living daylights out of me when they blithely cut through the traffic with inches to spare on an approaching bus. But again, they are hard to get hold of – they operate out of small side-alley depots.

The answer is to get my hands on my own transport – which means a bicycle. Shanghai is perfectly flat – a bicycle would be ideal. But where can I get one? Is it possible to rent one? Could I borrow one from the staff at the Jinjiang Hotel? With both of these ideas, I run into a dead-end. No rentals, and no-one is willing to lend a bike – not even for money. A bicycle is the most treasured possession of a local Chinese – it would be the same, in the west, as lending a car to a stranger. Besides, if a local were to lend a bicycle, he or she would have to face the terror of being a bus-commuter again.

*   *   *

HE IS CYCLING ALONG THE BUND, I am puzzling over a Shanghai busmap – we meet on a street-corner. His name is Wang – he speaks very good English, not the kind that comes from parroting phrasebooks. He is quite tall for a Chinese – he stands level with me, at just under six feet. He is dressed well enough that he could be mistaken for a cadre. His transport, however, gives him away –

his bike is old, rusted, and falling apart.

Within a short time, we have struck up a rather bizarre deal. I express my loathing for the packed buses, he expresses his loathing for his dismal heap of a bike – it all clicks. I will buy a bike at the Friendship Store, use it for my stay in Shanghai, and sell it to him. That way he can jump the ration-queues for new bikes, since I will be selling him what constitutes a 'used bicycle'.

The same afternoon we are down at Shanghai Friendship Store, and he is selecting 'my' bike. It's a handsome black tank – a prestigious Phoenix brand, with upright handlebars, chain-case, mudguards, rod-type brakes, fat tyres, and heavy-duty spokes. He would have to wait years to get his hands on a Phoenix – especially one with three gears, which is what he has chosen. I take the bike for a spin around the grounds of the Friendship Store – once the British Embassy. Then I pay for it, and we coast off into the streets, with Wang on his old bike.

Wang waves at me to slow down, but I'm off like a rocket, getting my revenge on the buses – overtaking everything in sight, revelling in this newly-acquired freedom. I have joined the orchestra – the crescendo of bells – what a blast! There is a the thick mesh of bicycles – it is difficult to manoeuvre. Cyclists alongside turn and stare, which does not make my progress easy, as some come in dangerously close. This gets my adrenaline flowing: dodging the heavy-laden tricycles and streams of bikes, we ride all the way out to Frenchtown. I give the bell one final flick before going into a café with Wang, and the top-part shoots clear off the handlebar into the gutter. Wang jumps down to retrieve it, with a startled look – for me it's just a bike, for him it's a status symbol. Instead of going to the café we go to a bikeshop, where all the nuts and bolts on this factory-fresh job are tightened.

For a foreigner to ride a bicycle in China is considered undignified: foreigners are rich and should travel by taxi. That's the theory. In practice, bicycles are considerably more dignified than riding the bus, and allow greater freedom than taking a taxi. The bike suits my own brand of random tourism – but much more than a deal now, it has sparked a tour-guide on wheels. Wang can give me the rat's-eye view of Shanghai – the gutters and the drainpipes. There's nothing I like better than poking around the streets, and in Shanghai that's where the action is anyway. Fortunately, it is a city devoid of proper tourist sights – there is the odd museum, but try as they might, the authorities cannot beat the streets as the main attraction. Wang manages to get some time off, takes me round the restaurants, the back-alleys, the old Chinese sector. For the reduced amount he can get a meal, I figure he's not an extra expense when I foot the bill. He can get a Chinese-priced meal – if I paid, I would be paying at a foreign mark-up. He insists, at least, on paying all the parking bills – two fen at a time – and dives in with grain-ration coupons for cakes in cafés.

Thunk! Pow! Boom! Kerrash! 'This is most interesting!' shouts Wang. 'Watch out! Hey!' He has just smashed up again – in a racing-circuit video-game. Never having been at the driver's wheel, he is gaining the wrong impression of driving – yelps of delight and frustration – and I glance around quickly to see if anyone has noticed the interloper in their midst. I have smuggled Wang into the Jinjiang Club – he is posing as my translator. And this is the first time he's encountered a video-game. He is dizzy from the steering-wheel; the simulation-experience is total. I try and steer him away from Space Invaders, lest he attract more attention.

At table-tennis, in another section of the Jinjiang Club, he is on more familiar ground. He cleans me out. Our roles are reversed now – I am his guide to the hallowed sections of the city where he is normally forbidden. Only foreigners and cadres can get into the Jinjiang. For Wang, what is forbidden is exciting – western video, jazz, pool, video-games, opulent decor – fuel for his insatiable curiosity. The man is simply bored out of his mind. Him and a billion other Chinese: a ready-made market for blockbuster Hollywood movies.

We'd long cancelled the English lesson components – nobody, however, had taught Wang any western table manners, and it was with considerable embarrassment that I rushed him out of the elegant Jinjiang Hotel 11th floor dining-room after attempting breakfast one day. To my horror he had leaned over and stuck his face right into the fried egg – and with one almighty slurp, polished it off. Still recovering from this, I gazed in wonder as he proceeded, egg all over his grinning face, to spoon jam on the toast, and then coat it with butter – using a left-handed knife. And *then* he looked around for a place to spit – common behaviour in

Chinese restaurants, but totally inappropriate in the Jinjiang.

I arranged another meeting with Wang in two days' time. Meanwhile, I roved around Shanghai on my own in the brisk winter air. Shanghai was becoming more familiar to me. I could discern three distinct towns – architecturally and culturally they were divided very much along the lines of the former foreign concessions. There was the downtown area – the commercial district around the Bund and Nanjing Road (the former International Settlement); there was the snappier Frenchtown area (the former French Concession); and there was the ghetto-like 'Chinatown' area.

In 1842, at the end of the First Opium War, a defeated Chinese empire agreed to open five treaty ports to foreigners – Shanghai, Canton, Ningbo, Amoy and Fuzhou. Treaty ports had their own administration, clubs, parks, hospitals, schools, trading houses, and courts – and the Europeans kept the Chinese out of those places. The British and the French steadily expanded their Shanghai territories. Shanghai was eventually divided into three jurisdictions – the British-dominated International Settlement; the French Concession; and the City Government of Greater Shanghai, which was administered by the Chinese, and encompassed (after 1927) all sections of the city outside the foreign enclaves.

'Chinatown' was my misnomer for the old Chinese sector – once walled in – that existed before the arrival of foreigners in Shanghai, when the place was a simple fishing village. But it was not the fact that it was the old Chinese sector that suggested 'Chinatown' to me. It was the smell of the place. It was the combined smell of incense, dried fish and rotting cabbage that linked it to a hundred other Chinatowns across the globe. One other scent – not at all pleasant – hung in the air. The smell of excrement. Chinatown had no plumbing, and no sewage – wooden buckets were used by the locals. The place was a maze of narrow cobblestone alleys and ramshackle wooden housing.

In Chinatown I learned the first lesson of bicycle ownership: mark your vehicle. It was useless to cycle over cobblestone; I had left the bike in one of the numerous bike parking-lots at the edge of Chinatown. Several hours later, after losing my bearings in the labyrinth of alleyways, I realised I couldn't identify the parking-lot again. I frantically searched for the attendant who'd given me the parking token. No sign of him. Eventually, by a painstaking method of retracing landmarks, I arrived at a parking-lot that looked vaguely familiar. There were a million other bikes parked there – all looking the same as the one I'd purchased. The attendant was different, which was what had thrown me off. It took another hour to find the bike that I had the key for.

I ventured further and further afield on the bike – until I was almost out of Shanghai. Marked on the map were ferry-crossings over the Huangpu River – there were no bridges. South of the Bund, I found a ferry-landing – I followed another bike-rider straight onto a ferry, paid a few fen for the trip, and tried to pay scant attention to the other passengers – who stood there looking gape-mouthed at me.

By now I was well and truly lost – but this didn't bother me. I had developed a new system of navigation. When the time came to find my way back, I would simply check the nearest bus coming past, and then consult my busmap. Buses always travelled down the major arteries, and the arteries went somewhere.

The east banks of the Huangpu were completely different – there was satellite housing, apartment buildings; lots of factories and pollution; and the most intensive vegetable farming I'd ever seen in a city. In one vast cabbage-field a knot of peasants were taking potshots at a target with 303 rifles. Lunchtime militia practice. By the waterfront I came across barges with giant vats full of excrement. This 'night soil' was being prepared for delivery from Shanghai to farmlands beyond.

'That is the way to Suzhou,' said Wang. We were standing outside the saffron walls of the Jade Buddha Temple in north-west Shanghai.

'How far is it?'

'Not too far – you can go there the same day on a bicycle.'

'Have you been there by bicycle?'

'No, by train. But I have friends who did.'

I was flabbergasted by this piece of information. Travelling to the city of Suzhou was something that I had only imagined possible by train. If the way was flat . . . I dug out my map. Wang had pointed to a road that followed the rail-line to Suzhou. There was something else that showed up on the map: the Municipality of Shanghai was so large that it extended half the way to Suzhou. What was there to stop me getting there by bike? And why stop there? Why not go all the way to . . . Nanjing?

Nanjing! I cruised along behind Wang contemplating this new information as he scouted out a likely place for dinner.

'Not this one', he'd say, glancing at the bike-parking, or a cluster of people out the front of the restaurant – 'Let's try another one.' At the next restaurant, a string of fireworks exploded on the sidewalk, and two figures in suits with red carnations in the lapels were at the door. The restaurant was packed – it was a wedding party. Wedding parties, it seemed, occupied all the restaurants in Shanghai. The statistics were turning over in my mind – if six million people lived in downtown Shanghai, how many births, deaths and marriages were recorded every day?

'The autumn and the spring are very popular for tying the knots – is that what you say? – *tying the knots*?' Wang was very proud of his grasp of the essential idioms of English – books one and two – and always eager to try them out on me.

Eventually, even Wang had to give up on the restaurants. We had to muscle our way into a wedding party, landing a small table at the fringe of the proceedings. Clustered round the restaurant were identical tables – with heaping plates of food in the middle, and a glass of orange soft-drink for each guest.

'This is one of the biggest expenses in the life, this getting married party,' explained Wang, 'Sometimes it can cost 3000 yuan or more. It can take many years of savings to make the day a success.' Wang explained that he had a fiancée, but he did not expect to marry just yet – he was still saving for the day. He had been engaged for four years.

The customs of bride-prices, dowries, and lavish wedding send-offs were severely criticised as being 'feudal' in the 1950s – and again during the Cultural Revolution – but they were never abolished. The palanquins that used to parade dowries through the neighbourhood were gone, but in their place, a minibus or a bicycle-entourage would be formed to show off the quilts, household appliances, cooking sets and furniture of the dowry. The majority of marriages were still arranged through go-betweens, the same as they had been before 1949 – the go-betweens being parents, friends, the work-unit, or, more recently, matrimonial agencies. Dowries and wedding-banquets were the major part of the huge expense on the part of the couple. Other costs involved clothing, and fancy wedding-photos. Although the actual wedding ceremony took only a few seconds in a registry office, the couple would be off to Nanjing Road to rent a western-style wedding-gown and suit for photographs. Then they would change back into rented matching suits for the wedding-banquet. 'The revolution,' Wang chortled, 'cannot abolish the getting married party.'

The guests were happily slurping and sucking their way through large amounts of food; Wang managed to divert some of the fabulous concoctions from the kitchen to our tiny table, and we feasted. There were sizzling prawns, pieces of spicy beef, plates of stir-fried vegetables, mounds of rice. By myself, I would never have been able to get food like this in such a restaurant – Wang knew what to order. And what a contrast with the Chinese food served in the tourist hotels. Here the place was packed, noisy and smoky – and the food was spicy; in the cavernous dining-rooms of the tourist hotels, the Chinese food was tasteless, and the tables were silent.

I remarked on this difference to Wang.

'It is good to make noise in the restaurant,' he shouted. 'The more the noise, the better the restaurant. That is the Chinese idea of the food – to have the big banquet with many people at one table, and talk loudly.'

It was therefore possible, I mused, to rate a restaurant by sound alone. A 75-decibel restaurant would be reasonable; a 100-decibel restaurant would be excellent; a 60-decibel restaurant would be lousy. This one was around 90 decibels – a noise level that afforded a certain measure of privacy if one wanted to say what one thought, in English anyway – as Wang did.

After dinner, Wang helped himself to one of my cigarettes, a 555, and sat back, puffing contentedly. The packet came from the Friendship Store – imported English filter-tips. I had to wonder if he didn't feel somewhat transformed by our meeting – in my company, he could have all the luxuries normally denied to him. For my part of the bargain, I could get the best food in the local restaurants, at local prices.

The bride and groom stopped by our table, flushed from the course of events, and – no doubt – from the frequent toasts to their health. I offered up a pack of cigarettes; Wang congratulated them; the groom evacuated his nose and throat into a nearby spittoon. The bride's face – coated in a thick powder – released a blissful smile. This charming couple had achieved their dreams –

everything in China is geared to a successful marriage day. It is the fixation of the entire generation in their 20s. The couple were off to Jiading, I was informed, for a five-day honeymoon. The bride had obtained special leave from her work-unit for the honeymoon: they would spend the time with the bride's mother, who lived in Jiading. Then they would return to Shanghai and set up house with *his* parents, since they might not be able to get their own apartment for another ten or so years. The groom – his tie loosened for action – nodded approvingly. Such is life – several generations under one roof – or even in one room.

'The husband is a lucky man,' Wang confided to me, 'since he is so short.'

'How's that?'

'The Chinese women are not interested in the short men.'

Wang obviously took great pride in the social advantages his own above-average height had.

'If the man is not tall but has finished the college, then there will be no problem; but if the man is short, and a little bit ugly, and did not finish the college, he will have to wait.' Women, according to Wang, were very demanding these days – they wanted a tall, strong partner with solid material wealth. If a man had his own apartment in Shanghai, he had his pick of brides.

Wang asked for the bill. A brief – and noisy – argument took place with the waiter, who was trying to make out a bill designed for me, a foreigner. Wang vehemently protested that I was his guest, and the bill was to be made out for a Chinese – much cheaper. I slipped Wang the money under the table.

Wang was proud to be able to pay – when he could – for me. Such an occasion was a visit to the Acrobatics Dome one evening. Tickets for locals cost a mere 40 fen apiece. Hoopla! The show was incredible – it was as if the sedate Chinese had sprung to life. They were juggling bottles, spinning plates, jumping through hoops, leaping through the air, clowning around. But it was what they were wearing that made them so different – here the 'packaging' of make-up, bare leg, spangled costumes and rouge was condoned by the State. Dancing and body-movement were the norm; contortionists tied themselves in exotic knots; even the music was brassy.

The acts needed no explanation, but Wang explained anyway, if only to hear himself talking English.

'There are the standard acts,' he said, 'We have names for all of them. In China there is the name for everything.'

The act we'd just seen was called 'The Pagoda of Bowls' – where a woman balanced a stack of bowls on one foot, and another stack on her head. These items had been passed up from below – by the man on whose head she was balanced. The act was at least 2000 years old, Wang informed me. This was followed by 'Balancing in Pairs' – a highly surrealistic act with a man balanced upside-down on the head of another, mimicking every movement of the partner below. This 'thing' sat down, crossed its legs (four), reached for two glasses of wine (one glass for each half), then drank the wine. I was enthralled.

'Balancing on a Stationary Bicycle' followed. It was a specially-constructed bicycle – but the pile of humans on it defied the laws of gravity. The grand finale of this segment was the formation of a column of three men on a moving bicycle – one on top of the other – to which were added five women on either side, hanging off the men, the frame, and the pedals. This gave a total of thirteen riders on the moving bike – and a fourteenth person jumped onto the front. Suddenly the women leaned out to each side of the bike, outstretching their arms. The strategic sequins on their pale green costumes – along with their tiaras – suggested something totally unexpected – for this delightful act was called 'Peacock Displaying Its Feathers'.

We were then treated to the spectacle of two female gymnasts in skimpy leotards hurling each other round on roller-skates – definitely not an act from the Han Dynasty.

'These women are very different,' I observed to Wang.

'Yes, they are very beautiful – lots of legs. Here is the best place to see the legs.'

'But how do the performers get away with it?'

'This is the People's Art,' explained Wang. 'The acrobats used to be the gypsies, performing on streets. So the State accepted them, and helped them.'

Other parts of Shanghai's 'nightlife' were off-limits to ordinary Chinese: they were strictly for the amusement of the foreigners in the tourist hotels. Wang begged me to take him to the bar at the Peace Hotel, along the Bund. We arrived at 8 p.m., when the music was just getting under way. It was dimly lit in the bar; Chinese cadres were allowed in – and I got Wang past the stooge at the door.

The bar was a faithful recreation of the glorious 1930s – from the fittings and furniture to... the band. The band members were old and wizened – soul survivors from the 1940s – but they were armed with drums, piano, trumpet and saxophone, and they were pumping out splendidly off-key renditions of 'When the Saints Go Marching In' and 'I Wonder Who's Kissing Her Now'. Wang was beside himself – intoxicated by the forbidden jazz; eyes glued to the foreign couples wheeling around the dance-floor.

'During the Cultural Revolution,' explains Wang, in the traffic, 'we had a lot of trouble even to go to the barber. There are wallpaper slogans in red over the shop windows, and your memory must be good to find the place. After you find him, the barber says – *Serve the People!* and then you reply – *Heart and Soul, Comrade!* And then he gives you the haircut.'

Such are China's great secrets – I promptly lost Wang in the sea of blue jackets and black bikes after a stop-light. I still had no idea where Wang lived, and he wasn't about to invite me home – our only method of contact was pre-arranged meetings at a café. It isn't healthy for his career to be in contact with foreigners – this is a risk he takes. Although he is close to 30 – the same age as myself – he still lives with his parents. In this he has no choice, since priority is given to married couples for apartments. Many couples actually postpone marriage because they can't find a room of their own. Late marriage is encouraged as a population growth measure – the minimum recommended age for marriage is 28 for men, and 25 for women.

I find Wang in the traffic again.

'You see that advertisement?' Wang points to a huge billboard showing Japanese TVs. 'We cannot buy it.'

'Then why do they advertise?'

'It looks good, and perhaps in the future we can buy it. But if you are a foreigner, you can buy it at the Friendship Store. We cannot buy the better Japanese one; we only can buy the Chinese one.'

'What about the ad over there?' I point at a billboard depicting Blue Sky Toothpaste, inexplicably in English.

'Oh yes, we can buy that. That is made by the State, here in a factory in Shanghai.'

'Why does the State have to advertise?'

'Because the products from Shanghai have a better reputation, so there is the competition between different work-units. And there is another reason.'

'Yes?'

'A lot of the Chinese do not generally brush the teeth. This will perhaps remind them, or start them on the road to brushing the teeth.'

The reason that the State sometimes advertises in English, Wang explains, is that English adds a touch of class to the product. The translation doesn't always take cultural factors into account: in Shanghai Friendship Store, I've seen such brands as 'Flying Baby' suits (logo of angelic baby with cherub wings) , 'White Elephant' batteries, 'Golden Cock' alarm-clocks, 'Double Bull' underwear, and 'Fang-Fang' lipstick. A decade before, posters here were of the revolutionary or heroic variety – those along Nanjing Road used to feature quotations from Chairman Mao's Thoughts – and I marvel at how easily the State has been able to turn around and justify the advertising of unobtainable Japanese products. We park the bikes and venture into a café.

Wang is, I find out, more highly educated than myself in a formal sense, and has a boundless curiosity. He relishes any contact he can make with foreigners – not just to brush up his English, but to inform himself about their lifestyles. He is growing more confident in his research into western mores and values – myself being the source. He inquires a lot about sexual customs – do people live together in the west? What does the government do about it? Is the government not concerned about what goes on behind these closed doors? The reason for this is related to his present dilemma.

'My girlfriend and I would like to conduct sexy experiment,' he tells me, 'to see if we fit, and if possible, to achieve the orgasms. Is that how you say it – *the orgasms*? But if the government finds out, I will get the criticism, so my girlfriend does not want to do the experiment yet – but we hear there are many others who do.'

This is actually a build-up to his next topic – will I assist in purchasing a pair of leather high-heel shoes from the Friendship

Store? It seems that these, like a string of other items – lightbulbs, bicycle tyres – are rationed, or in short supply, or both. His fiancée wants them.

We leave the café, rip down to the Friendship Store, and I smuggle Wang in. We have now developed a technique for doing this – I engage him in loud, concentrated conversation as we approach the forbidden door or gate, and we ignore any official who would think of stopping us. Wang dresses well – so well he could pass for a cadre. 'These ones,' he whispers. Feeling very foolish, I pick up a pair of high-heel shoes with furry backs on them, and look the saleslady in the eye. As we exit the store, walking back down the Bund to the cycle-parking, Wang takes my hand. Holding hands is common among Chinese – two men or two women, but not a man *and* a woman. In China a man and a woman holding hands is considered in bad taste; two men holding hands is perfectly natural. So here I am with a pair of high-heel shoes in a box, Wang holding my hand, trying to feel natural . . .

At night, couples become more daring and do hold hands. They court in the shadows in the parks, or loll around on park benches, doing what couples do all over the world on park-benches. In Shanghai's parks they go at it with quite a fervour, since bushes and darkness provide the only source of privacy in a city where apartments are chock-full of in-laws. By the eerie glare of sodium-lamps, I can make out women who've shed their drab Mao-suits and slipped into sophisticated home-made fashions, with a hint of make-up.

It is night-riding that I relish in Shanghai. With a scarf muffled round my throat, and my padded blue silk jacket, it is very difficult for the Chinese to pick me out as a foreigner. Since the street-lighting is dim, and since the cars rarely use their headlights, I can lurk in the shadows and blend in. This has its dangers – navigation at high speed means dodging meteoric objects from the shadows – other cyclists. They hurtle out of sidestreets right into my path. If a car does throw on its headlights, it is a signal for the bicyclist to get out of the way quickly. This is the rule of the road – the bigger the vehicle, the more clout it has. Thus if a taxi meets a bus, the taxi gives way; if a bicycle meets a truck, the bicyclist gives way. But it doesn't always work – and I turn a corner to witness a crowd gathered round a truck. A policeman appears with a mangled bicycle and puts it into the trunk of a taxi. No headlights, no insurance – and what has happened to the poor devil riding the bike?

It is freezing cold – I have to revive my hands with my scarf. I go back toward the bakery near the Jinjiang Hotel. It is open until 10 p.m., and caters to furtive couples who whisper in the corner-tables – there is nowhere else to go at this hour. I can get some take-out snacks there.

The neon of the bakery is visible some distance off. Hong Kong is probably ablaze with neon – ten days to Christmas. Here, not a sign of Christmas. By Christmas I will be in Hong Kong again. I will have to leave long-distance cycling to another time. It is cold, and my equipment and timing are all wrong. I'm not ready for it.

'We are good friends now,' beams Wang. This time he is riding the Phoenix, still in mint condition. He has paid for it, at a reduction – in amongst other deals like shoes, cigarettes and train-tickets. He is as proud as punch of the new bike – it is a lasting souvenir. The time has come for me to leave – he wants to escort me to the station. He parks his bike outside the Jinjiang Hotel. I go to get my gear. I can't really face a bus after all that biking freedom – I get the hotel to arrange a taxi. We stroll out the front of the hotel – and find a sleek Red Flag Limousine in wait. This jet-black hearse, with its two red flags fluttering up front, is usually reserved for high-ranking cadres or visiting VIPs, and not what I have in mind – but all the other taxis are out. The cost isn't too damaging, so what the hell . . . Wang puffs up like a general, strut-ting around like he owns Shanghai, finally getting into the vehicle and lighting up a cigarette.

'Look at the police!' he yells triumphantly. I peer through the curtained windows at the pole mounted over the street – the crow's-nest for manual light operation. Each time we pass a po-liceman, orders come booming down from the crow's-nest for cyclists to stop as we whizz by – and the policeman frantically phones the next crow's-nest along the route. Lights green all the way. Feeling very VIP-ish myself by the time we get to the station, I emerge with my backpack to find a crowd of several hundred has gathered round the Red Flag Limo. Wang takes it all in his stride and hustles me through to the station. On the platform he tells me that the high-heel shoes we bought don't fit his fiancée – but she'll wear them anyway – 'She is used to the tight shoe' . . .

*   *   *

FIFTEEN MONTHS LATER, I was back in Shanghai. By a quirk of fate, I'd gotten myself involved in writing a guidebook to China, angled for the independent traveller. I'd promised the publisher the earth, and now I had to deliver. The prospect terrified me – how could this monstrous country be sandwiched between the covers of a book? How would I find the time to visit all the places I had to visit, get back to Canada, research, write, and get all the material submitted without being five years out of date from travel-time to publication?

I had to start somewhere. That was the important part – getting started. There were two writers on the case – I'd exchanged a volley of letters with the co-author, Alan, on how to carve up the country. My half of the China pie included Shanghai and Jiangsu Province. Shanghai was the logical place for me to start: I was familiar with it, felt comfortable with it. And yet Shanghai, I knew, would be the hardest place to pin down on paper because essentially its values were not Chinese ones. Shanghai was unpredictable.

Apart from guidebook-writing, I'd returned with a few whims of my own to satisfy: cycling. I wanted to try getting out of Shanghai – as far as Nanjing if all went well. I'd brought along a cageless water-bottle that I could clip to the frame of a Chinese bicycle, and I had a few tools.

This hopelessly complicated mix of grandiose intentions was churning over in my brain as the CAAC flight from Canton touched down in Shanghai. Square One. Bristling with maps, books and plans, I made my way into Shanghai. My old haunt, the Jinjiang Hotel dorm, existed no more. I relocated to the Shenjiang Hotel, in the central area of Shanghai – sharing a room with an Englishman I'd met on the street.

It was not until I'd established myself in the hotel that my thoughts turned to Wang. I had his address on a piece of paper, but knew I could not visit. That left the telephone, or the postal system. A letter would reach him on the same day if posted in the morning. I decided the telephone was a better idea. By devious means, with the help of an Overseas Chinese, I got a call placed through to the man in the phone-booth that served Wang's neighbourhood, and we arranged a meeting.

Wang never got any of the letters I sent – and I never got any that he sent – but there was something else in the air. I was looking forward to this meeting – he, obviously, was not. He wouldn't tell me what had happened – I guessed his privileges and opportunities had been derailed for being in touch with foreigners. When I broached the subject, he shrugged and looked away. He didn't want to discuss it. I had some gifts for him – a solar-powered hand-calculator and a couple of Time magazines – he accepted them quietly, as if to say, yes, they're great, thank you – *but there is something I have to tell you*. Finally I found out what was at issue. He had a wife and son now. I congratulated him – the child, apparently, had been born six months after the marriage, so the 'experiment' had been a success. Now I got the gist. He had to protect them – he was not willing to take any risks. It was risky enough that he'd come to see me. There was nothing to be salvaged in this relationship anymore. I had lost a comrade.

Rather than allow this to make my blood boil, I threw myself solidly into the task at hand – guidebook writing. The last comprehensive guides for the independent traveller in China had been written in the 1930s, when a middle-class tourist-boom occurred – made possible by western-style hotels, by the foreign-built rail-system in China, and by ocean liners. Shanghai was the most sophisticated destination for travellers to the Orient in the 1920s and 30s; opulent hotels were built to provide safe havens for travellers and give them all the comforts of home.

Prior to my trip, I'd dug up loads of facts and figures on modern Shanghai. Ten thousand tons of night-soil were collected daily from older housing without sanitation in Shanghai; 28 tons of dust a month fell on the city; there were four million bicycles ... Shanghai was dubbed the East Gate of China – the largest port, the largest industrial city. It had more than 10,000 industrial enterprises, with heavy industry representing over half of that base – and accounting for most of the pollution. And yet Shanghai had been neglected by the Communist Government – much of the industry relied on technology and equipment from the 1950s.

In the city proper there were an estimated thirty square feet of living space for each person. As for public greenery, Shanghai had the equivalent of one page of the newspaper, *Liberation Daily*, as park-space per person. The statistics went on... but no Chinese sources would – or could – explain the tall European buildings along the Bund and elsewhere.

My guide to Shanghai's architecture – and the 1930s – was a copy of *All About Shanghai*. This guide was produced by a small press that started business in Shanghai in 1934, and sank without a trace in 1937, with the author remaining anonymous. The guidebook's fine detail gave a measure of what the place was really like – ads for clubs and hotels, listings of addresses. It gave me a good idea of scale in 1930s Shanghai – it listed 21 consulates, 9 hospitals, and 21 churches for instance. The 'monopoly board' had altered since the guidebook was written – some demolition, addition of Soviet-influenced sections, housing-developments on the fringes of the city. But very little of the architecture – or the sewage-system – in the former foreign concessions had changed. This was not out of a great interest in conservation, but simply because of lack of funds to develop.

Shanghai was a 1930s museum-piece: the central core had the same skyline, and the buildings of the Bund – Shanghai's legendary waterfront embankment – performed the same financial functions. The Bund was Shanghai's Wall Street: the Stock Exchange had been removed, the Bund had been renamed Zhongshan Road, but the trading and shipping continued along the waterfront. Customs House was still Customs House, although the clock – once known as 'Big Ching' – now played 'The East is Red' at 6 a.m. and 6 p.m.

I came across a passage in the 1934 guidebook describing an area of town close to my hotel:

> Bubbling Well Road begins at the Thibet Road intersection. It is here flanked on the left by the Race Course and Public Recreation Ground, and on the right by a number of impressive buildings, including the China United Assurance Society, which also houses a large apartment-hotel; the lofty Foreign YMCA, and the towering 22-storey building of the Joint Savings Society, containing the Park Hotel, the tallest building in the world outside the Americas.

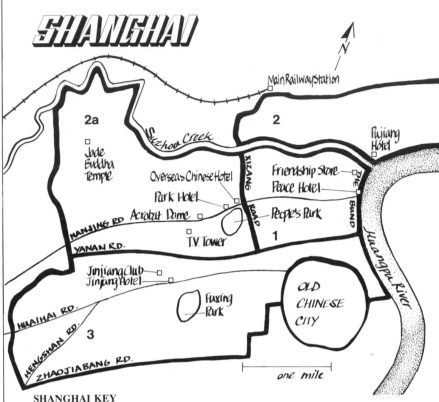

SHANGHAI

Main Railway Station

Pujiang Hotel

2a

2

Suzhou Creek

Jade Buddha Temple

Overseas Chinese Hotel

Park Hotel

Acrobat Dome

NANJING RD.

YANAN RD.

T.V. Tower

XIZANG ROAD

Friendship Store

Peace Hotel

People's Park

THE BUND

1

Huangpu River

Jinjiang Club
Jinjiang Hotel

HUAIHAI RD.

HENGSHAN RD.

ZHAOJIABANG RD.

3

Fuxing Park

OLD CHINESE CITY

one mile

SHANGHAI KEY

1 *Downtown* – comprising former British Settlement 1843-1863 (Central District)

1 2 & 2a Extent of former *International Settlement*, a merger of British zone(1) and American zone(2) in 1863, with an expansion(2a) in 1899

3 *Frenchtown* – comprising former French Concession, first settled in 1849, and expanded 1861, 1900 & 1914

After 1927, all sections outside the foreign settlements came under the control of the *Chinese Municipality of Greater Shanghai*. In 1937, the Chapei District(2) fell under Japanese control. In 1941 the Japanese invaded Shanghai; in 1945 it fell under Nationalist control; in 1949 it came under Communist control

SHANGHAI MUNICIPALITY & SURROUNDING AREA

Railway Lines

Road - Route Travelled

This corner of Shanghai was easy to locate, since the Park Hotel still bore the same name. The old Race Course and Recreation Ground, I knew, had been transmogrified into People's Park and People's Square, with Shanghai Library occupying the former raceclub. Bubbling Well Road was now Nanjing Road West, and Thibet Road was now Xizang Road – 'Xizang' being the Chinese for 'Tibet'. 'Bubbling Well' had previously referred to a bubbling eruption of carbonic acid gas at the western end of the road – the well had since been sealed over.

I was now at the intersection of Nanjing Road West and Tibet Road. There was an ad in the 1934 guide – 'China United Apartments, 104 Bubbling Well Road' – with a photograph: the building, with the clock-tower on top, was unmistakably the Overseas Chinese Hotel, now used by visitors from Hong Kong and Singapore. I went back to the original description: China United Assurance Society. That explained the lofty ceilings on the ground floor. I checked the numbering. 104 Nanjing Road West. It matched 104 Bubbling Well Road.

Where, then, was the 'lofty Foreign YMCA' mentioned in the guide? Under 'Sports and Entertainment', six YMCAs were listed – Chinese, Japanese, International, Navy – and the Headquarters of the YMCA at 150 Bubbling Well Road. Uncanny – I had pinned down the address to match Nanjing Road West. I could walk along and find that numbering, as though nothing had changed in fifty years.

The old YMCA Headquarters was the building sandwiched between the Park Hotel and the Overseas Chinese Hotel. There was no need to match numbers: on the stone facing of the building was the faded triangle logo of the YMCA. I walked up to the front. I had stumbled into the headquarters of the All-China Sports Federation.

A doorman accosted me. Somehow I bluffed my way to the interior and found a man who knew a few words of English. I got a short tour of the first two floors. Out the back was a full-sized swimming-pool – the original one, with a ceiling that extended to the second floor. Youngsters were splashing around, learning to swim. Upstairs were billiard-tables where youths were chalking the cues and smoking under the dim lights. The game of billiards, had, then, a clear mandate from the State as being non-corruptive!

As far as I could discern, the first two floors performed exactly the same function they used to – except that the State ran the show instead of the YMCA. The YMCAs in China were once for the prim, the pious, the proper – or the poor – arrivals in Shanghai. Or for the sports-minded. The seven or eight floors above were probably used as offices and lodgings for the All-China Sports Federation: instead of a copy of the Bible in every room, there was probably a copy of Mao's Little Red Book.

I passed a small movie-theatre on the ground floor. Some youths had just seen a film and were coming out. What was the sermon? Probably strings of production figures – on the ten-fold increase in pig farming, on the fifteen percent rise in steel output, on the staggering rise of manufacture of washing machines, refrigerators and fans – all courtesy of the benevolent State. The manager, my escort, seemed to think I'd seen enough. He showed me the front door.

With the more libidinous features of Shanghai, I had less success. Where was the Majestic Café? Or the Venus Ballroom? The opium-dens? The gambling halls? The cabarets stocked with Asian and White Russian hostesses? The alleys with such wicked names as 'Galaxy of Beauties' or 'Happiness Concentrated'? I wandered along Fuzhou Road – an alley with a bunch of book-stores, and profusion of small restaurants. In the 1930s, Fuzhou Road had numerous 'singsong houses' – so named because the courtesans within were also entertainers. These homely teahouses welcomed their clients with food and warm wine; a courtesan would light an opium pipe for her patron – reclined on a divan in a partitioned room. Such establishments came in several classes – the privilege of deflowering virgin courtesans was reserved for the wealthy.

In pre-1949 Shanghai there were an estimated 30,000 ladies of the night, and upwards of 200,000 opium addicts. In a city where prize racehorses were fed raw eggs, given champagne and silk blankets, there were tens of thousands of Chinese living on the streets in makeshift shelters. Thousands died each year from exposure and cold; in 1937, a particularly bad year, 20,000 corpses were picked off the streets. Somehow, the Communists, after their 1949 takeover, had eradicated prostitution, cleaned up the slums, and rehabilitated the opium-addicts. They did in a few years what the western missionaries had failed to do in a hundred.

There were lots of changes in the traffic, too – but not especially for the better: since 1949 not a single new main road has been built to ease the congestion of Shanghai's inner city. There were 16,500 cars registered in 1934 Shanghai – American, English, French, German – the most cars of any Asian metropolis at the time. They shared the streets with innumerable rickshaws – and with double-decker buses, trams, trucks, taxis, bicycles, mule-carts, handcarts and horse-drawn cabs. Cruising along in the thick of things – in a bulletproof limousine – would be the odd millionaire Chinese gangster with his bodyguards. Directing this downtown madness would be Sikh traffic policemen, imported by the British from India. In the French Concession, Annamese traffic police were employed, from the French colony of Vietnam. Chauffeurs could be White Russian or Chinese – perhaps the Annamese gendarmes just barked at offenders in Pidgin English.

The Japanese melted down a lot of the 1930s autos for ammunition when they invaded Shanghai in 1941, and interred all the foreigners. Odd to think of a Rolls Royce being turned into scrap, and shot back out some howitzer during World War II. The Japanese did similar things with the metal radiators used for heating in the hotels and apartment buildings (being of smaller stature, they also cut down the legs of billiard-tables in the hotels they took over).

Under 'Miscellanea' in the 1934 guide, I found this entry:

> The 'keep to the left' rule in driving is universal in Shanghai, and, indeed, throughout China and the rest of the Orient, save only in Tsingtao, a Summer resort city in Shantung Province.

The mind enters this piece of trivia into the left and right hand logic department: it's the kind of thing that an American movie-director will botch when making a movie about Shanghai. But how extraordinary – China must have switched over from left-hand drive to right-hand. Could it have been done when the Japanese dominated China? No, I reasoned: the Japanese had left-hand drive. Most likely it was one of those shattering Communist Party edicts: judge's decision final, and no correspondence entered into.

Private ownership of motor vehicles is outlawed in China – the bicycle fills the gap. In 1949 China produced 15,000 bicycles; in 1982, it produced 17,000,000 bicycles. With over 125 million bicycles in use, China has become the largest biking nation in the world. In every respect, the bicycle has replaced the car as the private transport option. Bicycle licenses are issued; drunken cyclists are reprimanded or arrested; there are billboards giving cycle-safety warnings; there is bicycle-parking and bicycle tow-away; some Chinese cities even have bicycle licence-plates to keep track of wayward cyclists; bicycles are colour-coded to designate a particular work-unit – such as the all-green bicycles which belong to the post-office.

For 1932 it was estimated that there were 60,000 foreigners living in the International Settlement and the French Concession, and 1.5 million Chinese in those areas. There were actually very few French in the French Concession – they were outnumbered by the British, Russians and Americans in their own sector. In the International Settlement, it was the Japanese who dominated the statistics, with the British second, then the Russian immigrants.

The foreigners had left – or been booted out – by 1953. By the 1980s, the foreigners – tourists, businessmen and students – were back to several thousand strong again. The large downtown apartment-hotels – the Jinjiang, the Park, the Peace – were again in use exclusively for foreigners, who were allowed the luxury of ample space. A luxury because there were now some six million Chinese living in a city built for 1.5 million.

Greater Shanghai had a population of 11.85 million according to the 1982 national census. Greater Shanghai encompasses a sprawl of 2400 square miles – which includes a dozen industrial satellite communities, and 200 agricultural communes. Shanghai Proper – the central core – covers an area of 90 square miles, with six million people. Families have been squeezed into every residence: the dilapidated European stucco mansions and tenement blocks are subdivided into multiple dwellings, with kitchens often shared by unrelated families. 'Kitchen' means a stove; the precious water-tap and toilet are also shared; bathing is done at public baths. Little maintenance has been done on the buildings: the paint is peeling, the plumbing is unrepaired, elevators have broken down, roofs are leaking, smashed windows are not replaced.

Thirty square feet per person of living space; an area of park-space per person equal to one page of the newspaper, Liberation Daily. In the parks, if not in the apartments, it is standing room only; the streets are choked with traffic; the Huangpu River is a fetid sewer. There are no bridges or tunnels crossing the Huangpu; there is no

40

rapid transit system. And yet most of the basic needs are filled – there is enough food, the buses run, and there are no squatters living in shacks.

*   *   *

THINGS WERE GOING WELL in the guidebook line, but with my other ambitious plan – cycling – everything had gone horribly wrong. When I went to check out the Friendship Store's stock of bicycles, I could not find any. They were locked up downstairs, out of sight, and only for sale to foreign students or foreign experts, resident in Shanghai, upon receipt of authorisation from a work-unit. In addition, I was weighed down with extra research materials – the biking idea had quite simply become impractical – even hopeless. I was totally frustrated.

I wandered aimlessly down Nanjing Road, chewing over this swift change of fortune. *Nanjing*. If I really wanted to pursue the project of riding toward Nanjing, there were several options still open – I could pick up a battered bike from a second-hand store in Shanghai, or I could try and purchase a bike further down the line, perhaps at Suzhou Friendship Store. Nanjing Road, with its seething mass of shoppers, its battalions of snotters and spitters and smokers, its advertising billboards, its tall buildings, its eye-catching department store windows – at least took my mind off things.

I stopped outside one of the department stores; the building was encased in an ingenious structure of bamboo scaffolding, over which construction workers in bamboo helmets were crawling. Then the tide of humanity surging along Nanjing Road picked me up again – and I bumped into a man called Zoubei. He and his very pregnant wife, Xiaomei, were headed off to a nearby restaurant – would I join them? They would love to practice their English. They had relatives in the United States, and many questions to ask. I complied. Zoubei was a short, thick-set man with a crew-cut and inch-thick glasses; his wife, slightly taller, was quite young – perhaps half his age.

Zoubei was an entertaining conversationalist, and not afraid to say what he thought. He worked in a factory which was clear across town from where he lived. It took him an hour and a half to get there by bicycle. There were plenty of factories in the area where he lived, but the powers that be had decided to give him lots of exercise by making him work across town. The factory had no windows, and was hot and boring. He got a demeaning wage of 40 yuan a month, no matter if he did the work or not. Today was his day off – a Wednesday. Why Wednesday? Days off in Shanghai are staggered, he informed me. If everyone had the same day off, the place would be a total mess – six million people on Nanjing Road at the same time.

The greatest honour I could do Zoubei was to visit his apartment, he said. It wasn't very big, but he wanted me to visit. When? Today? How would I get there? I'd get lost. We fell to talking about bicycles, and I asked him where I could buy a new one without attracting too much attention. Easy, he said, buy it at the Overseas Chinese Store. That was the Overseas Chinese equivalent of the Friendship Store, but the stock was a little different. Hong Kong and Overseas Chinese would come in, buy a refrigerator – using hard currencies – and give it to their relatives. Relatives happy, Overseas Chinese happy, Government happy, all other Chinese insanely jealous. Same thing with cooking oil. Rationed at the regular stores – but on sale quite readily at the Overseas Chinese Store.

It was a direct method of siphoning off foreign exchange from the Overseas Chinese. After all, a Chinese from Singapore or Manila was hardly likely to buy a new refrigerator in Shanghai and lug it all the way back home, where refrigerators were of higher quality and much cheaper anyway. So how far was this wonderful Overseas Chinese Store? Oh, just around the corner? Then, I told Zoubei, if I was to buy a bicycle, I could visit his apartment.

Zoubei looked at me quizzically through his thick glasses. 'You have *that* kind of money?' he asked.

'I will re-sell the bicycle,' I told him, 'later.'

We were down at the Overseas Chinese Store in ten minutes. I couldn't distinguish it from any other department store along Nanjing Road, except that identification had to be shown to gain entry. After changing American dollars into renminbi, purchasing some kind of ration-coupons, and using the RMB plus the coupons, I was able to get myself a brand-new Phoenix.

Two hours later, I was sitting in Zoubei's apartment, and the new bicycle was parked outside. Mission accomplished. Zoubei's was the first apartment I'd had the privilege of seeing. Basically, it consisted of one room – with a tiny kitchen off to the side. The main room had a television, small refrigerator (Overseas Chinese Store), bed, sofa, hotplate, wardrobe, chest of drawers, table. All the living was done here. On the way in I'd noticed that other apartment residents had put their hotplates in the hallway as a space-saver. Cooking was done in the hallway.

Suddenly there was an earthquake-like convulsion that almost caused me to dive under the sofa. We appeared to be right on top of some huge piece of machinery in a factory, and an awful hammering noise permeated the building at regular intervals – a thundering BOOM!, followed shortly after by a reactive KER-CHUNK! 'Ah, this is quite normal,' Zoubei assured me. 'I (BOOM!) don't notice it (KER-CHUNK!) so much now. When we were first here it was terrible, but now we don't take notice.'

'And does it stop at night?' I asked, my perceptive powers deadened by the traumatic sound.

'Oh yes. At 10.30 p.m. they close it down, and then it starts up at 8 a.m. the next day, but it goes on all week, even Sunday.'

'What is it?'

'It's the lathe in a box-factory.'

God, I thought, this has to be a sophisticated form of torture.

'We hope (BOOM!)' said Xiaomei, 'that with the baby (KER-CHUNK!) we can get another apartment, but there are long waiting lists.'

Xiaomei was a nurse – they'd only been married a short time. Zoubei showed me the honeymoon pictures from the seaside resort of Qingdao – Xiaomei looking demure in her revealing swimsuit. Well, things weren't *that* bad for old Zoubei, I thought. He showed me pictures of his relatives in America. They sent money when they could.

'And the baby,' I asked, 'Do you want (BOOM!) a boy or a girl?'

'Of course (KER-CHUNK!) it will be a boy,' said Zoubei swiftly, as if anything else was out of the question. With the 'one child only' policy, everyone wanted a male child. They would agree to having only one child, but only if that child were a boy. If they were to have a second child, then they could say goodbye to their dreams of a larger apartment, say goodbye to any job advancement, say goodbye to a decent education for their progeny. These were the economic penalties that could be levied once a 'one child only' pledge had been signed.

(BOOM!) 'I have a special treat for ourselves,' (KER-CHUNK!) announced Xiaomei. She brought out some Nescafé imported from the Bahamas.

'It comes from the Overseas Chinese Store,' said Zoubei wryly. Real coffee. Such things were extremely difficult to get in Shanghai. I remembered I had some spare coupons from the Overseas Chinese Store. I fished them out – they would be of no use to me, but Zoubei could use them. We went over the transaction I'd done to buy the bicycle. I still didn't fully understand it. What it boiled down to was that I'd used foreign currency to purchase the bike, so I'd actually paid more than I would have at a department store – if I'd been able to get the bike in a department store. The purchase receipt for the bike was now my proof of ownership – a valuable document.

Zoubei took out his tattered wallet to put the extra coupons in it. He could use the coupons to buy cooking oil and other rationed items. With his American relatives, who qualified as Overseas Chinese, he had access to the store – but he had to produce identification. What kind of identification? He had an Overseas Chinese Store card. I got him to empty his wallet. He had a travel permit card for visiting relatives in China, a work-unit certificate, a resident certificate, a bicycle licence, a swimming licence, a library card, a bus pass – the paperwork never ended. He also had ten different kinds of ration-coupons – for rice, for cigarettes, for grain, for cotton – as well as the special larger coupons for the Overseas Chinese Store. Having changed some money with me, he had two kinds of currency – renminbi and FECs. Seeing how bewildered I looked, Zoubei burst out laughing – he could see the joke in all this ID too. He had so many pieces of ID that he didn't have enough photos to go round – or else he couldn't afford the photos – so he would rip one photo off an older piece of ID and transfer it to a newer piece, as the need arose.

I passed the entire afternoon with Zoubei and Xiaomei, and the BOOM! and KER-CHUNK! of the factory next door. We drank more coffee, compared lifestyles in the east and the west, and poured over maps of Shanghai so that I could figure out my escape on the new bicycle. I became so engrossed that even I had started to ignore the shattering punctuation provided by the box-factory. Was this Zoubei's 'life sentence'? I hoped not – and I wished him and Xiaomei, and the forthcoming baby, the best of luck. Intrigued by my proposed bike-trip, they asked me to send a letter from Suzhou, the first stop. Zoubei wrote down his address in Chinese on an envelope – all I had to do was add a stamp.

Back at the Shenjiang Hotel, I took the bicycle up the elevator to the third floor, and wheeled it along the hallway to the room I shared with John, the English traveller. I set to work fitting the bike out with the waterbottle I'd brought along, and sizing it up for my backpack and side-bags. I had a couple of stretch-elastic cords to hold the luggage in place on the back rack. I still needed to get a supply of food and drink for the road.

The Englishman came back, exhausted from a hard day's tourism in Shanghai. He had brought very little clothing with him for the trip, knowing that he could buy it quite cheaply in China. So he had been shopping for clothes in the department stores. The clothing was of the ill-fitting military kind – khaki pants, canvas running-shoes, black sweater, black beret, and blue Mao-jacket. He now looked like a cross between a PLA officer and a deserter from the Foreign Legion. A droopy moustache added to the effect. In one of the top pockets of his Mao-jacket he sported a brand-new pair of chopsticks, ready for an assault on the next restaurant.

'Off somewhere then are you?' said John, pointing at the bike. He examined the tyres and the brakes.

'Yes, thought I might try a little trip.'

'Then you should go and buy some of this stuff.' He reached into his daypack and threw a jar my way.

'What is it?'

'Peanut butter, man. It's made in Shandong Province. Found it in one of the department stores. Thick and crunchy, no additives, completely natural. Full of protein. And really cheap, too. I swear by the stuff. You know, when I was in Africa, peanut butter kept me going for two months. That's all I had for two months – peanut butter.'

'Isn't it a bit heavy to carry around?'

'Depends if it's in glass jars or plastic containers.'

A picture formed in my mind: John with a battered suitcase, full of jars of peanut butter, sharing a meal with towering Masai tribesmen and their floppy-breasted women. John prised open a jar, and dug in a chopstick from his top pocket.

'Absolutely first class,' he pronounced. 'Here – try some, man.'

He gave me the other chopstick. The stuff did taste good. But for two months?

I got back to work on my baggage for the bike. There were two smaller bags that I'd purchased in Shanghai – one for books and research, the other for food. I could mount those on either side at the rear, and put my pack straight over the top of the rack.

John told me all about his problems back home. He had come to China, like the rest of us, to escape. He travelled on the Trans-Mongolian Express, the European escape conduit. Everybody in Europe dreams of being locked in a compartment on this train for seven days – sometimes longer – because it sounds like the grandest escape possible. John had lots of plans. He had an even better escape-trick lined up.

'I've got it all worked out, really,' he told me. 'You see, up in Xinjiang Province, they're Muslims. You know, the Kazakhs and Uighurs and those tribesmen. They don't speak Chinese. They speak Arabic and other languages. And you know the best part? Uighurs don't *look* Chinese either. They look just like you or me – they look like Greeks or Italians.'

'So what are you getting at?'

'What I'm getting at is this, man. If I can build up the right kind of ID, and wear the clothes that they wear, then who's to know where I'm from?'

'Kazakhs don't eat peanut butter.'

'Very funny, man. I'll find a way round that too.' He probably would, too. A new picture: chieftan John on a horse, surrounded by Kazakh women, his saddlebags full of peanut butter. Suddenly heavy metal rock came bouncing through the room. I jumped back, as if I'd touched a live wire. John had turned on the radio full bore.

'Groovy, man,' said John, snapping his fingers.

This was China?! I waited for announcements. There were none. The whole tape was being broadcast from *within* the hotel, at least on that station. And the same with the television – closed-circuit video, explicit Hong Kong movies. But where was the transmission? My curiosity was piqued: I dropped the tools I'd been working with and went off to find the manager.

Half an hour later, I found the room. It was fitted with four sophisticated stereo sets, and a bank of TV screens and VCRs. The screens monitored broadcasts by Shanghai Television, Beijing

Television, and the closed-circuit material – foreign and Hong Kong movies. The 'broadcaster', a young man, flashed a big smile – monitoring those screens and that music must've been the most coveted job in Shanghai. He didn't look any the worse for it, listening to 'yellow music' all day, and watching heady movies. In fact, he looked a good deal more cheerful for the experience.

The closed-circuit wizardry was there to pamper the tourists – or perhaps leave the visitor with the impression that the Chinese listened to hard rock, and watched naughty movies. In the process, copies of the material filter through – inevitably – to the ordinary Chinese.

Tourism has created a curious double standard in China: by opening to the outside world, China has reaped the financial benefits – but it has to stem the tide of 'bourgeois' ideas. The very presence of a foreigner is a threat: foreigners carry their cultural packages with them – ideas which are bound to invite imitation. Shanghai is especially open to such influences because it has never really been a Chinese city – its buildings, its tastes, fashions and attitudes are foreign to begin with.

In 1983 a nation-wide campaign was launched against 'cultural pollution'. Dancing was out; teenagers were being told how to dress, what hairstyles were acceptable, what music to listen to. Bookstores were raided by the Propaganda Department for 'yellow books' (banned western books and magazines were, however, still freely available to foreigners at the Foreign Language Bookstore). The cultural witch-hunt proved to be elusive – more often a ploy to attack another party-member. Was golf bourgeois? Was sex bourgeois? Was Picasso revolutionary? Teresa Teng, the pop-singer from Taiwan, was banned; on the other hand, *Jingle Bells*, a non-religious Christmas carol, was played year-round in a country that doesn't celebrate Christmas. It was called *Ding, Ding, Ding*. While many western movies could not be shown because of their sexual content, violent kung fu epics made in China under Hong Kong direction were standard fare at the cinema.

The sauciest video material, rumour had it, found its way through to special screenings for high-ranking cadres. Sexual privilege, like any other privilege, has always been the domain of the ruling class in China – the emperor was expected to conduct a vigorous sex-life, as a symbol of potency and creative power. For this reason large harems – with queens and concubines – were attached to the royal court. Mao himself had a well-earned reputation in the practice of concubinage: he preferred young women, as he thought they helped promote longevity.

Confucian ethics condemned physical love – and revolutionary China simply continued the tradition. It channelled morals into the single goal of marriage: this is a society where sex before marriage is tantamount to rape, where homosexuality is considered a form of madness (and officially non-existent), where adultery is gravely punished, and where divorce is taboo.

For all its 'modernisation', China still belongs to the world of the nineteenth century. Thus Charles Dickens is culturally acceptable: England is portrayed as a nation where children are most horribly mistreated. The Chinese can readily identify with Dickens – the dark, ill-managed factories; the crowded apartments with their foul toilets; the stern school-masters. In the movie line, Charlie Chaplin is acceptable since his films portray a backward, poor America of the 1920s, full of rusted cars and social injustices (and VD and millionaires).

George Orwell's *Nineteen Eighty-Four* comes much closer to capturing the real climate of China, so the book is banned. The Chinese who have read it claim it not as a work of fiction, but as reality – the doctoring of news and history, the forbidden sexual contact, the constant streams of economic statistics, the spying of neighbour on neighbour, the regimentation, the total subjugation of the individual to the Party – and the subjugation of art and literature to the cause.

*   *   *

THE CAKES ARE LOADED UP – nougat, chocolate and Cokes – high energy junk-food. One large jar of Shandong peanut butter, courtesy of John. Five-thirty in the morning. I have a vague idea of how to get out of the metropolis. I will head for the Jade Buddha Temple to the north-west, cross Suzhou Creek, make my way to the railway-tracks and follow those to the west. Then? I have little dots on the map – Anting, Kungshan. Once in Kungshan, I will be out of Shanghai Municipality: I calculate Suzhou to be a ride of 55 miles, or nine hours on a Chinese bike.

As I pick my way through the morning rush, my attention is drawn to a man with a large-wheel tricycle carrier bearing a heavy load – a phantom thrown up by the traffic. He has fitted an ingenious bell to the front hub, which is operated by a string from the handlebar. When he tugs it, the bell at the forks comes into contact with the spokes and makes an absolutely deafening clatter that surprises even the most seasoned ears – and they all allow him to pass. I follow in the slipstream, past joggers, people brushing their teeth in the gutters, street-corner *taichi* practitioners, and an old man spearing cigarette butts with a bamboo skewer.

Two hours later, I begin to wonder if I'll ever get out of Shanghai. Magically, I round a corner and there it is – the countryside, but not from the cage of a train. Beautiful, disturbingly beautiful. Fields of yellow rapeseed, brilliant greens, the smell of manure, waterways. Up ahead is a countdown milestone, along with the relevant destination – Suzhou – in Chinese characters. And then – heart attack! – there is a striped orange crossbar on the side of the road, in the vertical position. It is some kind of checkpoint, probably intended for cars, but I have no desire to be an extraneous variable in such a net. I move my legs into maximum gear and rocket on, not looking left or right – powered by pure adrenaline. Out of the corner of my eye, flashing by the post, I notice a uniformed officer in a small guardbox. He has seen me too – but is not concerned enough to want to stop me.

I follow a farmer with a dead pig slung over his rack for a few miles. He takes a small earphone from his pocket and plugs it in. A hearing-aid? What would he want to listen to the noisy trucks for? No, it's a small radio he's tuned into. Modernisation! The man has achieved rightist nirvana – two of the most treasured possessions, radio and bicycle, combined with a freemarket pig. Suddenly the pig falls off – and I dismount to assist recovery . . .

The landscape is soft – a tapestry of deep greens and misty yellows, calm waterways, and white-washed farm-housing. I'm in luck that the landscape isn't any softer – the Plum Rains are due soon. These rains come in the late spring and are responsible for the high agricultural yield of the region, particularly for rice. To my great relief there is not a hill in sight – the highway is dead level. I run parallel to the train-tracks for some distance; a black locomotive with fire-red wheels comes thundering by, belching clouds of smoke, and sending out a piercing whistle.

The farmer is due to turn off. I give him a cigarette – we must part company. He gives me some final directions, pats his bum and grimaces. My destination is several sore bums away. Is this actual farming jargon? (Ah yes, Nanjing – 100 sore bums to the north!). In quick succession, the oncoming traffic throws up a Shanghai Saloon with drawn curtains; a droning three-wheel samlor with passengers and luggage piled to the canvas roof; and two army punks at the helm of a Harley-sized Xingfu motorcycle. In the sidecar of this speedy number is a very pale-looking grandmother.

Soon after leaving the farmer, I find some new company on the road – two students from Shanghai. Though they speak no English, we manage to communicate our destinations – they are headed for Suzhou too. They have no luggage at all – just a handful of tools. They're probably going to Suzhou for an overnight stay and returning to Shanghai next day. We stop to share some cakes and drinks. The students watch in consternation as I fill one of the cakes with peanut butter, using a chopstick. What strange eating habits these westerners have! They donate a very nice Chinese map of the highway – something that I've been unable to find in Shanghai. Several hours later, I follow them straight into Suzhou, and they direct me to the gates of Suzhou Hotel. I have made it this far without problems – tired, but high from the rush of putting my off-beat plans into motion. The desk-clerk spits on the floor, then turns and asks me how I got to Suzhou. I tell him I put the bike on a train. I request a room with a large hot bath.

In central Suzhou there are sweetshops that make your mouth water and your teeth fall out. They sell candied fruit, peanut nougat, pastries, dumplings and steamed buns. I replenish my stocks of high-energy food for the biking ahead, and pick up some canned drinks from the Friendship Store.

Suzhou is a city that has managed to keep its traditional identity and lifestyles despite the tremendous pressures of the Maoist era and the Cultural Revolution. The city – once walled – is surrounded by a moat. It is a small city (meaning less than a million people) and laid out clearly in a grid-pattern. Calm canals crisscross the streets; plane-trees shade the walkways; there are numerous humpback bridges of stone. The back-alleys are made of cobblestone – the cyclist's worst enemy. Located within the city are garden-retreats which, in centuries past, were created to please retired scholars, doctors, merchants and officials. They vied with each other in the construction of ponds, rockeries and pavilions – places to read, recite poetry, have philosophical discussions, meditate, talk, or chase a local courtesan. A few of the gardens have been restored, and now masses of tourists and Chinese trample through the unkempt domains. Apart from gardens, bridges, temples and courtesans, Suzhou used to have numerous bathing-houses: Marco Polo reported that these baths used cold water – hot water was for strangers, such as himself, who weren't used to the shock of the cold water.

As in the past, the mainstay of Suzhou's economy is silk-production, and the classical art-forms still flourish. In one quiet gallery – in the garden of the Master of the Nets – I find woodblock prints done in the old style, alongside 'doctored' ones. The doctored ones have a few red flags waving out of a classical-style landscape, or a bright red tractor – or a factory-chimney. Some even show peasants with the Little Red Book. Like everything else, Mao decreed that art should serve the people, and therefore attempted to bend all the art-forms for propaganda purposes. As Lu Xun, the famous Shanghai writer, observed: 'All literature is propaganda, but not all propaganda is literature.'

Nearby – outside on the street – is some artwork with a more practical purpose. I stop to observe a painter at work on the wall of a building. He is adding some brushstrokes to a largish One Child Only painting. The Madonna and Only Child have been finished: the infant is a rosy-cheeked girl. Without exception, billboards like this depict a daughter in an attempt to convince would-be parents that having a girl isn't so bad after all.

I head out of Suzhou two days later. It is easy to find the way out: all I have to do is follow the Grand Canal and the railway-line to the north-west of the city. I have scouted the exit the previous day – I take my bearings from the large red door of a fire-station, and a huge One Child Only billboard. Shortly after, I stop on a bridge overlooking the Grand Canal for breakfast. It is an estimated 35 miles to the next open city, Wuxi, so I can afford to dawdle. A long line of barges passes under the bridge; the lead barge sounds a foghorn that makes my inner organs twang like bowstrings. If I had not located this waterway on the map precisely, I would not have known what it was, for the Grand Canal has nothing grand-looking about it at all. It is a plain, pint-sized canal.

Further on, a scene from a surrealist movie-set: I turn a corner and there, coming slowly along the road, are two men hauling enormous loads on separate handcarts. The loads are pulled by ropes over their shoulders; the weight is written on their faces – very heavy. There is nothing unusual in this back-breaking labour – except for the fact that the loads are half a car each. The man up front is straining forward with the rusted front end of a small car; the man behind him has the rear end of the same car. The car looks as though it was sliced in half for the ease of hauling – but wouldn't it have been easier to push the original car down the highway, and dispense with the handcarts? Surely the wheels on the car must have still been functioning. Absorbed in their horren-dous task, these scrap-metal merchants barely acknowledge my presence; I watch them as they crawl past...

On the road to Wuxi I overtake a posse of farmers cycling home-ward. The challenge has been thrown out – they quickly respond. A mad race ensues down the highway – they overtake, I pass again, they speed up, I shout at them, they yell abuse and encour-agement. All six of us are strung out across the highway, going hell for leather. The farmers put on a burst of speed, and it is then that I realise that they're due to turn off and wish to be in a position to say goodbye. All sweating profusely, we shake hands and grin.

Bikes break the ice – lost in Wuxi, I strike up a conversation in the traffic with a young Chinese, and before I know it, I am on the seventh floor of a grey concrete apartment block, and his dad is drinking me under the table.

'I hate factory!' my new-found friend proclaims.

'Me too!' I respond.

What he means is that he works in a hat factory. His girlfriend is a truck-driver; his sister is in the army – she arrives home in her khakis to prove it. Before I can protest, mum is up barbecuing dinner on the charcoal burner on the balcony – and dad is refilling my glass with a powerful brandy steeped in herbs. A resounding

'GANBEI!' for every glass I knock back.

The walls are bare concrete – six people living in two tiny rooms. Pots and pans hang in profusion off the walls. At dinner, an amazing bunch of dishes just keeps rolling through – duck-eggs, fried fish, snails, crispy chicken-skin, eggs with mushroom, bean-curd – it seemed impossible that so much could come from the burner on the balcony, and all entirely spontaneous. Feeling the effects of the alcohol, I get up to go to the toilet. Toilet?! We don't have things like that! Out, down seven floors, follow your nose, no lights – a communal one. I stagger back, tripping over the pile of shoes near the front door – and there is more of that evil brandy waiting for me, along with some delicious shrivelled coconuts. The members of the family insist that I stay the night, but there doesn't seem to be even floorspace for me to do so. My friend from the hat factory escorts me, considerably under the weather, to the gates of my hotel, where he can go no further . . .

The Shuixiu Hotel is a pre-fab building, imported in sections all the way from Australia. There is another of these in Suzhou, and in a few other cities in Jiangsu Province. The curtains feature koala bears, kangaroos, and aboriginal motifs; there is a fridge, television, phone, radio – and all the other creature comforts that the tourist is expected to need. I have battled my way into one of these expensive rooms at a student rate. Nearby is a second highrise hotel – the Hubin. It is even more expensive, and frequented by group-tours arriving by bus. The trouble with both hotels is that they are miles out of the centre of Wuxi – both are located over-looking Lake Taihu, which is billed as the main attraction. After the hubbub of Shanghai, and the pleasant streets of Suzhou, I find this isolation on the outskirts of Wuxi to be disheartening, and resolve to leave as soon as I can.

The town-centre of Wuxi, too, is dead. Wuxi is a town that was earmarked for industrial expansion by the Communist Party in the early 1950s. Before this it was a sleepy town of little note; now it is a boom town with no character. The process of industrialising the town actually started in the 1930s when Shanghai entrepreneurs set about expanding textile production; the process was acceler-ated under the Communists – hundreds of factories were flung up; the production of textiles was boosted; massive housing de-velopments were cast in concrete on the fringes of Wuxi. But the emphasis has been totally on increased production – there has been no concern for city-planning for people, and no concern for the environment. The new Wuxi is thus a mix of dowdy concrete and appalling pollution. There is no comparison to the clean, well-groomed, leafy streets of Suzhou. The only place where any soul remains in Wuxi is along the Grand Canal, which cuts through the middle of town. I go in search of the right bridge from which to observe the busy water-traffic, and think about my next move.

*   *   *

CONFIDENT NOW THAT I'VE COME THIS FAR, I decide to blunder into the countryside a bit more, but still within permit-limits. My target is the village of Yixing, about 35 miles to the south-west of Wuxi by road. I have a permit for the place, and it sounds interesting enough. It is in a tea-producing centre; close by is another village – Dingshu – which makes ceramic teapots. I leave Wuxi early in the morning, cycling along the shores of Lake Taihu. In the distance, large fishing junks with bamboo-battened canvas sails ply the waters. Skirting round Lake Taihu, I strike a series of steep hills – which oblige me to walk the bike. Once over these, pancake terrain appears again. Having cleared the last of the hills, I make a peanut-butter stop – gouging out lumps of the stuff from the jar for an instant snack.

Off the main route now, but it still doesn't get me away from the traffic. The trucks continue to come roaring down the centre of the road at breakneck speeds. One combination – a pair of overtaking trucks and an oncoming bus – forces me to ditch into the road-shoulder. The air-horns on that bunch were so loud they could be mistaken for those of a train. I do, however, get a closer look at the villages.

A different vehicle commands the roads – the walking-tractor. Little more than an engine with an easy-rider crossbar attached to it, this device hauls trailer-loads of produce, goods, and people. I pull over as one lumbers past. In the open driver's seat of this chariot is a man whose gaping lower mandible is stuffed full of rice; in the back, atop a load of produce, is his wife in haircurlers and a surgical mask, and a kid with toy binoculars filled with blue lemonade. The three of them gaze at me as they chug past – it is hard to say which party looks more stupefied.

54

My automatic reaction to any sound of double-barrel throat-clearing is to speed up. When I hear the sound on my left flank, I'm surprised to find the same farmer I passed fifteen miles back. He is waving as he lobs a big green ball of spittle into the side of the road. I smile back, we ride on a bit further – suddenly he cuts me off, dismounts, motions with a gnarled hand at a roadside farmhouse. We trundle off down a dirt path. Seconds later, I am guest of honour in his dark, dank hovel. Quaint from the outside; bare table, mud floor and chickens inside. And a giant cassette player. I don't think the farmer quite understands that my command of Chinese is about thirty words, and I get the tones on those wrong anyway. He keeps writing things down on the palm of his hand – hieroglyphics to me. I search through my phrasebook in vain – *'Do you take credit-cards?' 'I have diarrhea' 'Is there an elevator?' 'Do you have an ointment for diaper rash?' 'Can I make a reservation?'* Who writes this crap? The farmer brings out a book, a broken pair of glasses, and his daughter. She touches my hair – I guess to find out if it's real or not.

The neighbours quickly crowd into the hovel – filling every square inch – and the farmer offers me a sickly mixture of hot water in a grossly dirty jamjar. Then some cooked eggs – which I refuse. He can ill afford to waste eggs on a stranger. An argument breaks out between him and his wife. I throw in some shortcake from my saddlebags, and before the man can claim me as his long-lost grandson, I decide to retreat. I give the farmer my phrasebook – won't do me much good anyhow – he'll get many years of amusement out of it . . .

I reach Yixing in the late afternoon, and cause a sensation down the main street as I try to find the hotel. Crowds as deep as twenty congregate if I stop. I find the guesthouse, park the bike, and venture back out to buy some supplies. A curious commerce is in progress down the main street – sales of farming tools, sunglasses, zips, pigs' feet and noodles. Down a side-alley I stray across a comic-book rental stall, with the clientele stretched the length of the alley. The tiny comic-books are either out of print or too expensive, so customers are obliged to sit and read them on the spot. There is, however, barely a child among the readers – they're all farmers. Some of the stories are picture-by-picture versions of folk-tales; others are war-comics; others feature heroic deeds of the Communists, and some are adapted from cinematic stories. In an age where the bookstores stocked little else but the complete works of Mao, Marx, Lenin and Engels, who could blame the people for turning to comic-books for some imaginative action?

I buy some oranges at one stall, and turn to face a solid wall of perhaps 200 people, all silently gazing at me. This Pied Piper treatment upsets me so much that I am forced to run for the cover of the hotel-room.

The next day, cinema-sized staring-squads trail my every step down the main street. By lunchtime I've had enough, and shoot off on the bike – to the nearby village of Dingshu, famed for its teapots. I arrive at what must be *xiuxi*-time (constitutional siesta) – hardly a soul in sight, probably all dozing away in dormitories. Camp-beds are routinely provided at the workplace for this siesta. Out of a factory comes a man who speaks fairly good English; he escorts me back through the factory to the lab, where he brews up some tea. He then opens up a small kiln, which reveals not a scientific experiment in progress, but his lunch – being heated at 200 degrees. This he shares with me. Then he takes me on a tour of the idle pottery factory, and out to the canalside markets of Dingshu.

Dingshu is one of those delightful towns in China where the entire population is engaged in specialised production. Here it is pottery – of all shapes and sizes. Past the markets, there is a scene that could easily have come straight out of a 16th century painting: huge ceramic jars are being loaded onto barges, to be transported elsewhere. They are undoubtedly storage jars for oil or grain. The eye drifts, searching for more details. There are stacks of jars on a wharf; there is housing that is constructed from the base up from the same kind of jars, and from broken pottery shards. The rooftops are composed of bright orange or deep green glazed tiling – the kind that is seen on imperial buildings such as the Forbidden City in Peking. In the streets there are glazed ceramic garbage-bins in the fanciful shapes of frogs, lions or elephants. These I have seen in other parts of China, particularly in parks – so now I know where they come from. And there are ceramic tables, ceramic stools, ceramic teapots and cups that I recognise from my travels.

Dingshu is the Middle Kingdom that one imagines one might

see – traditional China. The great irony of tourism in China is that the Chinese guides fall over backwards trying to show off the achievements of the Party. They herd tired geriatric group-tourers through new soap factories, oil-refineries, steelworks, or fish-freezing factories. The tourists are not the least bit interested in such fare – they haven't come halfway across the globe for that. They are interested in the old, pre-Communist China – the ingenious handicrafts, the boatmen sculling along the Grand Canal, the Great Wall, the birthplace of Confucius, the old Buddhist temples – the very things that Mao Zedong tried to erase from living memory. Thus, all over China, to please the tourists, battalions of repairmen are rebuilding temples that have been demolished during the Cultural Revolution; craftsmen who can remember the ancient methods of hewing stone or wood have been conscripted. And the ceramic spare parts for the temples – the fancy glazed tiling for walls or roofing – come from Dingshu. I had seen, in a showroom, an entire Dragon Screen. This intricate fresco, done in multi-coloured ceramic sections, was the size of a small wall – it featured a full-length dragon, clutching wish-fulfilling gems. Such a piece would be placed near the entrance of a temple to scare off evil spirits.

Dingshu has made very few concessions to the upheavals of the Maoist era, mostly because its craft already had industrial applications, and was therefore in no particular need of revision. Building materials have been produced here for thousands of years – and now include sanitation systems and roof-tiling. For domestic use there are lampshades, flowerpots, and crockery.

On my way out of town I stop at a retail outlet. This shop has the most surprising collection of teapots: they are made of the dullish brown stoneware that is produced in Dingshu. It is unglazed – the tea itself will eventually give the inside of the pot a silky finish. There are ingenious designs – squarish teapots; gourd-shaped teapots; teapots with dragon or bamboo motifs embossed on them; there is even a teapot that is entirely sealed over – it has no lid. I immediately claim this bizarre masterpiece – at a ridiculously low price – and load up with some other small pots.

Enthused from a great day in Dingshu, I moseyed back to Yixing, looking forward to a hot bath in the tourist and cadre hotel. Down the hallway a hotel worker was busy spraying the walls with insecticide. Rooms aren't locked at Yixing Guesthouse. I turned the door-handle – still gasping from the insecticide fumes – saw four people in the room, and closed the door again, thinking it was the wrong room. It was the right room – full of the wrong people. Two were from the Public Security Bureau, one was a CITS man, and the fourth was the hotel manager. Unfortunately, the CITS man had a good command of English. In his capacity as guide for China International Travel Service (the official organisation for parting tourists from their foreign currencies), he had developed some fine-tuning for the nuances of the language. Nothing escaped him. I offered my guests a cup of tea from a thermos – they barked an instant refusal, in unison.

Formalities over, Public Security swung into full stride with interrogation – a fixed, bitchy face on the woman who directed it. As angelic as I could make myself out, it got me nowhere. They weren't so much concerned about the cycling – though this, they claimed, was much too dangerous for a foreigner. What riled them up was the visit to the farmer's hovel. Bicycle breakdown, I explained – the wheel was wonky. *'You left the highway – someone telephoned us'* – the phrase was repeated over and over again. They asked to see my receipt for the bicycle, my Alien Travel Permit, and my passport.

It took them a while to nail me with a technicality. To pass the time, I unwrapped the teapots I'd bought in Dingshu, thinking this might add weight to my claim to being an innocent tourist. I absent-mindedly poured hot water from one teapot to another, to check the spouts. Perhaps I could still talk them into a round of tea.

'You haven't got a bicycle licence,' said the CITS man, after some deliberation.

'Don't need one,' I told him bluntly. 'It's the same as ration-coupons – I don't need those either.'

'Your Alien Travel Permit isn't valid for travel by road,' said the Public Security woman. 'Car' had been struck off the permit.

She was right – it probably wasn't valid for travel by road. Public Security routinely crossed off 'Car' and 'Ship' on permits. The tourist was expected to travel by the modes of Train or Plane. But how was I supposed to have gotten to Yixing, which was on my permit, if there was no train? By taxi, of course, came the reply. By this stage we'd established that 'Car' was the same as 'bicycle', meaning 'road', but not the same as 'taxi' – and I'd given up on the logic of the situation. They were trying to tell me that a taxi was not a 'car', whereas a bicycle was.

My first concern was that they would impound the bike, which was worth 150 yuan, or try to keep my passport. But no, it seemed they had other plans. They wanted two things – to post me back to Wuxi, where the 'mistake' had been made, and a written guarantee that I would not do the same thing again. Fortunately they did not find out I had started cycling in Shanghai. The 'mistake' would cost 90 yuan – the fee to transport myself and the bike for 25-odd miles in a minibus back to Wuxi. I knew that the minibus rate couldn't have been more than 30 yuan for the trip to Wuxi: when I presented this fact, the driver said I had to pay for the minibus to return back to Yixing. I managed to bargain the original fee to a still-hefty 50 yuan, and immediately shoved the figure on my 'confession'. The PSB officer screamed that I shouldn't have done that.

'You will be met by Wuxi *Gonganjiu*,' I was gravely informed.

The CITS man would accompany me in the minibus to Wuxi.

There was no reception committee in Wuxi, as it turned out, and I demanded that the CITS man – a little more cowardly now that PSB was out of the picture – purchase me a train-ticket to Changzhou immediately. I wanted to put some distance between myself and the jurisdiction of Yixing PSB and Wuxi PSB. Within half an hour, the bike was stashed in a baggage-car, and I was demonstrating zips, velcro, runners and webbing to the assembled curious crammed in the aisle of a rail-car.

At Changzhou, a short way up the line, I got off the train, rescued the bike, and headed off for the hotel. I was free to roam again – and it had at least been determined with Yixing PSB and the CITS man that within open city-limits I was legal. So I could carry on hopping from open city to open city by train, and have the convenience of my own transport within a city.

At Changzhou Hotel, I had been in my room for barely an hour when there was a knock at the door. Two older gentlemen introduced themselves as being from CITS – they wanted to give me a map and show me around. They looked like twins – both short, both wearing the same thick glasses and Mao-suits, and sporting identical haircuts. They quickly brought up the subject of bicycling.

'Is that your own bicycle that you arrived with?' asked one.

'Yes it is,' I said, with a vague premonition of what was to come.

'We will advise you not to bicycle in this city,' said the official curtly.

'For what reason?'

'It is too much danger for the foreigner. There will be the accidents.'

'We'll see about that,' I mumbled.

Damn and blast them! I had reached the end of my tether with officialdom. I picked up the teapots I'd bought in Dingshu, still in boxes, and asked the CITS twins where the post-office was. They gave directions. I put the boxes in my daypack.

Suddenly I stood up, took the daypack, and marched out of the room – headed for my bicycle. Once out of the room, I broke into a run. The CITS men, hot on my tail, did likewise. I got to my bike, unlocked it, mounted, and shot off through the gates of the hotel at top speed. The chase was on – I ripped through the traffic, skirted round cyclists and pedestrians, accelerated down the middle of the road, avoided a car, turned a sharp corner, pitched to the right to avoid a bus, overtook another slew of cyclists, rounded another corner, and crunched to a halt in front of a squat green building – the post-office.

'G'day! How's it going?' Pulling up at the same time was another foreigner on a bicycle. The first foreigner I'd seen all week. Solidarity! The CITS twins arrived, both huffing and puffing, both red-faced – and furious – to find myself and Andrew on the foot-path. Andrew spoke Chinese, and had just started teaching English in Changzhou. He was living proof that foreigners were indeed allowed to cycle in Changzhou. The CITS men had been bluffing. Changzhou was a small city – the CITS men obviously knew Andrew, the Australian. Andrew spoke a few words of Chinese to them, and they quickly retreated.

I was greatly relieved to see another foreigner – it wore me down to face these officials alone. Parked over a pot of tea in a decrepit teahouse, I related the story of my 'capture' to Andrew. 'Dead set!' he would interject, 'No shit! Are they for real or what? Struth!' He defused the whole situation with his broad Australian accent.

Andrew had been thinking along the lines of doing an inter-city bike-trip himself, but he would have to shelve the idea until he finished working in Changzhou. If he got into trouble, his job could easily be terminated. He wanted to stay longer to polish up his Mandarin. Even though he was the only resident foreigner in town, he complained he couldn't practice his Mandarin as much as he wanted to. He could not become fast friends with the local Chinese as they feared being hauled over the coals for making contact. He could not go and visit anybody at home. Students could not visit him in his hotel – not even in the dining-room. And he had been told not to read the daily newspapers in Changzhou. The vendors, in addition, had been told not to sell him newspapers, so the only way he could get these precious bits of parchment was by buying vegetables in the markets. The vegetables were wrapped in week-old, top-secret Changzhou newspapers. For a moment I conjured up an image of Andrew buying some tomatoes – then taking them home, throwing them away, and saving the newspaper.

My confidence was restored in Changzhou – I had lost round one to PSB in Yixing, but won the second round over Changzhou CITS. It would take more than pieces of paper to dampen my zest for the highway. But I had a guidebook to write, so I couldn't afford to be thrown out of China. I got Andrew to help me with the process of booking the bike on a train out of Changzhou – a complicated rigmarole of labelling. Once mastered, this procedure enabled me to hop from city to city and have the bike for (legal) use within city-limits. There was no guarantee that the bike would arrive at the same time as myself on a train – so it had to be sent a few days ahead to the next destination. In its own way, all this tedious paperwork negated the freedom value of having the bike.

Although I indulged in several more 'test-runs' between cities, my heart was not in it anymore – the initial impetus had vanished. I didn't wish to face Public Security alone. I did a final cycle-trip from Tianjin to Peking – a distance of 80 miles in a single day. Although I used the bike extensively around Peking during my stay there, I had no intention of shunting it any further around China. As the end of my stay in Peking drew nearer, I asked a hotel staffer where I might sell the bike. He bought it off me on the spot.

It was in Peking that I met a young German named Helgard who had some similar experiences to share. She had done extensive touring around the globe, and thought she'd have a crack at China. She had brought her own 10-speed bicycle into China – she just declared it the same way as one would a camera. She'd put the bike on trains and boats to get as far as Wuhu, in Anhui Province; there, she decided to try her luck at cycling, with a first destination of Maanshan, which was about 35 miles away. Unfortunately she got caught in a heavy downpour, and took shelter in a nearby factory, where she was treated like the Fairy Princess. But princesses are not supposed to cycle, and Public Security descended on the scene, along with a CITS translator. They took her by taxi to the nearest town with a train-station (the CITS man rode the bicycle through the rain!). At the station they presented her with an outlandish taxi-bill, which she was obliged to pay if she wanted to get herself out of a tight spot. She also had to write a confession, saying she wouldn't do such a silly thing again.

It all sounded very familiar – PSB and CITS working in tandem, the rip-off transport bills, the confession. But PSB had not thrown me – or her – out of China for cycling between cities. There *had* to be a way round this rigmarole, and I was determined to find it.

I am turning these things over, on a northbound train from Peking. The countryside is whipping by. I am reminded of the poetic old Chinese adage that what the tourist sees is 'looking at flowers from horseback'. The surface meaning is that the tourist doesn't see things as they really are – just gets fleeting impressions. If you stopped the scenery long enough, maybe things would come out much better – or much worse. But in any case, to see things clearly, you have to go more slowly. Go slowly, and carry your own food – and then you are *really* travelling; then you will see something.

The days of 'flowers from horseback' are over in the main cities that China has opened up – the warts and pimples are there for the ordinary traveller to see. But in the countryside and backwaters, glossed over by the expanses of train-glass, travellers haven't even started. Only a fraction of China's population lives in the cities – the rural areas are the more interesting parts to visit. Yet only a handful of rural areas are open, because the countryside is poor. To see the rural areas close-up – with the smells and sounds – I need my own transport. I have to tether the 'horse', and look around; the challenge is to get further than I've got.

CYCLING TO
XIAN

SEPTEMBER, 1984: Tibet opens to individual travellers, astonishing all the skeptics, including myself. The Chinese have obviously decided they can pay their army upkeep bills in Tibet from tourism. I rush off a long letter to Robert Strauss: we have stayed in touch over the years since meeting in Peking. In the past Tibet has been impossible to get into, except for the well-heeled – an incredible opportunity now presents itself. Robert agrees to meet in Hong Kong early in 1985; he also agrees to come along on a bicycle trip from Shanghai to Nanjing.

My initial bike-trip was not, as far as I was concerned, a failure. Rather, it was a reconnaissance for another trip – a longer one. I'd learnt a lot: if you bought a Chinese bike, you were legal in the cities; if you biked 30 miles out of a city, the matter was up to the PSB Foreign Affairs Section – the regular police would not interfere, and neither would the army. Most surprising of all, the roads were in good shape, and were flat – at least around Shanghai – so having a gearless, heavy Chinese bike was really no problem. A western bike presented a spare parts problem, and it would attract too much attention. Chinese bikes were sturdy: Wang Dakang, a farmer from Sichuan, had notched up 44,000 kilometres on a four-year cycle-trip around China – equivalent to a complete circuit of the globe.

The greatest obstacle to a longer trip by Chinese bike was not physical but bureaucratic. You could virtually be anywhere during the day, but you had to be in a open city by nightfall to be safe from officialdom. In such densely-populated regions, there were no hiding-spots for camping out. A longer trip required a route with strings of open cities, and flat enough terrain for a gearless Chinese bike. The Yangtse Basin open towns from Shanghai to Nanjing were spaced 35, 45, 55 miles apart – within day-trip range. That route could be done in four straight days of cycling – but I wanted something meatier. *Strings of open towns; flat terrain.* I consulted a 1984 listing of places open to foreigners; I dug up a relief map – splotched with purple on the Tibetan Plateau, and a calmer green around the flattest part – the North China Plain, positioned between Peking and Shanghai.

Shanghai to Nanjing, and then ...the logical extension was to head for Peking – but there were vast gaps in the middle with no open cities. My eye drifted to other parts of the map – to Sichuan Province (fascinating, but too mountainous, too many mosquitoes); to Mongolia (rough weather, no shelter, problems with PSB). Again I came back to the Yangtse Basin. Shanghai had always been my lucky starting point. If I started in Shanghai, travelled north to Nanjing and then, well, cut across China... I traced a line across the map ...to ...Xian. Xian! The forgotten cornerstone of China travel – well-connected as a destination, yet remote enough to make the journey interesting. Best of all, Xian was a staging point for going overland to Tibet.

It all looked vaguely possible. I checked a rail-distance chart. Shanghai to Xian: 1511 kilometres – or 945 miles. By road it would be maybe 150 miles more. The relief map looked flat from Shanghai to Kaifeng, with some hilly sections after that. Between Shanghai and Nanjing there was a string of four open cities, but from Nanjing to Kaifeng, a distance of around 400 miles, there was only one open city – Bengbu. From Kaifeng to the west was another 'ridable' string — Kaifeng - Zhengzhou - Gongxian - Luoyang - Sanmenxia; followed by a large gap to Xian. In sum, this meant that half the route required camping out – not a pleasant prospect. Travelling light – no sleeping-bag or tent – would still work if the weather held, but could the authorities be dodged for a thousand miles?

Possible, impossible – here was a challenge – cycling to Xian. The idea was gathering momentum – I could see that long ribbon of road ahead... the opportunity to pedal through the countryside, the chance to get right off the track – these were the drawcards. The next step was to get Robert to agree to this 'excursion'.

Had such a trip been accomplished by a foreigner before? As I delved into who had actually cycled across China, I found, to my amazement, that I was a century too late for 'firsts'.

From 1890 to 1893 two American students cycled around the world by way of Europe, Asia and America. The pair, Thomas Allen and William Sachtleben, clocked up 15,000 miles on their travels, and published a book on the Asian section of the trip, titled *Across Asia on a Bicycle* (1894). I tracked the book down. At the front was a photograph of them in China. They carried very little – sleeping-rolls, an American flag, and a banner proclaiming details of their trip in Chinese characters. They rode one-speed Humber safety bicycles: these used the revolutionary chain-and-sprocket gearing to the rear wheel – standard on today's bikes, but an innovative design in the 1880s. And they used air-filled tyres, which made for superior suspension – the pneumatic tyre was patented by John Boyd Dunlop in 1887. For the skeptical, Allen and Sachtleben carried cameras – and brought back 2500 photos.

Against the advice of every official from New York to Teheran, they succeeded in wheeling 6600 miles across Central Asia. The route took them from Constantinople through Teheran, Samarkand, Tashkent, and across the Gobi Desert – via Urumqi, Xian, and Taiyuan – to Peking. From Tianjin they took a boat to Shanghai, and thence to Japan. They spent about four months crossing the Chinese Empire – covering a distance of 3100 miles. Their greatest problem was money – not the lack of it, but the *weight* of it. Since there were no banks in the interior of China, they had to carry silver to cover purchases – the silver was chopped up and concealed in the bicycle-tubing. They were not so lucky in concealing the bicycles themselves. Word would travel ahead quickly about these machines; chaotic crowds would gather at their approach – the American cyclists were forced to stage exhibitions of their riding skills to placate the curious.

Various nicknames were given to the new machine: some called it a 'two-wheeled cart'; others described it as a 'foreign horse' – and one peasant said it was a 'little mule that you drive by the ears, and kick in the sides to make him go.' In case of hostile attack, both cyclists carried revolvers. These were not used, although both men were involved in hand-to-hand combat with innkeepers over exorbitant prices – not greatly different from the situation of the budget-traveller in China today. But in general they were treated well for foreigners:

> To the good-will of the mandarins, as well as the people, an indispensible concomitant of a journey through China, our bicycles were after all our best passport. They everywhere overcame the antipathy for the foreigner, and made us cordially welcome.

They were the first westerners to cover this route since Marco Polo. They fired up my imagination: if they could get away with such an extensive trip – on bicycles of primitive design – through areas without roads – then *anything* was possible.

⋆   ⋆   ⋆

I BROKE THE NEWS to Robert on the plane from Canton to Shanghai, in April.

'We're going on a longer bike-trip than I told you,' I sputtered.

'How much longer?'

'Well, I was thinking Shanghai to Nanjing, and then... '

'And then?'

'To Xian,' I blurted out.

Robert sat bolt upright.

'Are you nuts?! I can't do that. It's been five years since I set foot on a bicycle.'

'Look, you don't have to be an athlete – you'll get all the training you need on the road –'

'But it's halfway across China – it's crazy!'

'That's exactly why we have to do it,' I reassured him.

'It's madness! If we get caught on those bikes, we could ruin our chances of getting into Tibet. They'll boot us out of the country. Where would we sleep, anyway?'

'Most of time we can get to open cities,' I lied. 'I'll show you on the map later.'

Robert was silent for about ten minutes. Then he turned round and said: 'Okay, I'll give it a try – but I'm not cycling in Tibet.'

Robert was silent for another ten minutes.

'How much is all this going to cost?' he asked.

'Not much – zero in transport costs, for starters.'

'I'm right down to my last pound you know. The flight into Hong Kong cost a packet. Leaves me bugger all for the road to Lhasa.'

'I can lend you some money.'

Robert was little changed from our previous meeting in Peking three years before. He'd shaved his beard off – replaced it with a moustache – but his head was full of wild plans, projects and assignments as usual. He was always searching for new directions, new challenges. He could easily have sat back on his master's degree in oriental languages, with his wife and three kids, and become a staid academic – but he'd thrown all that security away, and he was on an airplane bound for Shanghai instead. This is where he wanted to be – he loved travelling. Teaching had provided his meagre income – along with some freelance editing and translating. He'd packed in his teaching job in Portugal for this trip.

In a way, I felt guilty about the whole thing – but he was not terribly concerned. He thrived on taking risks, thrived on being down to his last pound – and not a job prospect in sight. Robert, although in his early 30s, was still on the loose, refusing to settle into the role that everybody expected of him. Over the last few years, when we frequently corresponded, he had shifted numerous times – Germany, England, Portugal. His life revolved around interminable financial problems – no sooner had he landed a job than he decided to move again. He studiously avoided the subject of wife and three kids, which had caused at least one of the moves, and a lot of the money-worries. His wife was obviously not prepared to accept his nomadic nature. Robert was a stubborn bastard. Once he made his mind up to do something, the rest of the world could go to hell.

Pujiang Hotel, Shanghai, April 15th, 8 a.m. A woman with black rubber boots, thick gloves and a mop waded into the men's dormitory bathroom to do battle with the porcelain and plumbing. The traveller from Manchester in the next bed smirked, and mumbled something about 'Vesuvius' erupting again – Vesuvius being the toilet. The plumbing in Shanghai, at least, had not changed – not since the 1920s, when the Pujiang was Astor House, a classy hotel. Perhaps the original plumbing was reaching its fatigue point, and was rusted out. Still, we could count ourselves lucky to have some plumbing at our disposal – older parts of the city didn't have any at all.

There were lots of surprises in store in 1985 Shanghai – largely in lifestyles. All the things western that were banned during the Cultural Revolution were now the latest status symbols – western perms, make-up, stockings, jewellery, tight blue jeans, high-heels, boots, short skirts. Who would've thought that the best way to blend in would be to wear a three-piece suit? These were all the rage, encouraged by Deng Xiaoping himself – something to do with conducting business with the Japanese. The Mao-suit had been mothballed, at least in Shanghai – it was only worn by the elderly. Uniforms were in – there were smart pantsuits with piping issued to hotel-staff and airline hostesses. Even army uniforms sported sharp new trimmings to denote rank. Communist China's first-ever beauty parlours were to be found along Nanjing Road, and the long-awaited Japanese electronic goods were sold freely in shops. In the early evening, teenagers in boots and blue jeans congregated in loud discos down Nanjing Road. The discos were playing all the music forbidden a few years ago – from Hong Kong and Taiwan. We, as foreigners, were not allowed into the discos – a curious role-reversal. And a come-back: it was rumoured that a few prostitutes once again walked the streets of Shanghai.

Gone was the consumer desire for cassette players, watches, bicycles, and sewing machines; now the big four were colour TVs, electric fans, washing machines and refrigerators. These were the prestigious dowry items, so the cost of weddings had risen to astronomical heights. Even bicycles no longer had top private transport status: people had their eyes on motorised bicycles, on motorbikes, and on trucks that could be purchased by collectives. An attempt to ban chopsticks (health hazard) and replace them with knives and forks didn't get off the ground, but free enterprise was off and running – encouraged by the State. 'To get rich is glorious' was the new motto; prosperity was the catchword. Factory workers, too, got incentives for working harder.

A new campaign was under way – nation-wide – against rats. It was estimated there were four billion rats in China, so mathematically speaking it was each citizen's duty to catch and kill four rats. Although not related to the anti-rat campaign, Deng Xiaoping's revival of an ancient Chinese proverb was the theme of the times: 'It doesn't matter whether a cat is black or white as long as it catches mice.' It was hard to believe this was the same China, such were the changes in lifestyles, attitudes and individualism.

A mammoth new Friendship Store was under construction on the Bund; on the opposite side of the river, a huge glass and concrete high-rise, the Seagull Hotel, challenged Shanghai's traditional skyline for the first time since the 1930s. In a back-alley, I noticed a gasoline station – with proper pumps and attendants – the first such station I'd seen in China. Usually the gasoline came from an unmarked window through a thick black hose.

The blackmarket had reached Shanghai, too; still, it must have been quite new. I found out from another traveller in the Pujiang dormitory where to change money. He recommended strolling slowly along Nanjing Road near the Peace Hotel. There, indeed, the blackmarket found us in the form of a very nervous woman who agreed to give us 340 renminbi for 200 FECs – a markup of 70 percent. She took us into a shop further up Nanjing Road and thrust a dirty rag into my hand. Was this a joke of some sort? No – inside the rag was a wad of money. I handed it to Robert. 'Count the RMB,' I said. 'I'll get the FECs ready.' The money-changer had disappeared. Where was she? Probably having a nervous breakdown – 340 yuan was a fortune for a local Chinese.

As we counted money, we tried to look interested in a hair-dryer in the shop. A counter assistant kept indicating to us that what we had in our hands was more than enough for the hair-dryer – he'd take either currency.

'140, 150, 160 – no, wait a minute, that was 170 – blast! I'll have to start all over again...' Robert, never very good at arithmetic, counted the money four times. We had now vaguely shifted our attention to a Japanese cassette player; the counter assistant again indicated we had more than enough money for the purchase. This was one of those products that had been advertised on billboards four years ago – and was now finally available to the Chinese over the counter.

'It's all here,' said Robert, finally. We walked out of the shop. The woman joined us out of a doorway. I gave her the rag back as we walked along. It had the 200 yuan in FECs, all crisp 10-yuan bills...

The main task in Shanghai was to get our bearings rapidly, and get out of there. The bikes were easy to purchase – the Friendship Store was now selling them without any strings attached. This was because there was far less rationing of products – the reins on free enterprise had been loosened. Grain and cotton, along with a dozen other items, were no longer rationed. Eggs, charcoal briquettes, and certain élite brands of cigarettes still required ration-coupons. Ordinary brands of bicycle were apparently easy to get; bicycles made in Shanghai – the Phoenix and Forever brands – were still rationed, but available to those with FECs.

Down at the Friendship Store we each selected a *Yongjiu*

(Forever). I purchased a few extra inner tubes. Those were the only spares we would carry – we were depending on the fact that we could find spare parts for a Chinese bike along the way. Otherwise, I had a few tools, a clip-on water-bottle, and back-panniers which fitted the rear *Yongjiu* rack. Robert didn't have the benefit of the panniers, which slung the load lower over the back wheel. He simply strapped his backpack to the rear rack.

With Shanghai Public Security Bureau we drew a blank. We knew that there was a list of recently-opened places. The list of open places had grown to over 200 – which was double the number open in 1981. Half of these places were now open without special permission: the 'big red door' had swung open much further – and faster – than the wildest predictions. It was imperative that we find out where the newly-opened places were – some might lie along our route, and thus save us the uncomfortable prospect of camping out. Shanghai PSB wouldn't even issue us with an Alien Travel Permit – they told us that Changzhou and Zhenjiang – along the route to Nanjing – were now open without permit. We had until Nanjing to find out what was open for the next long leg toward Kaifeng.

'Deng Xiaoping – here we come!' With this battle-cry we sallied forth out of Shanghai on a crisp spring morning. April 17th: exactly two days spent in Shanghai – a good turn-around period. The sun was rising like a red ball; we ploughed through dense traffic. At a roundabout, a cyclist clipped my back wheel – he went sprawling, and so did the load of noodles in his panniers. Off to a flying start. We helped the man to his feet. The noodles, however, were not so easy to retrieve...

We cruised straight along Beijing Road through downtown Shanghai, turned right on Jiangning Road, past the Jade Buddha Temple, over Suzhou Creek, met the rail-line, followed that. Breakfast consisted of chocolate bars. The bizarre nature of the whole venture hit home – two grown men, with very little mechanical know-how, setting off on bicycles across China. I had to laugh – out loud – this whole thing was out of control. It was totally irresponsible. I felt like years had been unlocked from me. I felt like a kid who'd just raided a fruit-orchard.

Ten miles of dirt road and dust: there were extraordinary changes on this highway since 1983. Building was going on at a furious pace; there was a large increase in motorised traffic. I was almost deaf in the left ear due to the truck-horns. Road-widening was in progress everywhere – hence the dirt road. And there was much more free-marketing in evidence. A woman with a pig in her bicycle basket crashed into the side of a bridge upon seeing Robert. We overtook a farmer with bamboo crates hanging off his bike, full of chickens, and later another with sheep heads (live) sticking out of baskets.

A skein of polluted canals took us into Suzhou by mid-afternoon. I arrived in Suzhou with a sore bum, a runny nose, and face burnt to a crisp. My hair and fingernails were clogged with dust and grit. At Suzhou Hotel, all the glass in the building was being changed over to tinted glass – a lunatic project that left rooms on the ground floors wide open to the elements. There were large panes of glass missing in the dining-hall, too. The restaurant staff paraded around in new uniforms – red piping, white jackets and red bowties. I collapsed on contact with mattress at the hotel in Suzhou. The mattress had, as I recall, the shape of a dead camel.

★　　★　　★

CHANGZHOU, APRIL TWENTIETH. Today it's raining – rather fortunate to be under cover. We're in the meeting-room – a disused video-game in one corner, a huge table with green velvet-covered chairs, a thermos of hot water, two more armchairs, a green telephone, some scroll paintings on the wall, two dim fluorescent lights, a couple of thin towels, and two camp-beds with quilted green covers on them. There's a TV in another corner of the room – considered so precious that it is clad in an embroidered green velvet cover.

The hotel – the same one I stayed at two years ago – turned out to be full on arrival. After twelve hours on the road from Suzhou, we were in no mood to go across town to the other hotel – and the staff, sensing that we would not turn back, threw us into the meeting-room. Which, as it turns out, is ideally suited for the purposes of planning and calculation.

Changzhou is my stumbling-block – the real trip, for me, begins here. This is as far as I got two years ago, when Yixing Public Security aborted the ride. So far, so good – we haven't been caught by rain or officialdom on the open highway. It has taken me two years to get this far – the first 125 miles. The bikes, resting outside, look like they're a hundred years old already – spattered in mud, caked in dust.

Spread out on the table at Changzhou Hotel meeting-room are five maps of various sizes – parts of the puzzle we must solve to get to Xian. I've just poured some piping hot water into a cup with a small brick of medicinal tea, for my heavy cold. It is difficult to stitch the Xian route together: two provincial maps give us a good idea of the roads and intermediary points in Jiangsu and Anhui Provinces, but no indication of surface-quality. One Chinese map vaguely shows elevations, which is useful for trying to design a route that avoids hills. From Nanjing we are going in blind – neither of us has visited the provinces of Anhui or Henan. We can console ourselves with the fact that we at least have some maps with thick red lines – promising roads of some sort. In the fall of 1934, when the retreating Red Army started off on its devastating Long March through south-west China, one of the biggest problems was trying to figure out where they were: there were no roads at the time, and their route meandered through atrocious swamps and mountain-terrain.

Robert is attempting to read distances off the maps at hand with a toothpick and a piece of string, measured against the scale given with the maps. From Nanjing to Bengbu, he gasps, it is two whole toothpicks, and there's nothing open between. That means one night out, and if we're caught in the rain? What if it's a dirt road with potholes, and we can only do 50 miles a day? That might mean two nights out – or worse. We still don't have the vital information on which new places are open. Two whole toothpicks to Bengbu – 125 miles – and then from Bengbu to Kaifeng is even worse – perhaps 180 miles without a legal place to stop the night. At a pace of around 6 miles per hour on a Chinese bike, Bengbu will take 20 hours of solid cycling from Nanjing; Bengbu-Kaifeng is estimated at 30 hours on the road, or three days of pedal-pumping. It looks daunting and cold on paper – if we can somehow clear the hurdle in the middle, then the way to Xian looks possible.

At Changzhou we follow the Grand Canal out of town. We stop to inspect a few ancient arch-span bridges. There is a long red banner with Chinese characters suspended along one piece of the canal: I become very excited about this. Is it some revolutionary message? Robert studies the characters for a few minutes. The banner says *Caution – Underwater Cable.* Further on, Chinese cyclists are using a two-minute barge-trip to get across the canal. We pause to photograph their progress – since they cannot escape once on the barge, they have become reluctant photographic subjects.

The Grand Canal has been the thread of our trip so far – in fact, the original canal ran all the way to Xian. It linked Luoyang to the old Sui Dynasty capital of Changan (Xian). Sui emperor Yang Di, using a force of over four million labourers, extended the project down to Hangzhou, making it possible for junks to go along the Yangtse, up the canal, and on to ports along the Yellow River. The original destination of the Grand Canal had thus been Xian; in the 13th century, Kublai Khan had remodelled the work of Yang Di and linked the canal to Peking.

Only sections of the original Grand Canal remain navigable; its role as a conduit for the transport of goods has been eclipsed by the railways. At the heavily-polluted sections near Changzhou, the canal does not look like anything out of the ordinary. Long fleets of barges ply the waterways, much the way they must have done in centuries past; in the Tang Dynasty thousands of tons of grain were transported from the grain-rich south to feed the hungry Tang armies in the north. In this era, Xian had reached its height as one of the greatest cities in Asia.

This is a time-worn route: the inaugural pleasure-cruise along the Grand Canal took place around 605 A.D. Emperor Yang Di's fleet, by early accounts, consisted of two thousand junks: the Dragon Junks carried a thousand consorts and wives for the emperor, as well as musicians and entertainers; following them were junks with palace maids, servants and stores; bringing up the rear were ministers and monks, eunuchs and scholars, and generals. In times of no wind or current, the Dragon Junks had to be pulled along the canals; plodding along the banks were thousands of trackers, their shoulders cut and bloodied from the tow-ropes. The emperor, on the leading Dragon Junk, passed his time below decks, drinking wine and most likely experimenting with the tiger and leopard skin furniture as it swayed around gently in the currents.

An early painting shows Yang Di in the company of three women, two of whom are auxiliaries to the main recipient of royal attention. The 'Dragon-Emperor' apparently had uncontrollable attacks of sexual desire, and his entourage had to be ready to accommodate him at any second of the day or night; partly for this reason, some forty palaces were built along the banks of the Grand Canal. Among these was the legendary Maze Palace, which was constructed near present-day Yangzhou. This labyrinth of bronze mirrors, lanterns and wine-fountains was populated entirely by seductive damsels on couches. Sound-effects were provided by groups of naked maiden musicians; the air was lotus-scented. Yang Di tore around the maze clad in a leopard skin. He took special pleasure in altering the edicts of nature; since there were no windows of any kind in the Maze Palace, he could turn one night into ten before emerging to deal with the pressing affairs of state. The affairs of state eventually caught up with him in Yangzhou when he was strangled by a rebel chief.

In the mist, out of Zhenjiang, the figure of a man beating up a tree can be made out. He is practicing his karate chops on a tree-trunk; I can only assume that the tree will win. We stop to observe this rare martial arts exponent, and to get our bearings in the mixture of fog, dust and pollution. It is necessary, at this hour of the morning, to quickly find our way out of the labyrinth of a large city; this accomplished, we can stop to wind up our knees for the long ride ahead. Our first destination is a tiny dot on the map called 'Stone Horse', according to Robert. These place-names are quite poetic – earlier during the trip we passed a place called 'Leaping Cow'. We've also passed a bikeshop called '10,000 Prosperities Bikeshop' – a rather elaborate name for a piece of tarpaulin over the footpath, with bits of flayed inner tube as a signpost.

Further on, stacks of bricks line the road. It is yet another brick-factory. It seems that the road from Shanghai has been lined with bricks – dumped along the shoulders to be picked up by peasants who are allowed to build privately-owned houses on their state-owned land. Deng Xiaoping's audacious agrarian reforms are translated into bricks: Deng replaced the commune-system with a contract system. Rent is paid by delivery of a set quantity of produce, and once that obligation has been met, the family with the land-lease can grow anything they want and sell it on the freemarket. Peasants are allowed to own their draft animals, and can even purchase their own farm-machinery; the land-leases can be extended up to 15 years. These new measures, virtually giving the peasants outright ownership of land, explain the incredible flurry of activity along our route through the countryside – the expansion in building, in transportation, in free-marketing, and in traffic volume. To accommodate the latter change, road-widening is in full stride.

The final stretch to Nanjing is mostly unpaved. The road-wideners must be working on it. It is firm dust and dirt on a side-track following the rail-line to Nanjing – the kind of road that makes the bicycle bell ring all by itself, and that makes your fillings do something similar. The building industry is in full bloom at the roadside but with an inexplicable difference: not so many walking-tractors. Mangy donkeys are carting the loads of stones, cement and bricks. We pass one duo where the load of stones is too heavy for the donkey: the handler is plodding along up front, next to the donkey, with a rope pulling the same load.

The next riders we pass are wearing suits – indicating that we are approaching Nanjing. Soon we join the waves of riders on the boulevards of the city. Cycling along in the traffic are young women in tight faded jeans, western hairstyles, make-up, jewellery, shiny boots – enough to turn a man's head and cause a serious accident.

We ride straight into the courtyard of a cheap hotel, the Victory. Looking at a cracked mirror in the Victory Hotel, I am astonished to see a species of raccoon staring back. The area around my eyes is whitish – protected by glasses – but the rest of my face is plastered with darker dust. The ring of dust around the edge of the eyes gives the raccoon effect.

The first task is to get the laundry in – we dump an evil-smelling load of sweat at the front counter. This accomplished, we saunter up the road to the Jingling Hotel, one of the tallest in China. Outside, local Chinese in suits stand at the gates, noses pressed through the bars, trying to get a glimpse of this wonder of the western world, and of those leaving it or entering it. For three yuan, locals can take a tour of the building. Even though we are wearing grubby pants and shirts, our foreign faces are our 'entry ticket' – the guard at the gate waves us through. I relish the irony of situations like this – in the west, we'd be knocked back for wearing the wrong shoes. We take the elevator to the 36th floor.

On the 36th floor: the Sky Palace, a revolving restaurant and bar, opulent furnishings and decor, waitresses wearing cheongsams split up the thighs. Here we can, in complete luxury, survey the afternoon's last routing into Nanjing. Along Zhongshan Lu, the main artery that took us in, people are crammed into concertina buses; the wide, tree-lined boulevard is packed with traffic; tall western-style buildings make their appearance again – department stores, hotels, offices, institutes, hospitals. In the distance is a brown haze – the haze of industrial pollution. What looks remarkable from this angle is the amount of tree-cover on the streets, and the amount of parkland. Partially this 'greening' of Nanjing has been implemented to alleviate the heat of the summer; and partially to beautify the city after it was overrun by the Japanese in 1937. The Japanese massacred over 150,000 Chinese civilians in Nanjing.

I begin to feel dizzy – not due to the revolving restaurant, nor due to the glass of wine in my hand, but due to the fact that we have gone from a stone-age village, two hours previously, to the space-age wizardry of the Sky Palace. It is a weird sensation – one minute out there with the donkeys, in the dirt, grime and dust of the highway, and next minute with an aerial overview, wine, classical music and waitresses in cheongsams. *This* is culture-shock – going forward in time. Going backward is easy. A small group of local Chinese, oohing and aahing, shuffle through: they have paid for the tour of the Jingling, paid for a glimpse of the future.

Revolving around Nanjing, we celebrate completion of the first leg of the trip. Robert, who was dubious about the whole thing at the outset, is now a confirmed long-distance biker. He has no qualms anymore. Gentlemen! Raise your glasses to Xian! We've had a great run of luck too – no rain, no mechanical failure, no leg failure, nobody stopping us. This calls for another glass of wine, and a few self-timer photographs, during which Robert discovers he has lost his lens-cap. To the great mystification of the waitresses, he spends half an hour upturning every cushion in the place, and moving apart all the sectional furniture. It's hard to replace a 62 mm lens-cap in China. In triumph, he emerges from between two pieces of furniture with the little piece of plastic, and a big grin over his unshaven face. He orders a couple of drinks in Chinese from the waitresses assembled to watch the lens-cap hunt. The waitresses gasp in disbelief: no tourist speaks Chinese like that.

At Nanjing Public Security Bureau, we get no closer to the mystery of the newly-opened cities. We still haven't got a complete list.

'The list is in the big green book,' says the uniformed woman at the desk.

'Which book?' I inquire.

'All the travellers have it – with a green cover.'

'She means your own bloody book,' cackles Robert, sarcastically. Indeed, she is throwing my own book back at me – the guidebook to China. The book has been out on the stands for only five months, and is already hopelessly out of date. The tome is the size of a cereal box – everybody complains about how heavy it is, but everyone has a copy. The brisk sales, unfortunately, don't bring me any money – in fact I have lost money over the venture. We leave the PSB office, none the wiser about open lists, and walk off in search of a noodle-shop.

I brood over the curse of the guidebook hack – getting out of date. Since it takes at least six months to write a guidebook, and at least six months to get it printed and on the bookstore shelves, any guidebook is bound to be at least a year out of date. Everything changes – prices, telephone numbers, museum-hours, bus-numbers – and now the list of open places. These minutiae, which make such a guidebook so useful, will change the fastest, sending unsuspecting backpackers off at a tangent to non-existent hotels, or causing them to argue with hotel-staff for hours over prices that went up a year ago. What kind of wild goose chase am I sending these poor travellers off on? Would it be better to have a map with hit-and-miss destinations, or no map at all? Why is the lazy PSB officer encouraging the outdated lists? Perhaps not all the PSB offices have received the new lists yet... The only valid guide is the one you make up yourself as you go along – the traveller network – word of mouth.

'What are we going to do now?' asks Robert.

'There are 109 new places open – remember that newsclip in Hong Kong?'

'Pity about PSB – next stop is Bengbu.'

'Listen, we *have to* find out what's on that list. I've got an idea.'

'What's that – check your own guidebook?'

'We're going back there tomorrow – to PSB.'

'What on earth for?'

'To ask again.'

'Are you nuts? We'll never get away with that.'

'It's worth a try. They won't recognise us. If we go back at a different time, it could be a different PSB officer.'

'Hmm. Well, I guess we could change clothes.'

'If we pick up the clean clothes from the laundry, we'll look totally different. And Robert – you could comb your hair.'

The following afternoon, we are back at Nanjing PSB. The same woman is at the desk, but she betrays no sign of recognition. We are two more foreigners. They all look the same. We are dressed in clean clothes, and have neatly-combed hair. Our luck turns. Robert tells the PSB officer that we wish to go on an extensive tour of Anhui Province – what is open? She goes into another office, comes back with a complete list for Anhui. Five places, including Bengbu, no longer need travel permits. Open with permit are: Huaibei, Tongling, Chuxian, Chaoxian, Xiuning, Shexian, Fengyang and Jingxian. I've never heard of these – so they have to come from the brand-new listing. Excitedly, I extract a map from my daypack. We check the characters on the map. Three of them lie on our route! These are Chuxian, Fengyang, and Huaibei.

Robert casually inquires about an extensive tour of Henan, the province to the west of Anhui. The PSB officer goes back to the inner office; there is a lot of shouting. Her superior doesn't like the idea. Nevertheless, she comes back with a list for Henan. There are two new openings – neither place lies along our route. All the same, we will need permit-additions for Gongxian and Sanmenxia in Henan Province.

For Shaanxi Province, the inner office explodes – we will get no more information. Robert writes out his list:

Chuxian, Fengyang, Huaibei, in Anhui Province;

Gongxian, Sanmenxia, in Henan Province

This list is accepted: we are issued with Alien Travel Permits, dated April 23rd – stamped, sealed and official. Clutching these pieces of cardboard as if our lives depend on them, we thank the PSB officer profusely, bow, shake hands, bow again, say goodbye, and depart. It is hard to describe how much childish joy can be derived from overcoming officialdom – we feel extremely lucky.

The map has altered now. Nanjing to Bengbu is plain sailing, with two open places – Chuxian and Fengyang – to see us through. There are now two long stretches left – Bengbu-Kaifeng, and Sanmenxia-Xian. It is unlikely anything will surface to break up those stretches, but we can keep trying. Robert learned from a truckdriver on a previous trip to China that a new guesthouse was in progress in the village at the foot of Huashan, a holy mountain to the east of Xian. If there is a new guesthouse, perhaps officials are preparing the place for an opening to foreign tourism. Huashan lies midway along the path between Sanmenxia and Xian. We'll have to keep trying for a permit.

There is no need to scout out an exit for Nanjing. We have to cross the Yangtse, and there is only one point to do that – the Yangtse River Bridge. Until 1957, there were no bridges at all across the Yangtse; now there are seven bridges at various points. The one at Nanjing was started under the supervision of the Russians; in 1960 they withdrew their expertise – and their blueprints – due to a falling-out with the Chinese. The Chinese plodded on with the project, completing the bridge by 1968. It is a major feat of engineering, since the Yangtse runs a mile wide at this point, with a shifting bed and fast currents. The bridge has nine piers that support a double-decker structure: four miles of railway-track on the lower level, and almost three miles of highway – including the approaches – on the top. It is high enough to allow 10,000-ton vessels to pass underneath.

We get to the bridge early in the morning, when the traffic is lighter. Coming the other way are farmers cycling to market – loaded up with record-breaking numbers of geese and chickens. The bridge itself must break half a dozen records – it is so lengthy that after a while you forget it is a bridge. Toward the centre, we dismount to inspect some statuary attached to a pylon, depicting workers, peasants and soldiers – the heroes of Mao's China. It was not far from here that the million-strong Red Army stormed the Yangtse to capture Nanjing from the Kuomintang in 1949. Thus the bridge is a symbol of heroic nationalism – and as the final link in the Peking-Shanghai rail-line, it is of supreme strategic importance. As if to underline the latter fact, a sentry with a fixed bayonet wanders over to check us out.

Across the other side of the bridge I am on new ground – from here on, as far as Xian, is virgin territory. This spurs me on, and with a slight tailwind, I'm rolling over hills, rocketing down the other side looking for potholes. For breakfast: bread and chocolate. The scenery has changed with the watershed of the Yangtse. Now there are flooded fields, hilly wooded areas, dried stubbly areas, better roads, less dust, less pollution, more water-buffalo. We pass an impromptu buffalo-market at the side of the road, and cause a sensation as we dismount to get in closer. The buffalo and their handlers all come over to scrutinise us – and fearing that the buffalo will trample our bikes, we make a hasty exit.

On the way to Chuxian, we approach a farmer walking along the road with a peculiar fishing contraption. He has a couple of long bamboo poles, fitted with a net, which he dips into roadside pools in a rapid butterfly-like manoeuvre. Strapped to his wrist is a wicker basket to hold the catch. God knows what kind of fish could live in the inky pools. Intrigued, we abandon the bikes, and creep up on the farmer to set about photographing this phenomenon. The pond-fisherman, startled, shouts in Chinese not to take photographs.

'I've never seen this before,' Robert tells the man, in an attempt to justify his picture-taking.

'What is there to see?' retorts the man, with the grace of a Buddhist sage. He's been having a quiet day, minding his own business, when along come two madmen with cameras. In a huff, he turns his back on us, and marches off, bamboo poles at the ready, looking for less popular pools . . .

Chuxian, for which we have a permit, turns out to be too close to be useful as a stepping-stone. It is only 30 miles from Nanjing – and we get there at 11.30 a.m. Chuxian looks pretty dull and dusty – we consult a provincial map of Jiangsu Province. About 60 miles from Nanjing, headed north-west, there are hilly contours marked on the map. If we can get to that spot, there should be enough tree-cover for us to wheel the bikes off the road and sleep out.

Toward nightfall, we reach the spot. We are just about to dive off the side of the road when we notice some PLA soldiers on manoeuvres. Closer inspection reveals that the proposed sleeping-spot is occupied, through the trees, by a sizeable military establishment. We hastily continue, ending our search for a sleeping-site near a mountain-top – where we trundle the bikes out of sight.

At 6.30 a.m. next morning, our luck breaks. A heavy downpour hits. We've been on the road for less than an hour, and Fengyang, our destination, is still some 35 miles away. After an hour of pedalling through the muck, we take shelter in a local shop. Here we amuse the locals by using chopsticks on a jar of sliced apples in syrup. The rain eases off – we hightail for Fengyang, arriving five hours later with wheels and baggage encrusted in mud, and soggy clothing.

★   ★   ★

THE GREATEST HARDSHIP for the traveller in China is undoubtedly Chinese breakfast. Here we have no choice. At the guesthouse in Fengyang there is no other kind of breakfast. So there are dishes of rubbery bean-curd, over-salted peanuts coated in thick oil, mouth-puckering pickled vegetables, and fat greasy dough-sticks that are draped over a plate like dead moray eels. Plus some other things I can't identify – they look like black cabbage-strips – and bowls of buffalo milk. All these things are the wrong colours, shapes, textures and tastes for the western palate. Over at the next table they are all happily sucking and clucking away, obviously enjoying their food. We order some extra *mantou*, a kind of white dough that approximates raw bread.

'Here comes trouble,' says Robert, glancing toward the door. It is the Director of Foreign Affairs: this ominous title appears on his bilingual business card, which he flourishes with great ceremony. He cannot, however, speak a word of English; hence his sidekick, the translator. The Director immediately inquires, through the translator, how we got to Fengyang. We tell him we have cycled in from the nearby railhead. He appears reasonably content with this explanation.

The Director of Foreign Affairs is a shifty-looking character with grey hair swept back like a koala bear. He keeps his arms rolled into his jacket-cuffs, and assumes the airs and posturing of an ancient emperor. If we are foreigners, then we obviously fall into his division – we are his charges. The pair of them fuss over us like a pair of old grannies, telling us what time dinner is on, where to go, what to see, what to do.

'You must be tired after your long journey,' says the translator.

'They're onto us,' I whisper to Robert.

'No they're not,' says Robert. 'They mean the ride from the railway station – the fifteen miles.'

'Oh'

'You must take a rest,' says the translator. 'You mustn't strain yourselves. Would you like some more breakfast?'

'NO THANKS!' we both cry out, in unison. Why is it that they keep telling us to take a rest? We probe. Although Fengyang is a shining new addition to the 1985 freelance traveller's list, it has been open to group-tours and Hong Kong Chinese since 1979. All the previous foreign customers have been geriatrics on group-tours – all on their last legs. We, by contrast, have arrived on bicycles, looking dirty and unshaven, thus confusing the Director of Foreign Affairs since we possess legs that are faster than his.

What is there to see in Fengyang? We are hoping the Director won't ask the question – not only does he do this, but he then proceeds to answer it. We have to make a pretence of wanting to see Fengyang, which doesn't look in the least bit interesting. We've seen the whole town on the way in – it's a small place, perhaps 10,000 people.

'There is an emperor's palace in Fengyang,' says the translator. 'It was destroyed again and again, but we think of rebuilding it.' Other than that, there are a couple of ancient statues out in the farmlands, and a chance to see a real live commune – a showcase one, to be sure. They will take us around. In a Toyota. It will cost us a packet. But we've come all this way. Perhaps it will be fun to throw ourselves into the role of molly-coddled group-tourists. We agree to half a day.

The Toyota takes us over muddy roads to a plain concrete building. Here we are introduced to a 'model farmer'. Statistics are spewed forth. Things are ten times better than in 1978. In 1978 there were just hovels and mud; now there are concrete villas – and mud, we notice. In this village, sixteen families are housed in concrete – two families in each two-storey dwelling. The pigs, the geese, the sheep, the chickens and the ducks now inhabit the old hovels and huts: this is progress. Each concrete house costs a fortune to build, but the farmers here have done well – they have met their quotas for the State, and then have made good off extra sales to the State, and to the freemarket. There is something amiss with the concrete housing, however. It doesn't actually seem lived in – more used for storage. Perhaps it is all for show – the model farmer doesn't greet us in his own concrete villa, but in a kind of conference room.

Our model farmer, we are led to believe, makes 9000 yuan a year, and has recently purchased a tractor and a harvester. On a big board, in English, are figures from 1978 to 1985, showing how many pounds of grain have been produced and sold. The fact that the figures are given in English immediately makes them suspect: if the figures are to be believed, average income has increased ten-fold; and the model farmer's income has increased many more times. He is now a man of consequence: the proud owner of a concrete villa, several TV sets and a tractor.

Ah, but what a turn-around in attitude – whereas in 1975 this farmer would have been placed on the chopping block and vilified for being a rampant capitalist, now he is a hero. He is hard-working; he has become rich and successful; he is a pace-setter of 'socialism'. Yet, as our model farmer is quick to point out, he has not reached the magic category of 10,000 yuan a year income. In other parts of China, he says, farmers have done this; the sky is the limit, in fact – one farmer, he's heard, made 40,000 yuan a year off orange seedlings. Another, a chicken farmer, made 50,000 yuan a year. These farmers have plenty to celebrate. For the first time in their entire history, they are getting a good deal. City folk, with the industrial sector still shackled by the State, are green with envy.

This reminds me of a headline I saw in a Chinese magazine: PRINCESS MARRIES PEASANT. The former princess, of noble blood, grows up in a world devoid of privilege under Communism; then she meets an up-and-coming peasant – they marry; the peasant gets rich by some superhuman boning up on chicken fertiliser manuals; she can suddenly afford a lifestyle befitting a princess – they plan to buy a truck. The burning question is, in this modern-day fairytale: was the frog that gave the magic kiss capitalist or communist?

On the wall of the building we are in there are two posters. I inquire about them. One is for family planning; the other is a poster about breeding pigs. There is, in fact, a connection between the two. By breeding lots of pigs, our model farmer becomes rich enough that he can afford to pay any fines levied for 'overproduction' of children. Having extra children thus turns into a kind of luxury, only affordable by the wealthier peasants. The model farmer, it turns out, has five children – but these, he insists, were born before the 'one child only' campaign was introduced in 1979.

I ask what he thinks about the best solution to the problem of having one child. The dilemma is that while the parents can be convinced to have one child, they are unanimous in wanting to have a male child. Traditional Confucian ethics dictate that only a son can uphold the family name. In Henan Province, there were two cases where the husbands filed for divorce on the grounds that their wives gave birth only to female children. In 1982, western demographers calculated that 230,000 female infants had been killed as a result of the introduction of the one child policy in the previous year alone; in some rural areas, Chinese newspapers reported the ratio of male to female children as high as 5 to 1. The farmer smirks: he has a solution. Twins. One boy, one girl. That way, the wily farmer states, no rules are broken, and the parents get what they want.

There are other cases where the one child only rule can be bypassed – for example, in the rare event of a remarriage, or upon the death of an only child, or if the first child is handicapped in some way. I wondered whether those in power could indulge in more than one child. Probably they could not afford to set a bad example: China has a population bomb on its hands. Between 1949 and 1979 the population of China more than doubled; in 1982, the population surpassed one billion. It was estimated that if no population plan were instituted, the population would double again by 2010, making it two billion. Part of the problem is that with better medical services – and a more stable food supply – the average lifespan had increased from 40 to 70. A major part of the problem is that Mao Zedong firmly believed that birth control was a capitalist plot to keep China weak, and that there was strength in numbers. He set about forming the largest army in the world: the enemy, he reasoned, would be overwhelmed by the sheer number of Chinese soldiers.

At best – with maximised agricultural yield – it is estimated that the land resources of China can only support 1.4 billion; thus Draconian measures – forced abortions and sterilisation – are called for. Abortion can be performed up to the ninth month of pregnancy – in which case it might well be a caesarian section. These are the sensational aspects that one might read about in the Taiwanese or Hong Kong press; not so conspicuous is the astonishing fact that by 1985 the Chinese family dropped to a two-child-per-family average, as contrasted with 5.8 children per family in 1970. Yet it is dubious whether the one child only campaign can continue to slash the birth-rates: in the mid-1980s, as the peasants prosper under the economic reforms, they are more than willing to pay fines imposed for having extra children. Peasant families defy the policy in many areas – producing three or more children. The vigorous one child campaign of the early 1980s has been effective in the cities; in the countryside, where 80 percent of China's population lives, it is difficult to change the ways of the peasants, who believe that the more hands they have, the greater their production – and the more children they have, the better the chances of being looked after in their old age. In Anhui Province, a new system was being tried: under the 'responsibility system', the peasant would be given double-sized plots of land if he had only one child, and no plot at all if the second child appeared.

Bengbu Hotel Registration Form. Date of Arrival: April 26th/85. Date of Departure: April 27th/85. Where from: Fengyang.

Bengbu was described by the desk-clerk as a city of two and a half million. Luckily for us, it had been earmarked by the Anhui provincial government as a food-processing centre. Half of its industrial output came from food-processing – wineries, canned foods, grain-processing, poultry, candy. So we set about replenishing our food-stocks. The trained eye scanned the shelves of the department stores. Immediately discounted were the tins of chicken or fish – these were sorely disappointing on the road. They turned out to be greasy, inedible collections of bones. The eye rested on some cans of lychee nuts in syrup. These, I'd found, were tasty, cheap, and – although quite heavy – very useful on the road. The lychee fruit provided a high-energy glucose source, and the syrup provided much-needed fluids – in the absence of a trustworthy water supply.

In the hotels, water was not a problem – thermoses of piping hot water were supplied with the room. To go with the hot water, we'd brought along packets of soup. Robert swore by a jar of a horrible black substance which promised, upon the addition of hot water, an extract of every vegetable under the sun. As a drink, it wasn't too bad.

I had a private piece of outfitting to accomplish in Bengbu. I had to buy underwear. I'd lost a few pairs in the hotel laundry-service in Nanjing. As I conducted my hunt through the department stores of Bengbu for western-style underwear, I couldn't help thinking that my previous supply had been deliberately appropriated by the hotel laundry staff in Nanjing. No doubt they sold it on the black-market. There was very little in the way of Chinese-made under-wear. Perhaps they made do without it. Chinese infants had a slit down the back of their pants to make matters easier on the streets, should the urge overtake them.

I found, in a department store, some heavier cotton long-johns, almost like jogging pants, in lurid colours – they would take a long time to dry if washed. Then there were flimsy boxer-style shorts, which promised a cold start in the mornings if they made it as far as the Tibetan Plateau.

My mind shifted to other plans – perhaps I could ask around and buy some off another westerner? Or steal some? This reminded me of a tale I'd once heard about a traveller on foot nego-tiating the swamps of the Darien Gap, linking Panama and Colombia. He'd been accosted by naked Indians in the swamps – held at knife-point – but all they wanted, to his astonishment, was his underwear. Perhaps that is what naked Indians dream of acquiring.

The quest for underwear continued – I scoured the drab depart-ment stores. Nothing. Till, in a larger store, I spied . . . women's underwear. Now here was a find – jockey-style, lightweight, strong, dried easily. I ordered three pairs. Large ones. Unfor-tunately, the salesladies realised they had great potential for live entertainment standing right there. They sniggered, and took their time about the transaction. Ah, how they tortured me. What colour did I prefer? Wouldn't another style suit me better? What about some patterned briefs? Was I really sure that the size was correct? Wait – there were larger sizes at the back of the store . . .

A crowd of some 200 shoppers had gathered to witness my agony. I turned every shade of red imaginable. What a weirdo big-nose, they must've been saying. He's either a transvestite, or he's getting gifts for an over-sized mistress – or maybe he's on a honeymoon and she ran out of underwear – you know, he keeps ripping the stuff off her.

The long and short of it was that I finally got to pay for the items. The tittering saleswomen, of course, prolonged the return of the change – and in the deepest embarrassment I stalked out of the store.

★   ★   ★

AT THE CRACK OF DAWN we left Bengbu Hotel, cycling toward Huaibei. The sun was hovering over the horizon by the time we found the ferry marked on the map. We marched the bikes onto the ferry, and soon were crossing the Huai River, another milestone of our passage. Off to a fine start; then swiftly up to our knees in mud. Such is the luck of the road. We were lost: we had struck a bumpy muddy road that killed the backside. Twelve miles of it. The wheels were completely choked up with mud. It had accumulated inside the mudguards. I was forced to stop; the bicycle refused to budge. I dug the mud out with a screwdriver. Fortunately, the chain was completely encased in metal, so mud could not affect it. Robert dug out his mudguards.

A group of local farmers gathered to witness the mud-removing ceremony. Robert asked for directions, but failed to make himself understood as these people spoke a thick dialect. So he proceeded to write down the destination in Chinese characters. The farmers were stunned – not so much by the fact that Robert could write in Chinese, but by the fact that he wrote the characters with his *left* hand, an aberration unheard of in these parts. The gist of the matter finally got through: one man pointed north; another pointed westwards; yet another told us to go back to Huaibei, the way we'd just come.

'It's no use asking them,' said Robert. 'They've probably never been out of this village.'

'Great. Well, we've got a choice of dirt roads – none of them look promising. Maybe the map is wrong.'

'Or else the road is being re-laid.'

'Let's ask which road is being rebuilt then.'

Robert did this; the farmers unanimously pointed at a road going west. We set off again. There was a loud crash below, an ominous sound like the snapping of a chain. My rear wheel had slipped off, and ground into the frame. A passing Chinese cyclist helped us right the wheel with a wrench. He conveyed to us the good news that there was a better road a few miles ahead.

On this road, smooth as a billiard table in comparison, we stopped for brunch: chocolate bars and bread. A passing truck added a nice coating of dust to the snack. On this paved section we could make up for lost time. Fanned by a pleasant crosswind, we rode off at maximum speed to knock off the halfway mark. By our calculations, Huaibei was approximately 75 miles from Bengbu, or about 12 hours in the saddle...

By 6.30 p.m. we stood at the turn-off to Huaibei, sweating, dehydrated, worn out. The sign said 18 *gongli* into Huaibei from the main highway. It was much further than we thought. It would take two hours to get there. Two hours in, two hours out – that meant four hours of back-tracking off the main route. Somehow we couldn't face the thought of camping out, however. I opened a tin of lychee nuts while we made a decision. The lychee nuts were carefully consumed in equal shares. Refreshed by drinking the nectar, we decided it was better to plough on than spend the night out. Besides, there were no suitable 'hiding-spots' in view.

Darkness descended; still one and a half hours into Huaibei. Soldered to the machine, pistons powered by lychee juice, I ground on – soles, palms and groin locked in, working away. Hazards increased – trying to pick out potholes. An even bigger concern was bricks lying on the roadside – they had fallen from the backs of walking-tractors. The road was pitch-black, illuminated occasionally by a passing truck. A terrific chorus of frogs. A bat dive-bombed me. Robert almost rode straight into a huge black hole. It was just lit up in time by an oncoming truck; Robert swerved to avoid it. The crevasse he had narrowly missed was about four feet deep, and full of large pipes. The pipe-people! This was a brand-new hazard – category A, more dangerous than road-builders. We rode very slowly after this.

Civilisation, at last. At 9 p.m. we stopped at a small shack to load up on Ma Ling peas, baked beans, and a jar of peaches. There was a huge audience gathered round a television set on the other side of the road – a kung fu movie. This was the local cinema.

Finally we found the hotel. It was a large, heavy building. Television must have been new in Huaibei – most of the staff was gathered round a colour set. There was a great commotion and ringing of telephones on our arrival. Where had we come from? From the railway of course, we replied. I glanced at Robert – there was a rail-head at Huaibei wasn't there? He'd forgotten. We stuck by the story anyway.

'I am from the Foreign Affairs Section of the PSB,' said a sinister-looking gentleman. 'Can I be of help?'

My heart skipped a beat. Had PSB caught up with us? We showed the man our passports and permits – everything was in order. The manager wanted 80 yuan for a double room. Robert had a fit. Eighty yuan! We showed him previous receipts for a double-room for 16 yuan. It appeared the figure of 80 yuan included all meals; we opted out of the meals. The figure dropped to 25 yuan – this included a bath, the manager claimed. The man from PSB mediated – we agreed to 25 yuan; five people picked up our bags and charged off. There were about eight of us now – each with various bits of luggage – heading off through a nightmare of corridors to an outer section of the huge hotel.

The room was like a funeral parlour – heavy velvet drapes, grey furniture, lofty ceiling, chandeliers, thick carpet. But after the day's ride, a Russian morgue wasn't such a bad idea. There was one saving grace: a monster-sized bathroom, with a huge tub to soak in. With no soft furnishings, this section had a horrendous echo when the plumbing was in action. We filled out the registration form: Where To/From: Bengbu. There was a little tussle over passports – I refused to hand mine over. The manager finally accepted Alien Travel Permits as security; we shook off the man from PSB; and we were left to our supper of baked beans, peas, and peaches.

In Huaibei, instant amphitheatres were created around us wherever we stopped – to buy bread (crowd of 50), peaches (crowd of 40), pears (street-market, prolonged transaction – crowd of 200), cigarettes (40), and a can of curried chicken (department store – crowd of 80). For the local Chinese, we were better than television. The program was 'The Alien'. Episode 1: the Alien makes a purchase! Episode 2: the Alien produces a map. Episode 3: the Alien opens his bag! Episode 4: the Alien changes film. Episode 5: incredible – the Alien speaks some words in Chinese! The glossy books, the exotic zips, the state-of-the-art webbing, the space-age shoes – these details enthralled them. Most of this derived from sheer boredom; some of it derived from curiosity. I once read about a famous western rock-star who said that China was great because nobody recognised him, and therefore he could avoid mobs. Obviously he hadn't ventured out of Peking – he would've been mobbed regardless of any recognition.

We did our fair share of observation too. One of the busiest merchants on the streets of Huaibei was the vendor of sunglasses. He had a large roadside stand with samples mounted on it. Sunglasses are the hallmark of China's youth – nobody over 30 wears them. Truck-drivers, students, factory workers – men and women – wear sunglasses because it is 'cool' to do so. It doesn't matter if the sun is out or not – Chinese youths will still wear their wraparounds. The second merchant of interest was the noodle-maker, whose performance took place in the window of his eating establishment. He took an ordinary piece of dough, pounded it up and down – and spun long, flat ribbons out of it – the noodles. These he whipped back and forth - and finally threw into a bowl of hot soup, ready for the customer. The art of noodle-making was unchanged from the days of Marco Polo. Doing a brisk business nearby was an open-air comic-book rental stand. It was near a staircase leading to a store: the clients – young and elderly – were scattered up and down the stairs with their noses embedded in the tiny comic-books. They were so engrossed that they failed to notice my photography of the scene.

At five in the morning we wheeled the bikes through the doorman's bedroom and out the front gates. There was a slight tailwind, light traffic; the push was on for Kaifeng. Kaifeng was several days away – if we could overcome this logistical obstacle, the way was open to Xian.

The road was atrocious – how on earth had we managed to negotiate it at night before? It was barely passable by day, with all the potholes, road-building and pipe-laying going on. We weren't the only ones leaving town. The streets were alive with cart-people hauling their loads along. Some were just getting up. They had been sleeping under heavy quilts on the handcarts; they each had supplies of firewood, food and coal. Some travelled in small groups: Robert managed to find out that these itinerant teams notched up to sixty *gongli* a day, taking local products and selling them in smaller towns. One team, a husband and wife, had a bicycle-assisted cart – she walked and hauled, he rode the bike with a tow-rope attached to the cart. Then we passed the most unusual conveyance we'd yet seen on the highways of China – a sail-assisted cart. There were two people up front pulling this vehicle – in the middle of the cart was a mast with a rough canvas sail flapping around in the wind. The haulers, bewildered by our scrutiny, were tacking down the highway at full speed – maybe five knots. We raced to overtake them, so as to be in a position to take some photographs.

We reached the turn-off; shortly after, along the main road, we triumphantly crossed the line into Henan Province. It was a difficult stretch ahead: from Huaibei to Shangqiu, a distance of over 80 miles, there was no rail-line to explain our presence if intercepted.

By nightfall, we were about twenty miles short of a place called Suiqui, and still a hundred miles short of the target of Kaifeng. We sized up a wheatfield as a likely resting-spot for the night. The plan was to wait till it got really dark and then shoot off into the wheatfield with the bikes, quickly dropping out of sight. The problem was that it *didn't get dark*. The stubborn moon was three-quarters full and glinted on the shiny bits of the bicycles. We hung around the wheatfield, trying to look inconspicuous. A couple of farmers stopped to ask us questions, obviously perplexed about where we would be spending the night. We would've loved to spend the night in some farmhouse – but that would most certainly have landed us in trouble with the authorities.

The moon, finally, slipped behind some clouds; the road was dark enough; we backtracked quickly to the wheatfield we'd staked out, and wheeled the bikes off the road into a small clearing. Like a pair of hunted rabbits we peered over the stems of wheat, to see if anyone was on our case.

'Do you think anyone noticed?' I whispered to Robert.

'Nope. We've disappeared into thin air,' he whispered.

'And tomorrow we reappear somehow –'

'AAARGH!' Robert flung his arms up in front of his face and dived to the ground.

'Jesus! Keep the noise down will you? What happened?'

'A flying black thing – it came straight for me.'

'Don't be daft.'

'Look, I swear it. It was like a huge spider.'

'How could you see it if it was black?'

'The moonlight.'

At that moment I turned around and came face to face with the same UFO that Robert had been talking about. It was travelling at high speed – straight for me.

'AAARGH!' I flung my arms up in front of my face and dived to the ground.

'See,' sneered Robert, 'I told you.'

'Bats,' I whispered. 'It was a little bat.'

'Oh, right. Little bats after the insects.'

With these unsettling creatures for company, we picked our sleeping-spots.

I stared up at the sky – it was chock-a-block with stars. This was the infinite roof for the evening – a dizzy display of distant worlds. Dreams, dreams...

I awoke shivering, damp and clammy. In the distance a rooster crowed, a frog croaked, a dog barked. I pressed a button on my watch. It was 3 a.m. If we got off to an early start, it might be possible to do the hundred miles to Kaifeng. The motivation for doing that was high – food, drinks, hot bath and a warm bed in Kaifeng. Going straight there had another bonus – no rationing of present supplies. Left in the larder were five tins of lychee nuts, three tins of meat, and one tin of drink.

By 4 a.m. we were out on the highway, walking along in the dark, trying to warm ourselves up. We were both frozen. The painted white bases of trees delineated the road. It was still quite dark. We were not alone on the road, we discovered. Strange forms loomed up – men dragging wardrobes on handcarts. Where the hell were they going at four in the morning? And others, like giant beetles, scurrying along the highway with unwieldy loads of white sacks, also on handcarts. By 4.30 we could finally make out enough of the road to be able to ride without falling into potholes, and off we headed, slowly, for Kaifeng.

By 8.30 a.m. we were stripped down for the heat. Still a good 90 miles to Kaifeng – if we worked at it all day, we could get there. The traffic presented some fascinating permutations on bicycles. We overtook a trio of cyclists who were completely obscured by their unwieldy loads: bright yellow rattan chairs. The chairs were ingeniously stacked to form a mobile mountain that would've been the pride of any circus. In all probability, the rattan chair cyclists were headed for Kaifeng, where they would be able to sell their furniture at a premium. In China's big cities, raw materials like wood are next to impossible to obtain – but in the countryside, peasants have ready access to such items. The strange spectre of a man pedalling a bunch of rattan chairs – or a full-sized sofa – down a highway for a hundred miles thus has a perfectly rational explanation.

Another balancing act: a family of four mounted on a single bike – the family car, so to speak. Dad was in the driver's seat, mother seated side-saddle on the crossbar, one kid dangling off the handlebars, the other mounted over the rear rack. Further along the road we overtook a tricycle carrier with a kind of wheelchair up front, and one wheel at the back. In the forward seat of this bizarre vehicle was an older gentleman with a crate of empty bottles; propelling him from a bicycle-saddle was a man collecting cowdung. The cow-dung was transferred to hessian sacks at the back of the trike. This bottle and turd collecting machine was moving slowly along the highway. We passed another series of the huge white sacks on handcarts, being pulled along by sweating men. Most mysterious – we'd been passing similar loads all day.

After lunch, with a good 55 miles to go, I settled into my afternoon trance. This was a kind of deep meditative state, in rhythm to the bicycle, during which I 'played' tapes of selected episodes from my life – or else the same injustices over and over again. These 'tapes' all related, of course, to life back in the west. When in China, I dreamed of the comfort of home; when in the comfort of home, I dreamed of travelling through China.

The heat was suffocating. Road-widening was in full swing, and there were only saplings and arid stretches down both sides of the road. The guard of thick trees had been removed in the road-widening process, thus fully exposing the road to the sun. In the middle, the road was a sticky mess of tar; I spun along faster, since the tyres were actually beginning to stick to the road. The road began to shimmer – a shifting mirage, a sea of tar. I experienced a peculiar sensation of everything being uphill – when I looked around at the wheatfields, I could see the area was dead flat, but looking straight ahead, it seemed like an endless uphill climb. The grade seemed only slight: my legs were trying to tell me something, and my eyes were translating that into a slope.

ILLUSTRATIONS, CHINA, LEAF 1 – LEAF 8

Front Cover – cycling along the Bund, Shanghai – police observation pole at left; Customs House clocktower to the right.

1 *Top left* – looking down Nanjing Road from Park Hotel. *Top right* – sign of things to come, Nanjing Road. *Mid right* – morning fencing exercises in Frenchtown. *Bottom* – view of former Chapei District.

2 *Top* – furniture removalist takes a break while his co-worker pedals tricycle carrier, Shanghai. *Mid left* – invalid cyclist cranks bike by hand, Nanjing. *Mid right* – fatal accident shown on safety display board. *Bottom* – traffic policeman mediates between cyclist and pedestrian after accident, Chengdu.

3 *Top left* – Chengdu tricyclist – hopefully the gasoline barrels are empty. *Top right* – slicing through Chengdu. *Middle* – stone-faced commuters at stop-light, Peking. *Bottom* – ferry-crossing over Grand Canal near Changzhou.

4 *Top left* – just married, in matching pantsuits, Shanghai. *Top right* – comic-book rental stand and patrons in Dingshu. *Middle* – old men comparing bird notes in a quiet Wuxi park. *Bottom left* – 'one child only' mural being painted in Suzhou. *Bottom right* – the family sedan, and man exceeding child quota.

5 *Top* – Grand Canal traffic, Changzhou. *Mid left* – puzzled students inspect author on solo trip to Suzhou. *Mid right* – duck farmer, Jiangsu. *Bottom* – rapeseed fields in the spring, Jiangsu.

6 *Top left* – young PLA soldier, Kaifeng. *Top right* – rural Chinese bag their first foreigner – Robert – on the way to Zhenjiang. *Mid left* – Classified area – the author in Fengyang. *Mid right* – friendly farmer near Luoyang. *Bottom left* – not quite the real thing – recycled soft drink bottles. *Bottom right* – breakfast surgery – greasy dough-sticks being deep-fried at a street-stall.

7 *Top left* – author on the Yangtse River Bridge. *Top right* – itinerant vendors with sail-assisted cart, Huaibei. *Mid right* – the road-wideners at work – rip up now, pave later. *Bottom left* – chickens on the move, near Gongxian. *Bottom right* – walking-tractor cruises past fresh truck wreckage.

8 *Top left* – Robert on the road past Sanmenxia. *Top right* – tribes of grannies tackle the slopes on Huashan. *Mid left* – part of terracotta army excavations, close to Xian. *Mid right* – vendor with his own terracotta army, outside museum. *Bottom* – Renmin Hotel, Xian: Robert on right, author at left.

酒醉骑车被撞死

大连电风扇厂工人林怀男29岁，于×月×日晚9时13分酒醉骑车，在友好广场东侧逆向交通、迎面同自行车驶驶的大客车相撞林当场被撞死。

THE FOREIGNERS ARE
NOT ALLOWED TO TAKE
A PICTURE HERE
禁止外国人拍照

Coke 可口可乐 Coca-Cola

7

Robert consulted the map. We stopped to split the last can of drink. I could've used another six of them. There was very little we'd been able to scrounge for road-maps for this region. Maps were classified information. There was a general map, but the detail on it was microscopic. Since Chinese characters can be written vertically or horizontally, Chinese maps pack in a lot more detail than western maps can.

'We're better off following road-signs,' said Robert. 'I'm burning up too many braincells trying to read this map.'

'You're just about due for a new brain anyway, aren't you?'

'Humph. You know, I just can't understand how they can get these characters so small.'

'Must be photo-reduction.'

'I'm not so sure – you've heard about those craftsmen who carve words onto the hair of a panda-bear?'

'No, but I've seen some who carve good-luck characters on eyeglass-frames.'

Place-names were a frustrating chore for Robert since the normal linguistic clues – the context of a sentence – were absent. But in a way he enjoyed the whole puzzle. Having decided on a career as a linguist, he wanted to tackle a totally alien language – and master it. For the linguist, this 'decoding' was the ultimate challenge. He had thought about doing Arabic, but it didn't appear so useful. It was the Chinese tones and characters that fascinated him.

So, many pairs of glasses later, here he was, cycling through China. It could have been different. If he'd taken up Arabic, he could've been cruising the desert on a camel, practicing his Bedouin dialect.

Most of our fluid consumption took place in the heat of the sun, when we could easily race through two water-bottles and three cans of drink. Now that we were down to cans of lychee nuts for fluids, we would have to rest out the mid-day sun. This put us behind schedule – Kaifeng looked further and further away. Opening a can of lychee nuts attracted a crowd of twenty silent on-lookers, plus a colony of ants. They gathered round as we shared the can. I couldn't make up my mind which was worse – the crowd of starers, or the ants. Finally it was the ant-colony that made us move on to another spot down the road.

In the afternoon, an extraordinary sight materialised. The huge white sacks on handcarts – the loads that we'd been passing all day – all ended up in one spot. It was some kind of processing factory, and the handcarts were coming from all over the area. The road was jammed with handcarts; bits of cotton floated through the air. Soon we found ourselves hemmed in by hundreds of cotton-pickers – a solid wall of faces. Eventually, a self-appointed leader came forward to break the ice. This done, it was discovered that Robert spoke Chinese, and the crowd – much larger by now – moved closer, shouting questions. Who were we? What were we doing in this place? How did we get here? How old were we?

Having fielded some of the questions, we decided to leave. But this seemed impossible – the crowds of cotton-pickers were too thick for us to extricate the bikes. The leader shouted something; a passage was cleared – an effect like Moses parting the waters. We made good our escape.

By 6 p.m., after battling the sun and wind all afternoon, we got to a place called Qixian. A signpost indicated 53 *gongli* to Kaifeng. Even if we could make it into Kaifeng, we would need another hour to find the hotel – we wouldn't get there till midnight. We would have to camp out. We clocked up another twelve miles and dived into an orchard by the roadside. Robert immediately sat down on something unsavoury in the dark, judging by the resulting smell – probably night soil or fertiliser. Cackling to myself, I probed for a fertiliser-free sleeping-spot, and threw my poncho on the ground.

*   *   *

KAIFENG, MAY FIRST. The worst leg of the trip is down. We have made it this far. Our arrival in Kaifeng coincides with May Day – International Labour Day – but no sign of any celebrations. The city is nevertheless bustling with street-markets – cobblers, tailors, shoe-salesmen, food-hawkers and vendors of sunglasses. The first thing that strikes us is the abundance of bright yellow bananas, which have not been sighted anywhere else along our route. Further investigation (eating half a dozen on the spot) reveals that they're imported from the Philippines – but why does the banana pipeline end here, of all places?

Kaifeng is one of the very few cities in China where population has actually decreased. A thousand years ago, Kaifeng was the capital of the Song empire, with a population estimated at over a million; the city remained a centre of cultural dominance for over two centuries. History has not been kind to Kaifeng – in the 12th century, the city was sacked by Manchurian invaders; in 1461, 1642, 1887 and 1938 the city was submerged by the Yellow River – twice deliberately to foil advancing armies (both times being total disasters for the people of Kaifeng). Kaifeng rapidly dwindled in importance.

Being relegated to a backwater has some advantages – the city has retained a lot of character. Its population has stabilised at around 300,000 – unchanged for the last seventy years. There has been little industrialisation; ramshackle houses and narrow lanes prevail near the city-centre; there are dilapidated temples and pagodas tucked into the older neighbourhoods; even traces of the ancient city-walls remain.

I awake at Kaifeng Hotel vaguely aware of a figure twirling arms and bobbing up and down. It is Heine, the Swiss traveller, doing strenuous limbering-up exercises. Heine is one of those athletically-fit and self-confident types who can go anywhere and do anything. He hails from Zurich, and has just finished a two year stint working on development projects in Bangladesh. This has turned him into a total cynic.

'If I were in the position of giving money from the Swiss Government,' he informs us, 'I wouldn't give any.' He claims that a third of the money never leaves Dacca. It is spent on the military and on wasted projects like the setting-up of a hi-tech factory that won't be used for five years. Training is the answer – training and technical expertise to help people to help themselves.

Talk about noses. Heine has a huge nose. It arches out in a large hook-shape, stops dead, and plunges straight down to the upper-lip level. It must delight the Chinese. Robert tells him he is a splendid example of the genus 'big-nose', or *da bizi*', the general Chinese term for foreigner. This term is somewhat derogatory since a big nose is considered quite ugly by the Chinese – along with full lips, big ears and rounded eyes. A Chinese had once gone to great lengths to explain to me how ugly I was, and how difficult it must be for me to endure life with such grotesque features.

For our amusement, Robert catalogues the other terms used by the Chinese for foreigners – some nasty, some not. Amongst them are *'waiguoren'* ('out-land person'), *'waibin'* (foreign guest), *'yangguizi'* (foreign devil – derogatory), *'hong mao guizi'* (red-haired foreign devil – the worst kind), and *'meiguoren'* (American – a large percentage of westerners being mistaken for Americans).

The third night in Kaifeng: it is still pouring. We go to the dining-hall for the usual round of slop, and are astonished to see the table next to us decked out with appetizing vegetables and meats, some deftly cut into the shape of birds and other animals. A group of westerners trots in. They are on a gastronomic tour of China; the food has been brought in from all over the province; the chefs have been preparing for weeks. There is no chance we will get any of it. All we can do is sit and drool, and eat Filipino bananas.

Utterly depressed, we go back to the hotel-room for the weather-report on the television. There is no need for any translation: the chart shows big black umbrellas all over Henan Province. There follows a special report on the travels of a diminutive CCP digni-tary to the South Pacific. The Chinese media loves to show its officials interacting with people of different races, even though the Chinese in practice detest such intimacy. The theory is in keeping with the party boast 'We have friends all over the world'. The tiny official is shown being crushed in a handshake by a six-foot Fijian, who towers over him. In the next instant, he is forced to drink *kava* from a coconut shell. He tries to smile for the camera. Then he is crushed in the embrace of an overweight Fijian wife, obviously related to the earlier giant of the handshake episode. And so it goes on. How can the man endure this treatment? For the past two nights he has been crushed and smothered by all kinds of Brobdingnagian South Pacific islanders, and forced to eat and drink all manner of disgusting food and drink...

We've been holed up in Kaifeng for four days now, getting more and more frustrated. The Swiss traveller has been replaced by a Hong Kong businessman who spends most of his time in bed, hooked up to a Walkman, staring at the ceiling. He's in Kaifeng to help set up a coil-winding works, or something esoteric like that. He doesn't know what to think of us. Last night Robert reached into his washbag for some toothpaste; a huge cockroach ran up his arm out of the bag and onto his neck; Robert danced all over the room, much to the amazement of the Hong Konger, who hadn't seen the cockroach. I cracked up – this was the funniest thing I'd ever seen; Robert was not amused; the businessman gave him strange looks. Maybe it's a case of too much coil-winding – the businessman is burnt out. He lies there with his Walkman, looking at us both with glazed eyeballs. He's convinced we're quite loony.

On the fifth day of rain, we *are* quite loony. We have reached an all-time low. I'm sick of listening to the elephant-like trumpeting of the plumbing in the bathroom, sick of looking at the Hong Konger staring at the ceiling, sick of eating bananas from the Philippines – we *have* to move. Still pouring out there. We decide to go to Zhengzhou by bus on a day-trip – see if they have any better food there.

For the first time, we have a sneak preview of the road ahead. It is appalling. The first thirty miles or so is like a swimming-pool – the bitumen has been entirely dug up, but the road-wideners have been caught in the rain – mud and slush, muck, piles of rocks, gravel, and pools of water. It has seen its share of accidents too – trucks that have slithered off the road, one with a broken front axle. There are crater-sized potholes in the road, and there are colossal traffic-jams at small bridges, where only one vehicle at a time can pass. The road-wideners have obviously not got round to this section yet. Perhaps this is China's future highway – a colossal traffic-jam of trucks, buses, walking-tractors, and cadre jeeps. The drivers look like veterans already, with that resigned traffic-jam look on their faces. On bikes we'll be run off the road all the way.

On the sixth day we crack – we're going to Zhengzhou come hell or high water. The sky has that sort of moody light that makes it impossible to tell if it's going to rain or not – or for how long either condition will last. We depart at 6 a.m.; the rain hits at 9 a.m.; we are only twenty miles out of Kaifeng, and have a full fifty-five miles to go. Our raingear is soaked through within an hour. Robert has his daypack under his flimsy poncho – looks like some sort of hunchbacked pixie. The rain doesn't let up.

We've taken a terrible beating – lashed by headwinds, splashed by passing trucks, hit by a constant stream of rain. Legs barely moving now – the rain and headwinds have knocked the stuffing out of me, made me weak, wet and miserable. We've done forty waterlogged miles in eight hours, and still seventeen miles to go to Zhengzhou. I'm wondering if my feet are decomposing. It has been a total disaster. Robert stops to squeeze a pint of water out of his socks.

The joke has worn a bit thin. It is times like this – at my lowest ebb – that I have to ask myself what I am doing here, getting a thorough drenching, when I could be soaking up the sun on the beaches of Thailand. What am I doing here, in China, where the food is terrible, and where a foreigner can end up as the main sight of the region, with locals gathering in unwieldy numbers to stare?

As the rain pours down in monsoonal sheets, I think of all the useless things I've done in my life – *with* my life. Is this trip another useless thing? No, I reason – it is a challenge, a risk, a test of wits and endurance, with a single goal of getting to Xian – under my own steam. It is something which, once achieved, can be said to be finished. That is all the satisfaction I will need. In other parts of my life, nothing gets finished. It doesn't really matter how idiotic the goal is – Xian or Timbuktu – what matters is that the goal has been set, and come hell or high water, it must be conquered. The known world disappears – all the sycophants, whiners, moaners and naggers who embroil one in the sense of responsibility to society. All that matters here is getting to the end of the road – a simple question of pitting oneself against the odds. *Come hell or high water.*

It takes a superhuman effort – and four chocolate bars – to gain the turn-off to Zhengzhou. At the turn-off, there is a sign – it is 27 *gongli* to Zhengzhou. I imagine a blazing fireplace and a hot beef sandwich at the end of the route: that is what keeps me going. Navigation through the swimming-pools and pouring rain is agonisingly tracked by the kilometre stones. Each k-stone is a battle; we gain them one by one. I watch the k-stones going down – 27, 26, 25, cracking 20; slowly, slowly, cracking 10; then – light failing – we reach the city outskirts at k-stone 6. It is at precisely this moment that the rain stops.

Zhengzhou is best described as a rail-junction. It stands at the intersection of the major north-south and east-west rail-lines in China. In the centre of the city, there are half a dozen buildings

devoted solely to the loading and unloading of train passengers –
together with the relevant cottage industries. People mill around
this area in search of hotels, or food, or a place to dump their
baggage while waiting for a connecting train. Taxi-drivers with
vehicles of all shapes and sizes rove around looking for victims.

Closer to the station there are several large display cases, featuring in graphic detail what happened to passengers who took the
wrong luggage onto the train – things like kerosene, combined
with a cigarette or two. These photographs of mangled bodies,
dismembered arms and legs, and horribly-mutilated faces are a
stern reminder to passengers. Inside the main terminus chaos
rules, with frenzied crowds pressing forward trying to buy train-
tickets. These are issued through heavily-reinforced windows,
where the ticket-sellers cannot be seen. Orders are shouted
through a small hole at the bottom of the window, and if the purchaser is successful, a hand duly comes through the hole to
dispense a ticket. This is held high in triumph by the purchaser.
Around the hole, passengers fight it out for more tiny squares of
cardboard.

The city of Zhengzhou mushroomed in size and importance
after 1949 due to its role in a newly-constructed rail-system, and to
the fact that it became the capital of Henan Province. It is laid out
in a style identical to hundreds of other Chinese cities – wide tree-
lined boulevards, mammoth railway station, impressive Party
Headquarters, concrete residential buildings, a selection of fea-
tureless department stores – and a plethora of factories. A tourist
brochure describes the place as 'a developing city' (sprawl of
factories and pollution) 'which has made great progress since
Liberation' (ten-fold population increase, number of factories
quadrupled); the city has 'many sights, typical of China's long
history and rich culture' (the Red Guards destroyed the tourist
attractions and they'll have to re-construct them); it has so many
sights that 'the visitor is reluctant to leave' (the trains are booked
out for a week). In point of fact, there's very little to see around
Zhengzhou, or any of the large cities of China – the old sites have
been vandalised, the parks are shoddy, the museums are poorly
maintained. In Zhengzhou, there is not even much in the way of
free-marketing or street-life. The place is a dead bore.

Like everyone else, all we want to do is get our business over
with, and get the hell out of Zhengzhou. It will take at least a day to

dry our clothing and gear out. This is spread over an entire room at the guesthouse; but it seems unlikely that we'll be able to salvage much of the printed material. The maps are beyond redemption; my notebooks are in bits and pieces.

We pay a visit to Zhengzhou PSB – they are all out to lunch. There is, however, one officer left, and Robert sets to work on him for a permit for the elusive mountain of Huashan. First off, the man says no Huashan permit. Then he starts to soften. Robert's Chinese impresses him. In Nanjing, Robert tells him, PSB said no problem – go to Zhengzhou, the capital of Henan Province, and they'll give you the permit. We've been to Emei Shan and several other sacred mountains – we have to get to Huashan. The officer takes our travel permits, goes to an inner office, and comes back with the new addition: Huashan. We cannot believe our luck. We have a pit-stop between Sanmenxia and Xian.

*   *   *

FORTIFIED BY A HEARTY WESTERN BREAKFAST, we decide to hit the road again, eager to make up for lost time. Such is our haste that wet socks flap off the back racks. The current destination is Gongxian, just 50 miles away. The sun has made a guest appearance – an opportunity not to be missed. The bikes have had some minor maintenance done on them. My saddle, alas, will never be the same after the deluge on the way to Zhengzhou – it sags in the wrong places. This is not good news for the posterior.

We stop to observe a man loading live chickens onto a bicycle. He ties them by the feet in clusters of four or five. Each 'bunch' is then attached to various parts of the bike – the handlebars, back rack – and this odd combination of man, machine and chicken is ready to roll. I count about 25 chickens on the bike, all suspended upside-down.

Making progress now – crawling across the map. About twenty miles out of Zhengzhou, the scenery – which has remained unvaried for the last 400 miles or so – suddenly is broken up, turning through hills composed of reddish earth. Sculpted into the hillsides are cave-dwellings; in the valleys below these rabbit-warrens are flat fields of wheat – staircase farming. Whole mountainsides have been bevelled, scalloped and scored into wheatfields. There are even stretches of grass along the winding roadsides, where goats graze.

I wonder whether the goats have their own caves. Here, at least, is a luxury unknown elsewhere in China – space. If a family wants to expand, to add a room, they seem to be free to do so. Multiple caves, and private bedrooms – unheard of in other parts. And the air-conditioning – cool in summer, warm in winter. All the cooking is done outside. Mao and his Red Army holed up in cave-dwellings like these in Yanan, to the north-west of our present location. Yanan was the Communist base for almost a decade after 1936; the cave-dwellings afforded a measure of anonymity in the event of Nationalist bombing.

We cycle along a most pleasant route – an excellent road, a slight breeze, no strong sun. We pass a bike-shop carved into a cliffside. It has electricity, which the other cliff-dwellings do not have. The bike-shop is dug out of the cliff, and fully lined with brick, constructed in an arch-shape, presumably to prevent cave-ins.

In the afternoon, we come across felled trees at the roadside. This is more bad news for the posterior – it indicates that the road-builders are at work up ahead. Further on, indeed, the tar is being ripped up in huge chunks and thrown to the side of the road. The highway is being expanded to accommodate four lanes altogether, with additional space for slower-moving bikes and handcarts on the road-shoulders.

We toil up steep hills, sweating profusely – and then coast down off the high points, with exhilarating downhill runs. Apart from the bone-shaking encounter with the road-builders, the cycling proceeds along paved roads – which have been with us for most of the trip. The same afternoon sees us into Gongxian, and by the following afternoon we are in Luoyang.

Little evidence remains of Luoyang's role as an ancient capital. The boulevards into the city-centre are long, straight, and leafy; the tourist hotel – the Friendship Hotel – is a dull Soviet clone; there has been a considerable expansion in industry, and an equal expansion of red-brick and concrete blocks to accommodate the workers. Luoyang was once the centre of Buddhism in China – only the Longmen Caves, ten miles to the south of the city, now attest to the fact. These caves and niches harbour countless images of Buddha and his disciples – large and small – carved into the cliff-walls on the banks of the Yi River. Over time, and more recently during the Cultural Revolution, many of the statues have been vandalised, with heads and arms hacked off. Having paid our respects to the caves, we turn our attention to the refrigerators lurking within the Friendship Hotel.

Dull as it is, Luoyang is an excellent place to quench the thirst – the local Longmen Beer is served frosty cold, and there is a plentiful supply of western canned drinks, fruit-juices, and Laoshan mineral water. However much we drink, the thirst cannot be slaked – the body remembers the tough times on the road when the water has to be rationed. To drink unboiled water from local sources while on the road is to invite a plethora of stomach ailments, or worse.

We pass the evening in the company of two long-legged Lufthansa hostesses on a lay-over from Beijing. They are on a whirlwind 7-day tour of China. For them, Luoyang has the allure of the 'real China' – a less-touristed spot; in actual fact, because of the Longmen Caves, Luoyang is crawling with tourists.

In four days the hostesses will be back in Frankfurt. Robert, the linguist, comes to the fore, with a rapid display of Chinese – for the restaurant staff – and German, for the hostesses. In between, he provides a running translation in rapid English for me. Robert is juggling the three languages at once, and having a whale of a time. He orders for the two hostesses; the Chinese staff come out of the kitchen to ask questions about the German women. The only thing that slows down Robert's pace is when Pake, the taller of the two hostesses, complains that she hasn't had any sleep for the last three days. She must be suffering from jet-lag; Robert takes a long look at her, with many other things running through his mind beside translation services.

Early morning. Down the street from the hotel, Robert finds some display-cases that are of interest, and he methodically sets about photographing them. These boards show criminals, tell of their crimes, and then of their means of demise – usually a bullet through the forehead. A crimson tick placed beside the criminal's portrait indicates that he (more rarely, she) has been paraded around town in the back of a truck, and that execution has been duly carried out.

'This one was executed for rape,' says Robert, 'And this one for bank-robbery, and this one – let's see – for murder, I think.' He sneaks out his camera and snaps off a few frames. Bullets are a cheap enough method of disposing of criminals; as a further humiliation, the bill for that bullet is sent to the criminal's family. The bill is 10 yuan.

It has been Robert's misfortune to be mistaken for a Russian spy in China. Indeed, he looks the part – his face, his build, his moustache. The Chinese deductions are not entirely groundless, as Russians in Moscow mistook Robert for a Russian and asked him for street-directions. What he is seriously lacking as a spy is the expensive snooper photo-gear – the lenses that take trick angles, unknown to the subject. I am beginning to think he even secretly believes in the super-snooper role – here, as he sets about methodically photographing these display-cases, I can't help wondering what on earth he is going to do with the photos, and what on earth a Chinese policeman would think of his activities. Still, everybody should be entitled to a hobby . . .

From Luoyang, Xian looms up within striking-range. Three solid days of riding to the west, I calculate – but our maps are poor, and we can only make guesses as to exact distances. We have no idea as to terrain. Out of Luoyang, on the road to Sanmenxia, we strike varied countryside, and lots of hills. These slow us down considerably, and we're starting to wonder if we'll make it to Sanmenxia the same day, since it is 140 *gongli* from Luoyang. This means at least 14 hours, and with the hills, possibly 16 hours or longer. We don't have 16 hours of daylight to play with. We pass an overturned truck; then another truck – its cabin bashed in and half-submerged in mud, a tombstone-like reminder to other (living) drivers. Better than 'Slow Down!' signs, which most drivers ignore.

I remembered reading some outdated statistics in a Beijing publication – Henan Province had the highest number of trucks and tractors owned by peasants – something like 11,000 trucks and 250,000 walking-tractors. That means that there are at least a quarter of a million maniacs on the road in Henan Province, all out there trying to overtake each other at 80 miles per hour. Up ahead, on the crest of a hill, we have a close call with three of them – a truck coming from behind us squeezes past an oncoming truck; a third truck tries to overtake at the same time; we rocket off the road and dive for cover.

A signpost for Xian! I know the Chinese characters by heart – 379 *gongli*, it says. This is followed by a sign for Sanmenxia – 108 *gongli* – or eleven hours from here. We set up a self-timer photograph at the signpost – balance the camera on Robert's backpack on the rear of his bike, trip the timer, and run for the signpost. Some locals gather round the camera in our absence, and, hands behind their backs like awkward birds, they amble over to view through the lens. When the shutter clicks, one of them flaps his arms in his excitement. How can a photograph be taken without the photographer being behind the camera? This is complete magic to them.

The crowd has swelled now, and we clown around taking more photos – of ourselves, of the locals. The crowd is in a good mood; we are in a good mood – it takes on the atmosphere of a carnival. Robert tells everyone that we are Muslims from the Chinese province of Xinjiang – a ploy that is often used to save us a lot of tedious explanations, and one that allows us to blend in. With Robert's excellent Chinese, nobody questions this anomaly further. A curious policeman drops by – and a fisherman dressed in a catamaran. Well, he is wearing rubber boots past his knees, and above those – balanced on bamboo poles connected to his shoulder – hang two flotation-pods, which, I imagine, make him amphibious. The crowd becomes so big that it generates its own ice-block seller. *'Binggun! Binggun!'* cries the hawker. *'Binggun! Binggun!'*

We toil up hills, then speed down the other side – but it is a poor ratio of toil to relief. Besides, these things aren't hills any more – they're bloody mountains. With a gearless bike, that is no joke. We end up dismounting and pushing the bikes uphill.

It is on a descent from one massive hill that we run into . . . bees. As I come whipping down, I notice the hooded figures of beekeepers to the left and right of the road, attending the bee-hives . . . and then the meteoric rain of bees falls. There is no point stopping – I shield my face as best I can, and ride through the bees, which crash into me at high speed. No doubt, as the bees slam into my person, there are casualties among the colony, and I am pursued by angry bee-comrades down the highway – which certainly does wonders for acceleration.

We've just gotten through the second hive-ambush when Robert calls for a stop. His face is flushed, a beet-red shade.

'Fuck these hills!' he curses. 'Hope it isn't like this all the fucking way to Xian.' I ignore the comment, knowing full well that it probably is that way – all the way.

'Did the bees get you?'

'No, it's the bloody tyre – gone right down.'

The rear tyre is almost flat, and we are miles from any repair-shop.

'We'll have to try that village,' says Robert, pointing off a ridge to a cluster of huts below us. The alternative is to hitch-hike to the first town along the route and find a bike-repair place.

We wheel the bikes down to the village sighted from the main road. Robert tries his Chinese on the villagers, but no-one responds. Furthermore, we notice, no-one seems to possess a bicycle. A village with no bicycles – it must be extremely poor. A pump – we have to find a pump. At least if we have a pump, we can try and replace the inner tube, and fix the punctured one later.

Not a soul in the village responds to Robert's questions – they all look at him like a pack of morons, wide-mouthed. Others hide behind doors. Robert has now resorted to the written language. Amazingly, my phrasebook yields, 'CAN YOU LEND ME A BICYCLE PUMP?' That's an unexpected bonus. Elated, we shows this phrase in Chinese to a knot of people. They shake their heads. Just our luck – nobody can read. They are illiterate.

Robert finds their dialect incomprehensible. Since Robert speaks a 'distorted' form of Chinese, the villagers immediately assume that he is one of the fabled Overseas Chinese they've heard about, as if going overseas elongates the nose, rounds the eyes, and provides a moustache. The concept of a foreigner is quite beyond them: their sense of geography ends at the perimeter of the village. Gesturing at the flat tyre, we eventually get our message across – a man arrives with a huge Chinese pump. It has the wrong valve fitting, but with a few adjustments with pieces of wire, we get the tyre pumped up again. Mysteriously, it holds – there must be a flaw in the valve on Robert's tyre. This comes as a great relief, as I'm not looking forward to trying to replace the inner tube. I collect my tools from various villagers who've been passing them around, and we make a hasty exit...

The last twelve miles into Sanmenxia are a gift – the road winds down out of the hills and into the plains. We overtake everything in sight, racing the setting sun – knowing that once it gets dark we will be facing unknown quantities of potholes. We get to Sanmenxia Hotel a little after dark, at 8 p.m.

Sanmenxia is a quiet place – less traffic, less chaos on the streets. I don't manage to get much sleep, however – spend the evening being interrogated and tortured by various giant mosquitoes which have slipped through the window-screens.

As a day-trip, we cycle off to pay our respects to the Yellow River, whose course we have vaguely followed for the last 250 miles, but which we have yet to see. It is a drab, murky affair, bounded by high cliffing on the Sanmenxia side. The Yellow River Valley was the cradle of Chinese civilisation, fostering the great dynasties. But these are fifteen or twenty centuries gone – now along the Yellow River's path everything is cracked, faded, neglected, peeling, stained, old and crumbled. The networking of river and canals is no longer needed; the area is poor and backward; the great metropolises have shifted to the east coast.

Far below us is a ferry-crossing. The ferry comes in to a wharf, swirling yellowish silt in its wake. The moving silt and mudbars are part of a complex problem that the Yellow River creates. Along its length – from its source in Tibet, journeying 3000 miles to the Bo Hai gulf – the 'river of sorrows' dumps millions of tons of silt, elevating itself and then overflowing its banks. In some places the river runs along elevated channels as much as ten yards higher than the surrounding countryside. It has flooded thousands of times, and changed direction dozens of times – destroying all in its path, and claiming millions of lives. Some 900,000 people perished in the Yellow River flood of 1887 – the greatest natural disaster in history; a similar number reputedly died of drowning and starvation when, in 1938, Chiang Kaishek's soldiers deliberately blew up the Yangtse Kiang dam to stall advancing Japanese soldiers. Building of massive dikes and dams is seen as the answer to controlling the monster: there is a huge dam near Sanmenxia, built in the 1960s to hold back the silt – and now steadily filling up with silt.

On the road from Sanmenxia to Huayin, the landscape is a lot more rugged – the highway cuts through windswept cliffing. We pass a petrol-dump where truck-drivers are loading up. Petrol is rationed; the drivers have to get coupons from their work-units. The coupons are given to a pump-attendant; a black hose comes out of a mysterious window. But I start thinking – the truck-drivers are a fairly friendly lot – if a traveller could get a motorcycle into China somehow, the drivers could be talked into donating petrol for the cause.

Robert gets a flat tyre. This time we are able to stop at a small village with a bike-repair place. To avoid further problems, we have decided to replace the inner tube with one of our spares, and then patch up the old tube. To our deep concern, the bike-mechanic takes half an hour to get the back wheel off – he has to remove a piece of the black case enclosing the chain, then he has to extract a link from the chain in order to free the back wheel. The design of the bike is such that the back wheel cannot be removed any other way except by unscrewing the whole chain-case.

'Good job we didn't try this back in the village of the morons,' says Robert.

'We'd still be there,' I sputter. 'How could they design the thing that way?'

'We can scotch any plans for changing tubes ourselves – we don't have the tools.'

'But we've made it this far with only one flat. We should be okay.'

By five p.m. we've covered all but six miles of the ninety miles from Sanmenxia to Huayin. We have crossed the border into Shaanxi Province, on the home run.

'We've been incredibly lucky today,' says Robert, referring to the fixing of the flat tyre, to our rapid progress under cloudy skies, and to our escape from an encounter with rain earlier in the day. In response to Robert's remarks, the sky suddenly opens up and rain pours down. We take shelter, hoping it will pass. It doesn't. Ah well, we reason, if we can go sixty miles in the rain, as we did before from Kaifeng to Zhengzhou, then we can certainly go six miles. We sally forth with umbrellas at the ready, like jousting knights ready to do battle with the elements. The rain wins. It comes down in terrific sheets, backed by thunderclaps; torrents of muddy water flow at top speed along the trenches on either side of the road. It gets so bad we take shelter in a cave dug into a mountain-side. A large rat scampers out of the nearby wheatfields to join us, and eyes us suspiciously. This is one of the four million that the Chinese are trying to wipe out, and it looks at us like it has heard all about the campaign.

At 6.30 we figure time is running out – darkness will soon descend. We have to risk another break for Huayin. We sally forth again. I slip face-first in the muddy wheatfield as we make a dash for the highway. My hands, face and shoes are completely covered in mud. Robert laughs his head off, the rotten bastard. We push off down a mountain slope. Robert stops laughing. His brakes don't work. Neither do mine. We are both out of control. No matter how hard I pump the brakes, my speed increases. The wet brake-pads refuse to grip the rims on this steep slope. I am seriously considering ditching the bike while the going is good. Around a hairpin bend, a level stretch appears...

There is a long uphill stretch after this. I am trying to work out what Robert reminds me of, with his strange yellow raincape that he picked up in Jiangsu Province. Yes, a bee caught in the rain. A big yellow bee, with no leaf or flower to hide under, far from the hive. Another couple of hair-raising descents without brakes – and we land in Huayin, sopping wet. The staff at the guesthouse go crazy trying to locate the best room for us. We don't care – all we want to do is change our socks.

*   *   *

HUAYIN IS THE TOWN at the base of the holy mountain of Huashan. The guesthouse opened May 1st – the plumbing still wasn't hooked up – so we were given an expensive room with lots of plumbing, not realising till later that none of it worked. The toilet didn't flush. After repeated inquiries, an attendant on the third floor pointed to an outhouse at the back of the construction site, about 500 yards away. There was no sign of any garbage disposal, either. Robert asked about a garbage bin.

'Oh, we don't have those,' the attendant said. 'Just throw it all on the floor.' She picked up an empty cigarette packet to demonstrate – someone would clean the floors eventually.

Huashan is one of the five sacred Daoist mountains in China. There are nine sacred mountains altogether – four of them are Buddhist, and five are Daoist. I visited two of the these mountains on previous travels in China – the sacred Daoist peak of Taishan, and the sacred Buddhist peak of Emei Shan – so I knew vaguely what to expect. There would be thousands of pilgrims, all set to climb the stone-stair trails to the top of the mount, and hawkers lining the route to keep those pilgrims supplied. Along the way, there would be temples and pavilions – depending on how much survived the fury of the Red Guards during the Cultural Revolution, and depending on how much a return to religious worship was tolerated. For the traveller, there was the pleasant prospect of getting away from the socialist concrete hotels, and staying in a rickety wooden lodge, teahouse or monastery.

For the moment, we were stuck with the socialist concrete. No point in trying to climb Huashan the same night – we'd set off in the morning. There were others with more limited time than us – they would arrive in Huayin at night by train from Xian, climb at night, watch the sunrise the next morning, and come back for the evening train. Thus, though it was 8.30 p.m., this place raged on while the rest of China slept – the hawkers were out in force to get the midnight climbers. I put on some dry socks, and we went to check the foodstalls. I'd quite forgotten the hotel was still under construction – I missed a piece of concrete outside the hotel and fell straight into a storm-drain. Up to my knees. I was lucky I didn't break my neck. Robert howled with laughter. I came very close to killing him – that was my last pair of dry socks.

The foodstalls yielded a few cans of ham, some unleavened bread, glass jars of preserved apples. Hawkers lined the entrance-gate to Huashan. There was a roaring trade in walking-sticks, hats, drinks, batteries, torches, maps, Huashan cigarettes, Huashan badges, and all the other paraphernalia that the climber was expected to need. And climbers were going up in droves. The streets, with fires burning and music blaring, conveyed the flavour of a mediaeval carnival; the comparison with the pilgrims of Chaucer's *Canterbury Tales* was irresistible. We'd had enough excitement and slippery surfaces for one day – we would join the pilgrims the following day.

Back at the hotel, I racked my brains as to how to silence the man with the blaring radio directly beneath the hotel-window. He was three floors down, but the radio sounded like it was right in the room. It was not even music – the man had the radio turned up to the point of maximum earsplitting distortion. Water would've been the ideal way to silence him, but the plumbing in the room didn't work. All we could really do was ask to change rooms to the other side of the hall, away from the street. However, we knew the staff wouldn't be sympathetic to such a change – they were all next door gathered round a TV set of equal noise distortion, watching a kung fu epic. I could hear each scream, chop, parry and thrust through the concrete walls.

In the morning there was a loud bang on the door. It was a visit from the local PSB officer. Obviously the man was not used to dealing with foreigners, as foreigners did not get permits for Huashan. This, indeed, was what has brought him here. Robert spoke to him in Chinese; he demanded to see our passports, bicycle purchase receipts, and our travel-permits for Huashan. The officer was astonished at the permits, and examined them for some time, convinced there was some kind of mistake. But there was no mistake – the permits and papers were in order. The date was May 12th – our visas and permits were valid for another two months. The officer had done his duty by inspecting the papers, and that was the end of the matter as far as he was concerned. All we had to do now was apply for a hiking-permit at the gates of Huashan.

On Huashan the plumbing was much better – clean, clear mountain streams where we could wash up. Angular chunks of white granite lined the way to the top; trees gripped the slopes along the route. It was a handsome mountainside. So quiet – no traffic, no pollution, no Jiefang trucks breathing down our necks, no blaring radios. Perhaps that's why people came to climb the mountain – to get away from the filthy cities.

Some beggars – legless, blind – lined the first section of the hike, along with food and drink stalls. Granite was being quarried to fashion walkways at the base. Robert asked one of the workers how long it would take to get to the top. Five hours up, he said. No dust, no diesel fumes – just the pleasant sound of running water and bird-calls. Birds?! I hadn't heard a bird for such a long time.

We trudged upward. The company was congenial enough. There were soldiers on a few days' leave; teenagers from Xian on a weekend jaunt; couples ostensibly going for a picnic – but actually looking for some intimate privacy; indolent young women being portered up on the backs of sturdy, hired porters; and tribes of wiry grandmothers who put us all to shame with their brisk walking-speed, singing to keep their stride. The grey-haired grandmothers came once a year to climb – supposedly this promoted longevity. They would make offerings to Daoist deities at the top. They all had stout walking-sticks. Their journey was made more difficult by bound feet – some were so old that they belonged to the pre-Maoist era when 'lily feet' were considered to be dainty. But the combined pull of superstition, legend, history and folk-religion would get them to the summit. There were no old men among these groups, which led me to believe that the grandmothers were widows.

A porter bearing two agonisingly-full crates of beer, balanced on either end of a bamboo pole, toiled up the slopes. The beer was for guesthouses and stalls at the top. The hunchbacked porter had a peculiar slow-motion gait, like a mime in a trance. Those legs had done the trip hundreds of times before, and knew better than to rush. Sign of the times – there were young men making the climb in three-piece suits. And ties. And bare feet.

I was beginning to enjoy myself – nobody was on home territory here – everybody was a pilgrim or tourist. So we blended in – no large crowds gathering to stare at us; they were all much too busy climbing the mountain. We had, too, a legitimate reason to be on the mountain – once we went up to the peak and came down again, our tourist obligations would be fulfilled. Everybody understood what we were doing here. Very few foreigners could have passed this way, since no permits for Huashan were normally issued, but everyone still understood why we were here.

Closer to the top there was a sheer rock-face, completely perpendicular, with chain and metal ladders provided to surmount the obstacle. One slip and serious injury could've resulted – most likely one of the reasons that foreigners were not allowed on the mountain.

Near the summit, tucked down pathways, were monastic lodges run by wizened grey-haired Daoist priests, with black garb and white leggings; hair swept back and held with a pin, and wispy goatees. It had been a seven-hour climb all told, to an elevation of about 6500 feet – which was not much in real climbing terms, but still enough to knock us out. It was getting cold – I grabbed some quilts from spare beds in the room, and made myself cosy. It was a tremendous change from the circus where we'd spent the previous night. Here there was no electricity – just kerosene lamps. And no traffic.

In the morning I was awoken by the sound of fireworks. The grannies were out scaring off evil spirits with these. There were three small shrines in the vicinity of the lodge – dark enclosures with candles and incense boxes, lanterns, lattice doorways, and the occasional soft sound of bells. The grannies visited each of the three shrines in a long involved ritual, burning bright yellow strips of paper with Daoist texts inscribed on them, and bobbing up and down murmuring prayers. Such behaviour was a return to 'superstitious rites', tolerated over the last few years by the State.

I went over to the tiny shop at the lodge, and found only two tinned items – luncheon meat and sliced Chinese gooseberry. The latter was a totally new product in the tin line: I snapped up three of them. With these, a few eggs, some steaming *mantou* and tea, we managed an excellent breakfast, a big enough booster to get us up and hiking to the top of Huashan.

Marking the summit was the frozen figure of the official Huashan photographer, lying in wait for summiteers. He was curled up in his green army greatcoat. From the top it looked like a clear, flat run to Xian. It was with great peace of mind – and completely ruined legs – that we returned to the task at hand: a descent from the mountain, and a final run to Xian. It was the tail-end of a scheme that had started with a few rude lines on a map. A bare 75 miles of that route was left to negotiate.

Among the maps I had compiled for the trip was, of course, one of Xian itself, but I had not perused the fine print on the back of the map till our stop in Huashan. I was looking for rainfall information. *Semi-arid and semi-humid monsoon climate,* said the map. Searing in summer, freezing in winter, and damp otherwise. Average rainfall for May at 9.4 days a month; even worse in July with 11.3 days a month, while September registered 13.1 days. No wonder we were getting dumped upon.

It was then that I noticed a prize piece of plumbing, one previously overlooked. Huaqing Hot Spring Guesthouse. It lay at Lintong, about 20 miles to the east of Xian, and was listed as a tourist location. How big was the jurisdiction of Xian? Xian

County, the map said, encompassed 2295 square kilometres – or 883 square miles. We were already in the county by that estimate, and Lintong was most certainly included in Xian County – no permit would be needed, since Xian was wide open. A further bonus – Lintong was right near the Tomb of the Terracotta Warriors, a major archeological find.

Hot springs, I knew from other parts of China, were usually channelled through to large private baths in hotels – and hot springs had the finest plumbing in the country. I scanned the fine print for details. *'A larger palace built on the mountainside in 747 BC; hot springs can hold 400 people at one time; Lotus Bath is said to have been bath of the favourite concubine of Emperor Xuan Zong... Huaqing Hot Spring Guesthouse has pavilions, corridors and hot spring baths in the hotel which can accommodate up to 40 guests. Tang Dynasty reconstruct, with garden-type villas.'*

The thought of plentiful hot spring plumbing was overpowering – aching back and knackered legs gained new life at the very mention. Huaqing Hot Springs rang a bell somehow. I thought about it for a full hour, taxing my storage systems of Chinese trivia. Then I found out which bell. The hot springs were where Generalissimo Chiang Kaishek was captured in his pyjamas – wearing one shoe, and minus his false teeth. He was captured by his own generals, in 1936, in co-operation with the Communists. They were intent on killing him, but decided that would cause too much upheaval. So Chiang Kaishek was finally released for a king's ransom – on the condition that the Nationalists join a united front against the Japanese. Chiang never forgave those from his own troops who took part in the bizarre arrest: one of the generals involved was later executed, and another was later thrown into jail in Taiwan – for life.

The trip from Huashan to Huaqing was a 60-mile race against the rain. There were no big hills to toil up, but each rise felt, for the legs, like a little Huashan all over again. My legs were as stiff as boards – refusing to flex themselves. Only the prospect of a hot bath could get those legs into gear at all. Fifty miles to a hot bath; forty miles and closing...

'The rooms are 32 yuan a double. That's the rule,' said the prim lady with thick glasses at the reception-desk of Huaqing Hot Spring Guesthouse. She spoke in clear English. One look at her and we knew it would be useless to try and bring the price down. She was one of those super-efficient types who knew the rules, and stuck by them. Whenever someone like that wanted to win an argument, they'd say it was a new *'gueding'* – a rule. Didn't matter who made the rule up – or why – it was a rule, and it had to be obeyed. Robert made a weak attempt to show her some of our previous cheaper receipts from hotels – 6 yuan a bed. She brushed them aside:

'It's 32 yuan a double,' she insisted. 'That's the rule in Shaanxi Province. It's the same everywhere. And you must leave by 12 noon or you pay a half-day rate charge.'

'Does the guesthouse have hot water?' I asked, to make sure.

'Of course,' she snorted. 'It's a hotel – it has *everything*.'

'What about dinner-time?'

'Dinner finishes at 6.15 p.m. That's a rule. There is a shop, but it closes at 5.30 p.m.' We had missed both, and I was quite ready to rip the glasses off her face and stomp all over them to see if there was a rule governing that kind of behaviour too.

'Have you ridden your bicycle from England?' she asked an astounded Robert. He was in bad shape, but surely he didn't look *that* worn down.

We were both barely able to walk, but still able to ride – so we cycled back into town to the nearest tiny shop, and bagged some peanuts, biscuits and beer. The hotel-room more than made up for the dearth of food. It was out the back, past some weeping willows, through a rose-garden. Real 100-watt bulbs. A plastic garbage can. And there, in another room was a bath as deep as . . . a swimming-pool. Robert had first option on the bath.

'Ah yes, just the right temperature – superb!' he shouted from the bath-tub, grunting and groaning as he eased his destroyed legs into place.

Everything was processed through the bath-tub in time – ourselves, sneakers, bags, raingear. Finally we felt a tinge of remorse for the bikes, still spattered in mud. I had thought of taking a wet towel to wipe my bike down, but a better idea came up. Take it into the bath. The bath was big enough, after all, and we had to prepare the bikes for resale. Besides, what better mockery of the rules could there be?

*   *   *

THE TOMB OF THE TERRACOTTA WARRIORS is a few miles from Lintong; on unladen bikes, it takes us only half an hour to get there from Huaqing Hot Spring Guesthouse. Upon arrival, we are besieged by hordes of black marketeers keen to change money.

The Tomb of the Terracotta Warriors is an anomaly. It was discovered by peasants sinking a well in 1974. While other tombs around China were being smashed to pieces by Red Guards, the site near Xian was acclaimed as a Maoist-era find, and thus not linked to the 'smash the four olds' campaign (old ideas, old customs, old culture, old habits). Instead, the Red Guards were brought in to help excavate this huge site – and they were suddenly promoted as archeological heroes. The fact that the site was the mausoleum of ruthless emperor Qin Shihuangdi, certainly representative of the 'four olds' that Mao Zedong was out to abolish, did not alter the course of events. Instead of being criticised, Qin Shihuangdi was happily lionized in the process.

Qin Shihuangdi rose to power around 220 B.C., and is credited with unifying China by conquering six independent states. One immediate benefit of this project was a fully-diversified harem, quite a large one. Qin Shihuangdi's reign was brief – thirty-six years – and his dynasty, the Qin Dynasty, collapsed shortly after his death. During this brief reign, however, an empire was consolidated – highways were built, irrigation-projects installed, and work on the Great Wall was done. The emperor maintained his power by brute force. He slew his critics, attempted to uproot Confucianism, burned historical writing other than official Qin histories, and conscripted hundreds of thousands of political prisoners for projects such as the Great Wall and his grandiose tomb.

Like so many other aspects of history under the Maoists, the topic of Qin Shihuangdi is studiously avoided. No-one can quite make up their minds whether he is a hero or a renegade, so the subject is best glossed over altogether – the same approach is taken when writing up Mao Zedong's reign. Only a fraction of Qin Shihuangdi's massive necropolis near Xian has been excavated. It is estimated that some 700,000 workers were employed to construct this underground palace, to the east of Qin Shihuangdi's former capital of Xianyang (close to Xian). The work took 36 years: palaces and pavilions deployed in inner and outer cities, and surrounded by a wall some four miles in circumference. Droves of labourers and artisans were executed to keep the tomb's secrets: their mass graves lie amongst the underground splendour, along with Qin Shihuangdi's unexcavated tomb. In other sites large numbers of horse-skeletons have been found. Reports of other objects buried include bronze-chariots decorated with gold; a ceiling inlaid with pearls to simulate the sun, stars and moon; and a section composed entirely of live animals meant to simulate a zoo.

It is unlikely that these palaces will be excavated in their original splendour: the roofs and ramparts have collapsed, and materials have corroded. To restore a single terracotta statue from the pieces can take several months of painstaking assembly. Here one sees originals, however, of the terracotta warriors. In other museums around China, invariably the tourist is looking at copies or reconstructs of original items – the originals are housed in a vault somewhere, deemed too valuable to be on view. In the largest burial pit are an estimated 6000 terracotta figures of soldiers and horses, in full battle array, making sure that Qin Shihuangdi will be well defended in his afterlife. That is what the ancestor-fixated Chinese have, in the past, tried to do for their kin – ensure an auspicious burial-spot. To disturb such a place would bring bad luck.

It is amusing to note that in a nation that claims to have eradicated wastage of land for burials (the Party insists on cremation), and that claims to have put an end to ancestor-worship, a high proportion of tourist attractions in China consists of tombs and the accompanying gravestone art. Around the country the hapless group-tourist is shunted from burial site to burial site to see a couple of engraved *steles*, or six-foot tombstones; large areas around Peking seem to consist of nothing else but the tombs of emperors; in the vicinity of Xian there are hundreds of imperial tombs. Mao himself has become part of the cult of ancestor-worship: his body, embalmed in a crystal sarcophagus in a building in Tiananmen Square, has been preserved for future generations.

I gaze at the only vault at Qin Shihuangdi's tomb that has been excavated: several hundred soldiers whose torsos, heads, feet and limbs have been carefully glued together. The find would have been quite ordinary had it not been for the scale of the site, and the nature of the statues. Each terracotta statue – originally painted – is composed of a hollow torso, while the limbs and head are solid; each figure is individualised to the point of being a portrait. It is not known what sort of kilns were used to fire these lifesized pieces, since nothing of this size or degree of realism is known from before this era, or for long after.

Row upon row of terracotta soldiers, facing eastwards. They remind me – can it be? – of the ticket queues at Beijing Main Railway Station. Rows of commuters, waiting their turn, pressing forward, never getting what they want. They have the same vacant expressions on their faces. Train-travel to the next world. The building that houses the warriors itself reminds me of Beijing Railway Station: the same Soviet-style arched roof, the same guards patrolling to make sure you don't break the rules – in this case, no photos. What is it about this 'modern' Chinese architecture that has the extraordinary ability to turn every building into a military museum or a railway station?

Outside, I wander off to a side-room and encounter a group of geriatric western tourists. The room is identical to a first-class waiting-room at any Chinese railway station: the same floral-patterned armchairs and couches, the same antimacassars, the same lace doilies on the tables, and, it seems, the same large tea-urns and soft drinks, and uniformed attendants. These exhausted geriatrics are seeking relief from the crowds, and from the strenuous schedule of tomb-viewing.

In market-stalls nearby, the locals have their own miniature armies of terracotta warriors for sale. These are one-foot high versions of individual soldiers and horses, and they are pressed upon me by very aggressive touts. I pause to witness the sale of several pieces to westerners who are quite willing to pay the outrageous price demanded. There is a distinct buzz running through the stalls after this transaction – the news is quickly communicated to the other share-holders in this cottage-industry. A record kill has been made; there are suckers who want to pay more; Comrades! Raise your starting-prices!

May 15th. Twenty miles of cycling now brings us to the gates of Xian. The road is level, and the cycling should be easy – but every muscle and joint still remembers the climb up Huashan. Pedalling is agony. There is no great sense of elation on the entry to Xian. Relief, but no jubilation. We are too tired, too hungry for that. We have reached the eastern gate to the city, where a road bridges an ancient moat, now reconstructed, and pierces the old city walls. Xi-An: 'Western Peace'. It is odd that we have no energy to celebrate; the truth of the matter is that we have arrived long ago – the mind travels ahead. In Lintong, at the hot springs, we were already in Xian County, and we knew the target was accomplished. We slip into the traffic, headed for the Renmin Hotel. No crowds to cheer us on; no welcoming committee; no champagne or wild parties – just the satisfaction of knowing we've made it.

Did I say no champagne? A late-night bar at the Renmin Hotel stocks ice-cold Qingdao beer, and other fine liquors. We are back in the lap of luxury again – time to catch up on news, food, drink, laundry, and contact with other westerners. The bar is packed – Americans, Europeans, Australians – some on group-tours, some travelling on their own. This is the only lively part of the palatial Renmin Hotel – a gloomy, cold, cavernous abomination designed by Russians for Russians. The traveller network is in full swing in watering-holes like this bar – over a few bottles of beer, crude maps are drawn up, and addresses are jotted down.

I join a table with an Irishman who's come all the way from Kathmandu, by road, via Lhasa and Golmud to Xian. Next to him is an American woman who has trekked through the wastelands of Tibet – and lived to tell the tale. Sitting beside her is a Swede who's had some incredible adventures in Tibet, but since he contracted a bad case of laryngitis there, his deeds are only partially comprehensible. A Swiss woman recounts her trip in a hired minibus around Lhasa, banging her head on the roof of the vehicle a dozen times. She warns against extortionate Chinese drivers, rude Tibetan hitch-hikers, and rip-off hotel managers. What emerges from all this is a much freer picture of travel in Tibet than either myself or Robert thought possible. There is a buzz of excitement in the air. The overland route through to Kathmandu is viable, with an official opening barely a month ago, and an unofficial opening six months ago. The places along the way – Gyantse, Shigatse, Sakya – slip through my fingers. They are only names. To cement them into place, I have to go there in person – then the geography will stick. For the moment I have to content myself with tapping into the 'traveller network'.

'Well, a toast to Xian!' says Robert, raising his glass.

'To Xian!'

'And one for Tibet.'

'To the road ahead.'

'You know, Lhasa doesn't interest me so much. It sounds like an inevitable point to be reached.'

'I'm with you – it's what's along the way that will be more like the real Tibet.'

'The problem is how we're going to avoid officials if we go in by road from Chengdu.'

'How about fear of airplanes? You know, clogged ears – get sick if you fly.'

'Doesn't explain why you'd want a vacation at 17,000 feet, does it?'

'Ah well, a slight flaw in the alibi.'

* * *

XIAN, THE DUSTY TERMINUS of the journey, is an uninspiring place. Perhaps this does not do justice to a city that was once one of the world's greatest; but the fact is that its glory is long gone. In better days – from the 2nd century B.C. to the 10th century A.D. – the city was known as Changan – a cosmopolitan crossroads, an imperial capital, and starting-point of the Silk Road. At its height, as the capital of the Tang empire (from the 7th to 10th centuries A.D.), the city had a million inhabitants – and was alive with traders in silk, porcelain and precious stones. It covered an area of 30 square miles – a Mecca for scholars, entertainers, merchants, priests, soldiers and bureaucrats. The present city covers much the same area, but the city walls and gates now to be seen are not the Tang ones – they belong to the 14th century, and cover a downtown area of only five square miles. The few pagodas, and the handful of run-down towers and temples are also from the 14th century Ming era.

Now Xian is the economic centre of north-west China. It has a population of over 3 million, half of whom reside in the urban area – a wasteland of brick and concrete buildings, strangled under a thick mesh of trolley-bus wires. The streets are polluted and dusty, the restaurants are abysmal, the traffic is chaotic, the people are inhospitable. Outside the city walls is a heavy concentration of factories, running the full industrial gamut from fertilisers to electrical components.

Since modern-day Xian is totally devoid of colour, tourist authorities have dug deep into the past to keep their charges entertained. And what have they come up with? Tang dynasty song and dance! They've gone through all the tombs and museums, and patched together instruments, melodies, costumes and dance from a thousand years ago – a dubious piece of research. Through a contact at the hotel, one evening we join a tour-group of Germans, and are driven across town to a theatre. There, a dozen other tour-buses pull up, each identical, and the group-tourists traipse in. I have no idea where the theatre is on the map – but it has been the most comfortable bus-ride I've had in China.

The theatre is the imperial court for the evening – tourists become emperors. The fare is quite stunning – we are treated to scantily-clad Tang maidens going through their paces; we are treated to a Tang orchestra that has so many instruments it takes up the entire stage; and we are treated to acrobats with heavy make-up. The man next to me, Homo Ektachromo, fires off two rolls of film: he has a telescopic lens, and a strobe that is lethal up to fifty paces . . .

At the front gates of the Renmin Hotel we inquired of the security man where we might sell the bikes. Within a few minutes an older gentlemen in a scruffy Mao suit and dirty sneakers materialised, summoned over the telephone. He made us an offer – about 30 yuan less than we'd paid for the bikes in Shanghai. We neglected to tell the buyer we'd put half a year of wear on the bikes in the last month – he didn't even bother to inspect them. He just checked the brandname, squeezed the tyres, and handed over a thick wad of 10-yuan bills. Shanghai-brand bikes were rationed, and hard to come by in Xian. Although his threadbare clothing smacked of some sort of welfare case, the buyer was in fact a bigshot in charge of construction of a new 14-storey wing of the Renmin Hotel, with 800 beds. Our man was happy now – with a toothy grin he shook hands. He left one bike in the parking-lot opposite the gates, and rode the other bike home.

The bikes were gone – the receipts, the parking tags, the adventure. For a long time after, I absent-mindedly reached into my pocket, searching for the bike-key.

OTHER
EXCURSIONS

TRAIN 237 chugs out of Xian station. We're already missing those bicycles, when faced with the prospect of 18 hours in the confinement of a hard-seat carriage. We've been unable to get hard-sleeper tickets for Chengdu, and with the train packed to the gills, it's unlikely we will do so during the trip. The problem is that Sichuan is China's most populated province; it also has the fewest rail-lines. The Xian to Chengdu line, completed in 1956, was the first rail-line to link Sichuan province with the rest of China. It sliced months off travel time in China's south-west: we can't complain too loudly about the 18 hours ahead.

In our section, there are six passengers on facing padded seats. A similar configuration occupies the opposite window, with an aisle separating the two sections. Sharing Robert's seat, at the window, is a man dressed in a suit, silk tie and trenchcoat, with the suit-leg rolled up past his knees, presumably for air-conditioning. Robert is on the aisle-side – right next to him is a young woman attired exactly the same as the man at the window, which would indicate a recent marriage. What a way to spend a honeymoon! On my side are two dirty old men – well, old men in dirt-encrusted collars with stains on their pants, black fingernail ends, and yellowed fingertips. They're smoking like Trojans, and have an unlimited supply of hard-boiled eggs. By the time we get to Xian there promises to be an entire carpet of eggshells. Much to the embarrassment of the 'bride', Robert keeps nodding off – using her shoulder as a support. Dirty old men and snoring foreigners on the honeymoon – very romantic.

The cackle of the speakers commands my attention. Have I heard this music before? This is a game that rivals any western name-the-song TV quiz. The songs have been completely transformed by Chinese traditional musical instruments: on previous train-trips I've identified *The Yellow Rose of Texas, Swanee River, Auld Lang Syne, The Sounds of Silence,* and even *Rudolph The Red-Nosed Reindeer.* China does not recognise international copyright, so anything is fair game. But the melody-line now playing eludes me – what can it be? I'm certain I've heard it before.

Somewhere aboard this train – sitting in a tiny room with a couple of turntables, a microphone and a radio – is a broadcaster, whom, I'm sure, the passengers would love to throttle. The broad-caster gives news, tells passengers not to spit, reminds them not to bring explosive substances onto the train, reminds them to get off the train with some rhyming ditties: *'Those getting off at the next stop, please do so! Make sure you've got all your luggage, mind your step, don't drink unboiled water, don't spit.'* On the latter score, nobody has paid any attention. The floor is the garbage-bin – a receptacle for sunflower seeds, eggshells, spittle, nasal discharges and cigarette butts. There is no restriction on smoking anywhere on the train: China is a haven for smokers. Every Chinese male over the age of 15 seems to have the habit – a habit condoned by chain-smoker Mao Zedong and heavy-puffer Deng Xiaoping.

As darkness descends, the broadcaster announces that the dining-car is now serving – the richer among us leap to our feet. We thread our way through the cars, made hazy by chain-smokers . . . people playing cards, chatting, reading. In egalitarian China there are no classes – it's just that some sleeping arrange-ments are far more comfortable than others. We pass through the aisle of a soft-class compartment – inhabited by snooty cadres, plump army officers, and other privileged folk. There is a hushed reverence as we tread on a thick pile carpet – carpet that means no spitting.

We explode into the dining-car: the place is packed. I am thrown over a table as a waiter bustles by, juggling four dishes. The com-motion is incredible – diners are snaffling up food at an alarming rate; others are queued up around the tables waiting for them to vacate. We are propelled to the front of the car where beer and food tickets are thrown at us – the waiter plonks us down and thrusts chopsticks upon us. Before we finish the meal, the Chinese diners opposite have changed three times, leaving a mountain of bones and cigarettes as souvenirs. The waiter comes along and yanks the tablecloth – bottles, bones and all.

Dinner over, the passengers jockey for sleeping positions. Robert can sleep anywhere. Others, inured from years of practice, can sleep in impossible positions – crammed into the small spaces between the cars; one man has his head on his bag, which is sup-ported by a washbasin at the end of a car; others are propped up against vibrating windows; some are nodding off bolt upright. As for myself, I know I won't get a wink until I get good and tired, so I produce a Chinese chess-set, and line up opponents. This at least breaks the ice. I won't have to face a wall of sullen starers all evening. It is of little use to try and win, as heated discussion has started on the opposition side as to how to nail the big-nose. Each move is monitored by a committee of players – some ten of them by now.

Having been thoroughly wiped over the floorboards in several games, I hand over to another player, and get up to revive my muscles. I bump into a Tibetan bound for Chengdu. He's wearing a grey fedora, and he shoots off a brilliant smile. It is a salute from one minority to another – we recognise this much about each other. I get him to give me some Tibetan lessons, naming objects around us.

Train-journeys through China never fail to produce at least one English language 'leech' desperate to practice on a live foreigner. Chang, a middle-aged Chinese, wanders over to introduce himself. The conversation proceeds in fits and starts: Chang inquires about my financial affairs back home, a topic of enduring fascination since an hourly wage in the west can exceed a *monthly* one in China.

'And what is your job?' I ask him, to shift the topic.

'I do punctuation,' he replies.

Now here's an oddball job – a professional punctuator: hand him a freestyle draft and he'll riddle it with commas, semi-colons, brackets and question-marks. You never need worry about punctuation again. Unfortunately, no such luck – he does acupuncture. We fall to talking about Norman Bethune, the best-known doctor – and foreigner – in China. 'Bai Qiuen', as he is called in Chinese, is revered as the Canadian surgeon who fought alongside Mao, serving with the Eighth Route Army in the war against Japan. A widely-circulated poster depicts Comrade Bethune talking to Mao Zedong in Yanan; the doctor is also the subject of a popular comic-book.

Chang asks if I have any foreign stamps – he is a collector. He shows me a Chinese stamp with Comrade Bethune on it. Some foreign stamps, he tells me, cannot be brought into China – meaning stamps that bear 'anti-Communist designs', such as those from Taiwan. Here, an innocuous conversation produces a twist: I ask Chang about rare Chinese stamps, and he tells me a strange story.

In 1966, Mao Zedong launched the 'Great Proletarian Cultural

Revolution' to re-kindle revolutionary zeal: over a million were to die in the next decade from the fierce faction-fighting that resulted. At the height of 'Mao-mania', the Great Helmsman was venerated as a god: China was inundated with Mao posters, Mao books, Mao statues and other Mao junk. There was even a Mao Zedong alarm-clock with a Red Guard mounted on it waving a Little Red Book in time to the tick-tock sound. In 1968 a large bright red stamp was designed – featuring a great crowd of peasants waving the Little Red Book, and bearing the slogan, 'The Whole Country is Red'. At the last minute the stamp was withdrawn from circulation, prior to public issue, due to 'design inaccuracies'. However, such was the confusion of the Cultural Revolution that certain post-offices had begun selling the stamp two days before the official date of issue. It has, according to Chang, become the rarest of all Chinese stamps.

As a compensation prize for our close confinement, morning brings lush ravines, gorges, mountain-ranges, terraced farmlands, buffalo, wisps of smoke drifting from thatched cottages – and the soothing sounds of Chinese snakeskin fiddle, somehow seeming to match the rhythm of the train. *Bonanza!* The music that had eluded me the previous night – it was the theme-music from the television western, *Bonanza*. My mind must've wrestled with this puzzle all evening.

A rail-staffer trundles by with a large brass kettle – the first teawater of the day. The entire population of the train is up at 6.15 a.m., busy with tooth-brushing and other mysterious ablutions. The smokers set to work on the next packet. The spitters fire off a few rounds down the aisles. And I gaze out the window at the finest train-ride scenery anywhere in China...

By noon we're in an industrial zone, with chimney-stacks, haze, braces of cyclists at crossroads, concertina buses... and the train pulls into Chengdu North Station.

Chengdu is a pleasant enough place, as Chinese cities go. It has broad, leafy boulevards as main thoroughfares, and side-alleys alive with all kinds of hawkers – basket-weavers, cobblers, wart-removers, callous-removers, sidewalk dentists, tailors, streetside florists, poultry merchants, butchers, spice-vendors, comic-book renters and fruitsellers. After the stagnancy of Xian and the Yellow

River cities, Chengdu is an explosion of life: there is an extraordinary amount of trading and free-marketing. The abundance of fresh food comes from the lush Sichuan Basin, which forms the eastern part of Sichuan Province; the marketing is explained by the fact that Sichuan is Deng Xiaoping's home province. It was in Sichuan that Deng's economic reforms were first implemented, allowing peasants a free hand in planting crops, allowing them to sell surpluses on the free market, and allowing them to supplement their income with handicraft production.

The remains of Chengdu's city-walls were demolished in the 1960s. Areas with traditional half-timbered housing remain at the north end of the city – these overhanging structures are strangely reminiscent of Tudor cottages. At the height of the Cultural Revolution, in the late 1960s, the 14th century Viceroy's Palace – at the centre of Chengdu – was blown to smithereens. In its place, a four-storey Soviet-style Industrial Exhibition Hall was thrown up, with a gigantic statue of Mao plonked in front. If there were any pigeons left on the streets of Chengdu, they would surely take their bearings from this statue, amongst other uses. The 'Old Man' stares down on hundreds of peddlers hawking wicker furniture, pots, fabrics, meat, fruit and vegetables in nearby alley-ways. A short distance from the Mao statue, there is a roundabout where giant billboards exhort the populace – in English – not to go forth and multiply. Chengdu has a core population of over 1.5 million, with more than four million in the city limits. Sichuan Province is the most heavily populated province in China – over 105 million at last count. So there is a very aggressive 'one child only' campaign in progress.

As a counterpoint to the hubbub of daily life, there are quiet teahouses to be found in Chengdu's back-alleys and parks, its downtown streets, and even tucked into its old temples. These oases are where people go to meet, talk, or just relax; they are filled with bamboo armchairs, bamboo tables, ceramic teasets and sooty kettles. Some specialise – they cater to chess-players, or those intent on smoking themselves to death; one or two feature story-tellers, or plain-clothes Sichuan opera at night; others are more open, catering to families and couples as well as old men. The teahouse in China is the equivalent of the British pub or the French café, and since fierce debate has always taken place in the teahouses, they were closed during the Cultural Revolution as dangerous meeting-grounds.

I had fond memories of these places, from a visit two years previously. I had found the perfect guide – Shun Min – by chance in the traffic one day. Chengdu is one of the few cities in China where foreigners can rent bikes – at a stop-light an older man had pulled up alongside me and started talking in English; shortly after, I was cycling after him – down a back-alley to a teahouse.

Over a cup of stone-flower tea, I found out he was a teacher at a middle school in Chengdu, and he was 60 years old. At my request, over the course of a few days, he had taken me on a delightful tour of the teahouses of Chengdu, and more than a few of the restaurants. In between, he took me back to his apartment, which he shared with his wife and a number of in-laws.

He insisted on showing me off to those in the neighbouring apartments, and I had to ask him why he had no fear of associating with a foreigner. He was an old man, he said – he didn't care what happened to him anymore. I inquired whether it would make life difficult for his children. He shrugged: his daughter was grown up, and lived in Guilin, and he didn't know where his son was. I pressed the latter point. During the Cultural Revolution, Shun Min said, youths turned against their teachers: he didn't really care what happened to himself, but was terrified that something might happen to his son. So he left his son with another family for safe-keeping. The surrogate family left Chengdu – and Shun Min never saw his son again.

There isn't much time to explore Chengdu the second time round: Robert and myself are flat out getting the next leg of the trip under way. The plan is to make it from Chengdu to Lhasa overland. Many foreigners have failed to get started on this route. But we have a secret weapon: Robert. Robert's Chinese, we hope, will break the ice with the right truck-driver. From what we can work out, there are two depots in Chengdu where truckers congregate, and which will take paying passengers toward Lhasa – though they balk at taking foreigners. One specialises in the south route via Markam to Lhasa; the other runs trucks only as far as Chamdo, on the north route. The Chamdo truck-depot is further out of town, more obscure, and, we surmise, probably more receptive.

The third day in Chengdu, May 19th, we get up early, collect some bicycle rentals, and cycle off to the Chamdo trucking depot.

At the depot we are shunted around from office to office, told to wait. We wait. And wait. And wait. They seem to be ignoring us. Robert asks again. We want to pay for a ride as far as Chamdo, he tells a woman hiding behind a ticket-barrier. She nods. We wait. Two more hours go by.

A driver comes in to collect his truck-delivery schedule. He is going to Chamdo tomorrow. We both jump up – we're going too!

'No, not with that one', says the woman at the ticket-barrier. 'He flies!'

'What does that mean?'

'He drives like a madman,' translates Robert.

We sit down again. Another hour passes. A driver comes to get his schedule for the following day. The woman at the ticket-counter talks to him, points at us. *Those are the ones,* she seems to say. The driver turns around and scratches his head. Robert starts talking to him in Chinese.

'How much luggage do you have?' asks the driver.

'Hardly any,' says Robert.

'Can you be ready at 7 a.m. tomorrow morning?'

'Of course!'

'Then I'll see you at the gates.'

The driver turns around and walks off. We are dumbfounded. We have found a ride! Robert goes over and pays the woman for the fare to Chamdo: 60 yuan each. We grab the tickets and run out as fast as our legs will take us, in case they change their minds.

10 oranges	1 case of chewing-gum
20 chocolate bars	20 sachets of coffee
10 bags of instant noodles	20 cans of pineapple juice
10 cans of mandarin segments	6 cans of pork and tomato
1 case of medicinal brick-tea	8 packets of nougat

We shovel these things into cheap vinyl bags at the Jinjiang Hotel shop. They are our supplementary food rations for the ride to Lhasa. For bribes, we get four cartons of western cigarettes. All Chinese drivers smoke – heavily.

'It's good to have a bit of food when you're travelling, isn't it?' says the counter-assistant in the shop, as she tallies up the bill with an abacus.

'Yes,' I reply, 'Yes, it is.'

'Very much so,' says Robert.

We're both thinking of the great hardships in store for the stomach in the next few weeks. But not much time to dwell on that – there is more provisioning to be done. A xerox machine has to be located to run off copies of a vital discovery in Robert's German book about Tibet – a black and white portrait of the Dalai Lama. Western film has to be found – no easy task, since supplies seem to have been bought out. We go to Public Security to get a permit for Lhasa: at the same time a year earlier, that stamp had been impossible to obtain. The PSB woman asks how we intend to get to Lhasa. 'Plane', we tell her.

★   ★   ★

WE HAVE IGNITION! The Dongfeng truck rolls out of Chengdu, on the road to Tibet. The driver flicks a switch – it is a device that truck-drivers dream about – an automatic horn, which sounds at one-minute intervals. The driver's name is Zhang; in the back of the truck is a load of Japanese TV sets. Zhang has done 350,000 *gongli* – this is posted on the front bumper of the truck. He's been at it for fifteen years. Fortunately, the truck has only 163,000 *gongli* on the odometer – it still has plenty of heart left from the sound of the engine. It will need it – Chamdo is 1285 *gongli* through rough terrain – 800 miles. Chengdu to Lhasa is double that distance.

Zhang makes a stop to pick up a small overnight bag with his toothbrush and tea-mug in it. We pass a steady procession of slaughtered pigs on the backs of bicycles, slung on racks, and then a bus with its entire rooftop crammed with live geese. I ponder why no-one in China has yet devised a method of moving a cow or a water-buffalo around on a bike.

Our first objective is the town of Kangding, about 230 miles from Chengdu. We're anxious to put on distance – on the theory that the further we get, the greater the chance of continuing unhindered.

Among the first to describe the Tibetans was Marco Polo, though he never set foot in Tibet. His travel-patron was the Mongol chieftan Kublai Khan. The Great Khan was, apparently, bored stiff with official reports, but fascinated by minority customs in his far-flung empire. The Mongols themselves were a minority – a minority that the Chinese had attempted to keep out with the lunacy of building the Great Wall. Astutely, Polo endeavoured to fill small notebooks from his travels for the Khan's amusement. Many years later, when Polo was dictating his story to a scribe in a Genoan prison, he had access to his original notebooks – which bought the past into sharp focus. His notes on Tibet:

> Finally, after twenty days' journey through country roaming with danger-ous animals, the traveller reaches houses and castles built on mountain slopes. The people here have strange customs concerning marriage. No man will marry a virgin on the grounds that if a woman has not had several lovers she must be undesirable to men and unloved by the gods. So when foreigners or strangers pitch their tents in the area, as many as forty young girls may be brought by their mothers from the village and offered to them. The more attractive girls are welcomed and the others go sadly home. A traveller may keep a girl with him as long as he stays in the village, and when he leaves he must give the girl a jewel to prove she has had a lover. If a girl has twenty jewels, she has had as many lovers. The girls with the most jewels are then chosen as wives because, by common accord, they must be the loveliest. Once they are married their husbands cherish them and regard it as a great sin to touch another man's wife.

The Tibetans had somehow managed to reverse the rest of the world's logic. A contemporary of Polo's, the Italian friar Odoric of Pordenone, was the first European to give an eye-witness account of Tibet, based on his journey in the early 13th century. He described a sky burial in detail – how the body was chopped up and fed to the birds, and how the son of the family made a drinking-goblet from his late father's skull. And yet these same people, so easily given to chopping up a human body, could not bring them-selves to kill a flea, on religious grounds.

I return now to my own notebooks for the first mention of a Tibetan, inspired by my reading of their bizarre customs. Here is the entry:

From Kangding, the road climbs up over a pass of 13,200 feet, heading straight for the Tibetan Plateau. Being banged around the cabin of the truck from arsehole to breakfast-time – the road could use a steamroller. Pass a village with distinctly Tibetan architecture – squat housing with ornate windows and doorframes, and prayer-flags. Behind that, alpine tundra, docile yaks and towering snowcaps . . .

About 320 miles from Chengdu, approaching Qianning: the locals are under the spell of Polaroids – if they let you take a photo, they rush over

*expecting a print on the spot. The number of wildmen is in-
creasing — bright red shirts, heavy thick belts, daggers, felt hats, and
women with bright red head-dresses chasing wayward yaks. Pulled into
a truckstop yard for refuelling. Robert, trying to stretch his legs, moves
to the driver's seat. A Tibetan pops up at the window, mistaking him for
the driver, and hangs in there trying to wheedle a lift. Robert talks to
him in Chinese. 'I know all about you — I read about you in my history-
lesson,' says the Tibetan, with his hand through the window, testing to
see how soft the seat is. He reeks of alcohol.*

*There are two Tibetan hitch-hikers — one with a broad-sword
hanging from his belt, grey hair, shaggy black sheepskin jacket, and a
noble demeanour. He immediately breaks the ice — comes over and com-
pares hand-size and foot-size. No Chinese could break the ice like that.
He, too, stinks of alcohol, and I notice an empty bottle of spirits coming
out of a long, floppy sheepskin sleeve. They look like Apaches — with
high cheek-bones. The Chinese are the settlers; the Tibetans drift into
town to buy their liquor and try and get a ride. The liquor he is holding
is San Jiu, rotgut stuff made in Sichuan — it has a taste somewhere
between rocket-fuel and airplane distillate, and it's just as lethal. Why is
it that all the Tibetans we have met so far stink of alcohol?*

The Chinese idea of the 'minorities' is to keep them that way.
Since they live in the far-flung parts of the empire, mostly in
border-areas, they are a potential security threat. So now, in
Mongolia, Chinese settlers vastly outnumber the Mongolians.
And large areas of former Tibet have been annexed to neighbouring Chinese provinces. We are passing through one of them —
we're still in Sichuan, but actually already on the plateau — in an
area that once fell under Tibetan domination. The Chinese are the
settlers; the Tibetans are the nomads. There is no mixing — the
Chinese have a low opinion of the Tibetans — this much is already
clear.

I have no preconceptions about this route — I have no idea what is
round the next bend. This creates a certain rush of adrenalin — it's
like riding a wild horse. Very few foreigners have passed this
way — I have read nothing in print about it, nor seen any photos.
There is only one place I have any information about: a monastery
at Derge. It is hard to convey my astonishment at the geography
lesson that unfolds at each corner — there are 1500 miles of blind

corners before we get to Lhasa! There are times I am so enthralled by the vistas that I forget to take notes, and even forget to take photos . . .

The Chinese have plenty of words for 'No'. I have heard them all hundreds of times in the course of my travels. The main one is *'Meiyou!'* meaning 'none, we don't have it, get lost, get out of here, it's not possible.' There is, however, no Chinese word for 'Yes'. Or so Robert informs me. Instead, there are approximations. There's *'Dui Dui Dui Dui Dui'* (pronounced 'Doy-Doy-Doy-Doy-Doy,' very quickly), meaning 'Have got it', and there's *'Hao-Ba Hao-Ba'* (pronounced 'Hubbah-Hubbah!') meaning 'All right'.

I leave communication with the driver up to Robert. Once in a while I donate a cigarette to the cause, or throw in a couple of *Hao-Ba Hoa-Bas*. At a truck-stop hotel, I even manage to get across to the driver a question about the next day's departure-time.

'Mingtian - women - chidian - zou?' I inquire. ('Tomorrow - we - 7 - o'clock - go?'). This is backed up by sign-language, including seven fingers in the upright position, thrust in the driver's face.

'Dui dui dui dui dui,' confirms the driver.

'Big White Chief has spoken!' says Robert, doubled up in the corner with laughter.

The evenings are spent in small truck-stop compounds, for a nominal sum of money. Conditions are primitive – electricity until 9 p.m., but no running water. We inevitably share a room with spitting, smoking, farting and belching truck-drivers.

Zhang, our driver, is small in stature, but has a big heart – he keeps buying us dinner at the truck-stops. Each time, we have a furious argument about this – insisting that he is not obliged to buy our meals. Out of politeness, the Chinese routinely reject an offer at least twice – but Zhang will not even accept money on the fifth try. Each time, he manages to grab the bill for the meal – and we end up chasing him all over the truck-stop compound, trying to stuff money into his shirt pocket. It is not much to pay, but it is most generous of him. When we can, we try to even things out by forcing packets of chocolate or imported cigarettes on him (which he accepts after the third attempt).

*   *   *

THE TRUCK IS GROANING UP the Chola Shan mountain-range. How many passes are there on this route? We seem to spend all our time either going up a pass or down one. The truck sneaks up on yaks grazing by the roadside – these comical creatures take one look at the vehicle and thunder off at high speed. The scenery floats by, dreamlike – a huge grasslands area, yaks loaded up with goods, yak-hair tents with smoke coming out of them. Behind all this is a magnificent set of snow-capped peaks – who knows if they have been named? We stop for a closer look at the ingenious structure of some yak-hair tents, and a small group of Tibetans clusters round. Among them is a woman with an elaborate hair-do – a jewelled stud near her forehead – a ton of jewellery around her neck, and a waistband dangling half a dozen pairs of Chinese nailclippers. This area must be amongst the most remote on the face of the earth – and yet these people have contracted the Polaroid disease. They keep pointing to our cameras – where is the picture?

To placate them, Robert produces a Hong Kong guide, written in Chinese, with lots of colour pictures – of temples, Buddhist images, other iconography. A man with a huge piece of coral round his neck immediately claims the book as a trophy of the visit, and heads off back to his tent with it, presumably to peruse it at his leisure with a cup of tea before ripping out the photos to plaster on the walls of his tent.

'You can't have that – it's out of print!' howls Robert, running after him. I am in stitches. 'Out of print' means little to a man who's probably never seen a bound book before, still less a glossy photo – and who can't understand English anyway. All three of us – Robert, the driver and myself – give chase. The Tibetans think this is a great game, and pass the book around like a football as they run. With the altitude, I just about collapse, and stop to catch my breath. If it is possible to die laughing, I've come close.

'It's got maps in it!' wails Robert.

'We'll get lost without it!' says the driver.

'GIVE IT BACK, YOU MORONS', shouts Robert. He has tackled the main culprit, and they're in the scrum now, trying to get it out to the other players on the field. Robert has it – he flips it out to the driver, who runs back to the cabin as fast as his legs will take him. I'm already back in the cabin – Robert arrives, we close the door, lock the windows, fire up the engine, and thunder off, leaving the disgruntled opposition team to their yak-hair tents.

Just before Derge we cross a snowbound pass – up there at 15,000 feet. This time I get altitude sickness – I throw up my entire lunch. Not to mention last year's Christmas pudding. Reach deep inside yourself, the mind says. There is nothing left, the stomach replies. Robert, the budding mountaineer, is in his element, ravenously devouring chocolates and oranges. The higher we go, the more he seems to thrive. I spend most of the climb over the pass with my head between my knees. Every time I look up, there is the tongue of some glacier or another poking out at me – or, from the left of the truck, sheer drops of hundreds of feet, and a dizzying ribbon of road. The sun is strong, but next to the window, I am half frozen. If we stop, however, I get roasted. The road is absolutely spine-jangling – bouncing my shoulder into the door, or pitching me forward into the dash.

'Hey, will you look at this, Mike!' Robert shouts ecstatically. 'Look at the snow – it's magnificent!'.

Mercifully, we reach Derge...

Derge, May 24th. Due to my sickness – real or imaginary by now – we have persuaded the driver to stop for the day in Derge, home of a famous printing lamasery. Another cogent reason for stopping is that both the driver and Robert have massive hangovers, due to an all-night whisky-drinking session. The driver, instead of being grumpy about being behind schedule, turns into a first-class tourist guide, getting us through the monastery doors and lining up a meeting with the Abbot of Derge.

Derge Monastery is built like a fortress, with a few monks in wine-coloured robes visible along the battlements. There are two storeys; along the top rampart is the sculptured symbol seen on most Tibetan monasteries – the Wheel of the Law.

Around the walls of the monastery there is a constant procession of pilgrims – some prostrating the full length of the circuit on their hands and knees. What fascinates me, however, is a mop dangling from the second floor. It is dripping a gooey black substance – and down below, on the ground, the pilgrims congregate to smear it in their hair, or wash in it. But what is it? We draw closer – it can only be one thing – *the ink used in printing*. Makes sense – the books produced here are holy, the ink is holy – have to give the pilgrims a souvenir. One of them – spare me – is drinking it.

There are actually two kinds of ink – the black goo we've already seen in action, and another red ink used for medical texts. Upstairs we get to see the production of a text. There are rows of monks working in a machine-like rhythm, bobbing up and down with alarming rapidity – one inking a woodblock, and the other rolling a strip of paper. Both in a see-saw motion; both chanting an incantation. The assembly of one of these loose-leaf oblong books must be enormously complicated. The *Tenjur*, or commentary on Buddhist law, runs to 25,000 double-sided leaves. That means 25,000 separate woodblocks have to be run off. Then the work has to be sorted, separated, collated and bound – and shipped to the place that ordered it. Everything here is done to direct order – the completed books go to temples in Qinghai, Gansu or Sichuan Provinces, as well as to Tibet itself.

The Abbot continues the tour: we are led through musty halls, smelling of the rancid yak-butter used in lamps. We are shown the guardian deity of the monastery – a splendid green Tara statue. She protects the monastery against earthquake and fire – since everything here is made from wood, her vigilance is much needed. Further up the slope from the monastery is a section where logs of wood are cut to size, ready for woodblock-carving. Though none of the carvers wear glasses, I can only assume they are all going slowly blind since their work requires great detail, and their workplaces are badly-lit.

There were once three great woodblock printing houses in Tibet – Derge, Narthang, and Kumbum. Only Derge survives as a large-scale printing works, and it is the only monastery that possesses brass printing plates. Narthang was razed to the ground by the Chinese; Kumbum maintains a scaled-down printing operation. Derge is one of the handful of monasteries in Kham, or eastern Tibet, to have survived Chinese occupation – for it was in the Kham region that armed resistance grew in the 1950s.

After taking over Tibet in 1950, the Chinese had set about disbanding the monasteries, organising communes, disarming the Khampa tribesmen, and colonising the border-areas. The Chinese told the Tibetans that the lamas did no work, and spread lies about religion. The Chinese took inventories of valuables in the monasteries for tax-assessment. Then, around the mid-1950s, the Chinese tried to force the lamas to work in the fields, and on road-building. In several parts, armies of lamas formed, deciding to fight the Chinese rather than change their way of life. The local people joined the lamas – the start of the Khampa resistance movement. At Litang, the monastery was bombed and strafed by Chinese aircraft, as were others in the region. Numerous reports of Chinese atrocities filtered through, with the main source being Tibetan refugees escaping to India. They told of monks being deliberately burned to death, buried alive, shot, or tortured; they told of monasteries being stripped of their treasures, and burned. Scriptures and books were thrown on the streets; large copper and gold images were sent back to China; other temple images were removed – and the people told that these would be melted down to make bullets. One report said that attempts had been made to convert monks into laymen by forcing them to marry.

From Derge, it is twenty miles to a bridge spanning the Yangtse River. The Yangtse marks the Tibetan border, as delineated by the Chinese; previously the borders of Tibet extended much further east, encompassing Derge. The bridge is manned by a Chinese sentry; on a rock on the other side of the bridge 'Tibet' is engraved in Tibetan script. I shake hands with Robert and the driver – Chamdo, our destination, is only 200 miles away. The driver is only going as far as Chamdo – he will be making a run back to Chengdu after a few days' rest. Just before Chamdo we motor over a pass of 15,300 feet, and we cross the upper reaches of the Mekong River.

It is in Chamdo that we get our first taste of yak-butter tea. *'Don't let it get too cold – it'll give you the shits'*, says our hostess, matter-of-factly in Chinese. I try to empty as much of this disgusting stuff as I can on the ground when no-one is looking. With the Tibetan barley-beer, *chang*, we fare slightly better. Even get tipsy on it. Our hosts, a bunch of charming Tibetan women, have taken it upon themselves to ply us with biscuits, sweets, tea and *chang* – for no other reason than that they are having a picnic, and we happen to be passing by. These maidens have no fear of us, no shyness like the Chinese women. And manners equal to the men

– one of them, a delicate-looking Tibetan lady, takes a bottle of Chinese beer from Robert – a bottle that he has failed to open with his pen-knife – and blithely takes the cap off with her teeth. We try to reject food – but this obviously is most impolite – they will have none of it. So we allow ourselves to be force-fed by these damsels, and lounge around in the sun listening to the music they have on a portable cassette player.

Chamdo, May 26th. Robert has been attacked by bed-bugs during the night. He has bites all over his ankles and wrists. But the bugs have left me alone. This is only fair – he gets the bugs, I get the altitude sickness. We are wondering what our next move will be: we will have to go and start talking with the truck-drivers at the various depots around town. Zhang, our former driver, has been asking around for us, but so far has come up with nothing headed for Lhasa.

The answer walks straight into our room. A party of four men from Sichuan is given beds in our dormitory. They are bound, we discover, for Lhasa, and they have a couple of spare seats.

The new crew for the Lhasa run: first, the Boss, a thin character with leather jacket, binoculars, sunglasses, pointed shoes and a weedy little moustache. Hanging off his person is an expensive Japanese camera with a long zoom lens. This phallic appendage never leaves his person – all show, as we later discover there is never any film in it. In the front seat, next to him, is the mechanic, a young man who spends most of his time making derogatory comments about Tibetan women. At the wheel is the driver, the only stable and rational force in the vehicle. In the back, next to us, is the startling character of the accountant. He is dressed in black – – black sweater, black pants, black shoes. He has black hair that sprouts in a mop over his thick glasses – thus making direct eye-to-eye contact impossible. Then there's myself and Robert – since nobody can pronounce our names properly, we are referred to as 'Uncle' and 'Robot' respectively.

The truck: a private car cleverly disguised as a truck. The four-door passenger cabin takes up half the length of the truck; the cargo-carrying capacity is minimal. In China, however, one cannot have a private car at one's disposal unless one is a cadre or an army officer. This mob seems to have found a way round it – looks like a truck, acts and performs like a car. The music: dreadful Chinese opera with earsplitting high notes. Something will have to be done about the cassette player installed in the dash. Perhaps the tapes can be de-magnetised? The cargo: this has not been quite determined as yet. Certainly contraband – mostly video recorders and a small library of kung fu tapes from Hong Kong.

Supplies for the next leg: very sparse in Chamdo. We have been through every shop selling canned food. The only thing we've been able to find, of any nutritional value, is mandarin orange segments. How I hate those mandarins! I am sick to death of them. They *make* me sick – the syrup they come in is too sweet. Robert buys some anyway – he insists that we will get scurvy without a supply of vitamin C.

The scenery out of Chamdo: lichen, mosslands, snowcaps, treeless windswept plains – a desolate landscape of great majesty. After the crowded, polluted cities of China, this is a tonic. We pass two dusty horsemen, slouching into the wind – they're wearing felt stetsons, boots, wide leather belts and have wooden saddles padded with faded carpeting.

Bamda Army Base, elevation 14,400 feet. My head has settled down – no longer spinning from the altitude. I give the Boss a roll of film. Have to show him how to thread it into the camera. He runs off, photographing all the army officers. With that zoom lens he has to back off half a mile to take a shot – which impresses the hell out of everybody, except me and Robert. Still, we will be thousands of miles away when he gets those useless pictures developed – and we don't want him to lose face by giving him a few photography lessons.

We go to the officers' mess for dinner. Large khaki-coloured army-ration cans are opened. All our favourites: pork and tomatoes, bright green peas, ham, and mandarin segments. Robert attempts to pay for some food, but the Boss waves him away. Everything has been *fixed*. The Boss has been busy selling cassette players and cigarettes to the officers; negotiations continue as lunch progresses. Our trip is not exactly legal for a foreigner, so it comes as a surprise to find that the army officers don't give a damn about providing us with food and lodgings. Perhaps they are too remote to be accountable for such actions: certainly in the middle of China such a situation would not be possible.

A further surprise is the concrete squat toilets — they are the only approachable ones I've encountered so far in Tibet. The others had been so filthy as to repel any advances. En route to the room we've been allocated, I pass the mess-hall again. Strange things have happened to the mess-hall — it has been converted into a theatre, with rows of chairs facing forward. The place is packed, not just with army officers and privates, but with locals from villages near Bamda. Down the front is the Boss, digging his video wizardry out of boxes.

The lights go out, and after some false starts, the kung fu begins. The main character, a shaven-headed monk from some obscure monastery, has developed a peculiar brand of the martial arts that involves only fast wits and a sinister sense of humour. He has no weapons, but uses whatever comes to hand, or turns the weapons of others against themselves. In one scene, where an imperial orchestra is featured in the background, the bullet-headed monk makes good use of musical instruments — with one of the villains killed by a drumstick through the ears, another sent deaf by two cymbals clapped over each ear, and a third and fourth beheaded by the same cymbals — sent spinning through the air at high speed like frisbees. All this takes place, of course, while the hero is being attacked by countless numbers of opponents armed with swords and spears, in a choreography of violence.

Close-up of the heroine: she is tall, beautiful, proud, scantily-dressed, and getting up in the morning. Sighs from the soldiers in the mess-hall. The heroine is a martial arts expert too — and there are gasps from the audience as she is captured, still scantily-dressed, by an evil emperor, and tied up. No doubt is left in the minds of the audience that when she is tied up in this helpless state of undress, there is much more than interrogation at stake. Suspense. The tension builds. The emperor is slapping her around.

In a nick of time, the bullet-headed monk arrives from the ceiling somehow. What are the weapons at hand? He quickly sizes up the physics of the situation — how gravity and force can be applied to the objects in the room to maximise lethal results. He settles on a large vase, which is inserted over the emperor's head in a tight fit down to his neck. The emperor lurches around the room trying to get the vase off; the monk comes back — in between bouts of fighting – to strike the vase on the outside, deafening the poor emperor encased within. And so the story goes on . . .

Between Bamda and Baxoi there is a section of dirt road called 'The 72 Bends'. Along this stretch of hairpin switchbacks, over a high pass, the driver plays chicken with a long army convoy – composed of at least 30 Jiefang trucks. One by one he overtakes them. Nothing fazes him. We shudder every time he makes a move – there are horrendous cliff-drops to the left. We are overtaking from the left side. There is one kind of mistake here. Fatal. I am being thrown around like a rider on a bronco. The cabin is full of dust – from the army trucks. Suddenly the driver stops and pulls over – after all his hard work overtaking the trucks, risking life and limb, he's decided it's time for tea. All the army trucks that he's overtaken now pass us.

The Boss was a man who could fix anything. We stopped at Rawu – went into a shop – I saw some biscuits. *'No, No, Uncle – not fresh!'* said the Boss as I swooped to purchase them. He said a few words to the shopkeeper – out came the fresh biscuits, packets of them, for us. No money had changed hands. Mysterious.

Past Rawu, miracles! A few miles before we'd ventured through a splendid alpine scene – forest, meadows, snowcaps and lake – very reminiscent of the Canadian Rockies. But here, just past Rawu, was a *beach*. The lake was so big that it encompassed its own sandy beach – a strip five or six yards wide along its shore. Who on earth was going to believe me if I was to tell them I'd seen beaches in Tibet? It was incredible. Beaches with rain-forest and snowcapped mountains.

From Rawu onward, the road got steadily worse. The potholes got bigger; the road was gouged by streams of water crossing it. Minor landslides blocked our path at times, and we all piled out to clear the rocks. We had begun to notice many more Tibetan road-workers along this stretch. Sometimes the road would be rudely diverted through a piece of forest while the main road was reinforced. Reinforced because the road had become so muddy that the workers had to dig it up and insert slabs of stone under the surface, so that trucks wouldn't disappear into the morass. As we rounded a corner near one such stretch, three men came running toward us, waving red flags. Then they dived under a small stone bridge. Most peculiar behaviour, I thought.

'DUCK!' shouted Robert.

A loud explosion rocked the cabin of the truck – everyone dived to the floorboards. They were blasting a section of the road. Cautiously, the driver peered over the dashboard. The men were still under the stone bridge. BOOM! There was another horrendous report that echoed through every bone in my body. After this one, the road crew emerged from under the stone bridge and happily waved us on, past the pile of dust and rubble left by the dynamite.

Further on, about four landslides later, an unidentified obstacle on the road. There, flat on their faces in the dirt, were three Tibetans. The driver honked. They ignored him, completing their movement of bowing in the dust. Then they got up and moved to the side of the road. They were pilgrims. But between Chamdo and Lhasa there could be no big monastery. Where, then, were they going?

They could only be bound for Lhasa, which was still a good 400 miles away. No luggage, no food, nothing – the coral and turquoise they wore would defray costs. Prostrating all the way: spread-eagled in the dust, hands forward, getting up and moving to the spot where their fingertips last touched the dirt, and flinging their bodies to the earth again. The truck passed, and I looked back to see that they had resumed their inch-worming method of locomotion. Over a road like this, in its pitiful condition – 400 miles of it – how long would that take them? At least a month, I calculated – possibly two or three.

Just near Bomi a roadblock popped up. There were four army officers standing there, looking very mean indeed. *This is it*, I thought, *we're not going to make it to Lhasa*. Two of the officers peered into the front cabin. They glanced at Robert and myself. No great surprise registered on their faces. They were much more interested in the Boss and his Sichuan crew. *Contraband video*, I thought. *The Boss isn't going to make it to Lhasa*. Two officers were checking out the load in the rear of the truck. The Boss became quite animated – talking at an absurd speed to distract the officers. Luckily, the accountant had been sleeping in the back of the truck, and his rude awakening – the spectacle of his dust-covered person and his wildly unkempt hair – had provided more than sufficient distraction. The officers waved us on.

At Bayi, we pulled into an army base for the night. The soldiers, who'd been busy playing basketball, trotted over to welcome us. The Boss immediately announced that there would be a video-show that night. The soldiers cheered. Bags and equipment were unloaded; we were shown our rooms.

Bayi is a fair-sized town – meaning it has more than one street, and even has a shop. Apart from being an army base, it has a tex-tiles factory. And it has a junkyard. I went over with driver to get our horn fixed – this being the most important piece of the truck. In a yard not far from the army base were scores of abandoned Jiefang and Dongfeng trucks – some previously used by the army, others once used by logging and transport work-units. The mechanic on duty got the horn functioning again, and even started to look at the cassette player mounted in the dashboard. Luckily, after the player chewed several tapes and spat them out, he gave up.

How long would it take us to get to Lhasa? We'd crossed a dozen rivers, and negotiated 15 passes at last count: it seemed like we'd been on this road forever. Fuzzball, or so I had christened the accountant, looked more and more Neanderthal as the trip wore on. His white shirt was no longer white – the collar ring of dirt so ingrained now as to be a living advertisement for having used the wrong washing powder; and his black sweater was coated in dust. He never once changed this outfit. Nor brushed his hair. But it was his high raspy voice that elevated him to the ranks of an im-mortal comic-strip character. He was general dogsbody, luggage handler, landslide clearer, kickbag, tea-boy, the brunt of all jokes. Fuzzball was definitely not a traveller. It was his first trip away from home.

'*This place is full of dust!*' rasped Fuzzball as we sped down the highway. Silence for half an hour, while he picked his nose. '*This place is a mess of pine trees!*' Silence for another half-hour. '*This place is a bloody desert!*' Silence. '*We're being tossed around like a sack of potatoes!*'

'*Shut up you silly arsehole!*' snarled the Boss.

There was a long silence again. Fuzzball picked his nose. The me-chanic tried to get the cassette player working again. Fortunately, the player refused to co-operate. The driver announced a pit-stop.

The doors flew open; everyone went for a strategic position – each to irrigate his own patch of the desert. This done, it was time for a tea-break. The boss opened a large army-ration can. Just my luck – it was mandarin segments in a sickly syrup. They all attacked the can with chopsticks. Gloomily, I got back into the truck.

The driver motored off again.

'*Robot, you have naked women in England?*' asked the Boss.

'*Sorry?*'

'*Naked women on the television.*'

'*Oh – yes, sometimes.*'

'*In the evenings?*'

'*Late at night, yes, sometimes.*'

'*Next time you come to China, will you bring me some?*'

'*How can I do that?*'

'*Very easy, Robot. You bring me the video-tape.*'

What a dealer! The Boss was light years ahead of other business-men – he was already sizing up the porn-market for his VCRs.

Another long silence.

'*Robot, tell me about the Iron Lady,*' said the Boss. '*Is she really beautiful?*'

'*No, actually she's quite ugly.*'

'*But I heard she is very rich, and she controls all of England.*'

'*I think you're getting the two mixed up.*'

'*There are two of them, Robot?*'

'*Yes, one Prime Minister, and one Queen.*'

'*Then which one came to settle the question of Hong Kong?*'

'*That was Maggie Thatcher, the Prime Minister.*'

'*So she is the Iron Lady?*'

'*Exactly,*' said Robert with a finality that indicated he was not willing to discuss the subject of female English stereotypes any further.

May 31st. I had gotten so used to the banging around in the cabin of the truck that I slept through a morning session of potholes and rough roads. What jolted me gently awake was the *absence* of bronco motions. We were cruising – level – a paved road. Be-wildered, I checked out the window. Black tar – we were bowling along it. The first thing that caught my eye was a huge black Chevrolet. What kind of hallucination was that? Then bicycles, and women in fancier clothing . . . then a bridge . . . and then – my gaze shifted up, up, up in the distance – and there, head on, was an enormous white castle. The Potala – the palace of childhood dreams! And though I'd seen hundreds of pictures of it before, none came close to the awesome impact of reality. It soared out of the centre of Lhasa – a project of great daring, of great labour, of great imagination.

Soon we were in Lhasa, a dull-looking Chinese town. There were other foreigners here – we saw a few on the streets – we stuck our heads out the window and waved madly. We hadn't seen another foreigner for ten days. We were glad to see them, but we were also glad that we'd come the route we had. Flying into Lhasa would've been too easy – no shroud of mystery to be torn away. Fifty years earlier, an English traveller might have taken a month on the road to get to Lhasa on horseback from Sikkim. And now, coated in dust, caked in dirt, tired and hungry, we could appreciate the splendours of the Holy City. Like a hot shower, at Number Two Hotel.

★   ★   ★

TRADITIONALLY, PILGRIMS ENTERING LHASA after their epic journey would perform three clockwise circuits to gain merit. These were the Lingkhor, or outer circuit; the Barkhor, or inner circuit; and the internal circuit of the Jokhang Temple, at the heart of Lhasa. The Lingkhor circuit, some five miles in length, is no longer used – it has been intersected by Chinese buildings and roads, except for one piece near the Telegraph Office. The Barkhor, which doubles as the bazaar, is very much in use – although only since 1980. During the Cultural Revolution, any form of worship was banned. The Chinese still take special pleasure in moving against the grain – by walking anti-clockwise on this octagonal half-mile circuit. The doors of the Jokhang, closed for a lengthy period during the 1960s and 70s, are freely accessible.

Surging around the Jokhang are waves of Tibetans – bigger waves than usual along Barkhor Bazaar because it is approaching the full moon festival of Buddha's birthday. At a hearth along the Barkhor some pilgrims are burning juniper as an offering: smoke and flames fill the air, mixed with the rancid smell of yak-butter. I stand transfixed at the spectacle of the prostrators making their way around the Barkhor. Buddhist belief holds that man revolves around the Buddha in the same fashion that the planets move about the sun. The greater the number of circuits, the greater the merit acquired; the greater the merit acquired, the higher the level of incarnation in the next life.

Here in Lhasa is a force that attracts pilgrims from the far-flung parts of a broken empire. There are Golok nomads from deep in Qinghai Province – wild-looking pilgrims swathed in greasy sheepskins; there are nomad women from eastern Tibet, their long tresses smeared in yak-butter; there are Khampas – the tribesmen from eastern Tibet – with their daggers, leather belts and braided red hairbands; there are Muslim, Nepali and Kashmiri traders; there are lines of beggars, their clothing tattered, but their begging bowls full – since donations increase around Buddha's birthday. There are roving hawkers, there are story-tellers, sutra-readers, old women with pet sheep, younger women with hair bedecked with coral, carpet-dealers, and curbside dentists with foot-drills. There are vendors selling plastic shoes, hopeless Indian batteries, and cassettes of screeching Indian music. And working their way around the circuit are the prostrators – droves of them. They come well-equipped with rubber knee-pads, padded gloves, thick-soled shoes and even rubber aprons. Must be hell on the clothing.

In addition to this biblical cast of characters, there are large numbers of Chinese civilians and soldiers, and small numbers of westerners. Better than that, there are rare westerners – dinosaurs from the 70s – hippies and mystics, dope-smokers, visionaries and revolutionaries. Plus writers and photographers busy selling the plateau to the rest of the world. It is an extraordinary re-creation of the Kathmandu hip-scene of the 1970s. Kathmandu, in those days, was the end of the road overland from Europe – an exotic Asian cul-de-sac where (until 1975) drugs were legal. In 1979 with the turmoil in Iran, and the invasion of Afghanistan, the overland route had been disrupted. But now a new overland route of sorts has been created, in the most unlikely place – Tibet. With the opening of the Lhasa-Kathmandu road, the way is open from Japan or Hong Kong through China to Nepal and India. Lhasa has already become a crossroads for the various routings; it is a place that needs no publicity – it already has a mystique.

There are six beds in our room at Snowland Hotel, near the Jokhang Temple. The longest resident in this Spartan accommodation is John, from America. John is in his thirties – long hair, gaunt, laid back. He plans to be in Tibet about six weeks, then go on to Nepal, make his way across India – *slowly*, he emphasises – and maybe go to Burma after that. John shows us around – tells us where to change money on the blackmarket, where to buy yoghurt, where to get eggs.

He has worked out a routine for himself – getting yoghurt in the markets in the morning, doing a few circuits of Barkhor Bazaar, chatting with merchants – he's made friends with some Nepali shop-keepers. In the afternoon perhaps a hot shower over at the Chinese hotel, followed by a dinner of yak-burgers at the Banak Shol Hotel. After dinner, he goes for a Tibetan lesson, arranged with a man he met in the bazaar. Before turning in, he indulges in some quiet reading, and smokes a couple of joints. Yak-burgers? A westerner had taught the kitchen staff how to make them: mixing ground yak-meat with onions and canned mushrooms – and putting it all on a bun when done. There was no ketchup available in Lhasa. That was next, I thought. In the meantime, canned tomatoes served as a substitute.

I, too, have settled into Lhasa. It is a resting-spot, with plenty of travellers for company. Letters are written; mail is received. Urgent washing gets done. Money is changed, profitably, on the blackmarket. Reasonable food is eaten. New plans are made.

Both Robert and myself have hired hotel bicycles for the duration of our stay in Lhasa. The streets of Lhasa are paved and dead flat. It is less exertion to ride a bike for a fair distance than to walk it. Since we've taken ten days to get to Lhasa, we're acclimatised to the high altitude, so the bikes surprisingly have little effect on us. In addition, Lhasa has little traffic, so getting around is easy. It makes me feel good, this cycling two miles up from sea-level. I start to experiment with how much cycling is possible. Half a day in the saddle – slow riding – does not have much effect. Going up a slight hill – or sprinting on a level piece of tarmac – makes my heart race like a trapped pinball, being knocked round at the back of the machine.

When Lowell Thomas and his son visited Lhasa in 1949, at the invitation of the Dalai Lama, there were five foreigners working for the Tibetan Government. Heinrich Harrer and Peter Aufschnaiter had escaped from a British POW camp in India during the second world war, and had been granted asylum in Lhasa; Reginald Fox and Robert Ford were former British radio operators, now working for the Tibetans; Nedbailoff was a white Russian who had been imprisoned in India during the second world war, and had decided to apply to Tibet for asylum rather than return to Russia. A sixth European resident in Lhasa was Hugh Richardson, who had been head of the British Mission, and became head of the new Indian Government Mission.

These men were dedicated to helping Tibet modernise itself. They worked on numerous projects – a hydro-electric plant, an irrigation-canal, a radio network – and Harrer even helped construct a movie-theatre at the Dalai Lama's Summer Palace. They all lent their skills – teaching, surveying, translating, engineering – to the cause. It was too late. Tibet, a country that had been left to its own devices for centuries, was suddenly faced with invasion by a power with far superior technology. In 1950, China invaded, and the foreigners slowly departed – with the exception of Ford, who was captured at Chamdo and held by the Chinese for five years on charges of spying.

The Thomases, who were American radio commentators, had been invited to Lhasa by the Dalai Lama in 1949 because the Tibetans were getting jittery about the Chinese, and needed some international sympathy for their fragile status. The Tibetans could still not grasp the reality of what was about to befall them. In Lowell Thomas Jr's book, *Out of This World*, which was published in 1950 – before the Chinese invasion – there is an entry on what to bring as gifts in the rare event that one got an invitation to Lhasa:

> Incidentally, Reggie Fox, who runs the Dalai Lama's 16 mm projector, said that 16-mm Tarzan films or Marx Brothers films would make a big hit with the Dalai Lama and those around him. They most certainly don't want to see any pictures where human or animal life is taken; amusement and adventure are the things they are interested in.

Here was a city with no electricity (save for the generator at the Dalai Lama's private cinema!), no watches, no radio, no newspapers or magazines (except those imported from India), no automobiles or wheeled vehicles (horses and mules were the main means of transport), no movies, no advertising, and no plumbing. Rubbish piled up on street-corners and was removed once a year; dogs and ravens fought over the dead animals tossed in the garbage; the infant mortality rate was over 50 percent. There was no census taken in the Lhasa of 1949 or earlier, but the population was estimated at 25,000. There were an additional 8,000 monks at Sera Monastery, and 10,000 monks at Drepung – both of these monasteries being close to Lhasa. This brought the figure over 40,000 – and probably double that number would be in Lhasa during festivals.

There is very little left of the old Lhasa now. The population has grown to 150,000 – with the Tibetans being far outnumbered by Chinese civilians and soldiers. Drepung Monastery is deserted; Sera has a skeleton staff of perhaps 100 monks; the Potala is a museum. The city of Lhasa has mushroomed to an area that is eight times larger than it was in 1950.

During the March 1959 uprising, which saw heavy fighting in Lhasa for several days, the monasteries – including the Jokhang – were shelled. The monks had joined the rebels in fighting the Chinese; the Dalai Lama and his entourage secretly departed Lhasa to escape to India. The Chinese, at various stages, claimed the Tibetan rebels were being backed by 'American imperialists', 'Chiang Kaishek agents', 'Indian expansionist elements' ('heirs to the British imperialists'), former Tibetan nobles ('upper strata reactionaries'), and an assortment of other traitors. Estimates of Tibetans killed during the fighting in Lhasa ranged from 2,000 to over 5,000. The revolt was ruthlessly suppressed, with all able-bodied men who survived the fighting being rounded up and shipped out of Lhasa – nobody knew where. The Dalai Lama's Summer Palace had been reduced to a shambles by artillery fire; entire sections of northern Lhasa were flattened by shelling.

Now only around the Jokhang and the Potala do some traditional-style buildings remain: the rest is a sprawl of dull Chinese concrete structures. The Tibetan quarter, with its distinctive house-facades, is run-down. It is riddled with crooked alley-ways – where, failing a proper sewage-system, Tibetans crouch down to defecate. The Chinese slice of town – much larger – is paved, more orderly, better-lit, better cared-for. Lhasa has electricity, telephones, television, video-theatres, bicycles, motorcycles, trucks, Landcruisers, the odd bus, a few taxis, stores, hospitals, post-office, bank – but no soul. Modernisation under the Chinese has resulted in material benefits – but it has caused the destruction of Tibetan temples, language and culture.

The Tibetan pulse of things is strongest at the Jokhang Temple – but here, too, things are being transformed – right before my eyes. In front of the Jokhang the Chinese are building a vast square, which is, or will be, surrounded by two-storey shops and restaurants. The square is of Soviet proportions – it is too big, and it fully exposes the Jokhang, previously tucked in behind ramshackle housing. The new square gives full tourist – and military – access to old Lhasa by allowing vans and buses to drive right in. Old Lhasa was never laid out for four-wheeled transport – and even now trucks have trouble squeezing through the alley-ways. The buildings were constructed close together, probably to keep the vigorous cold of winter at bay. Whole acres of old Lhasa have been demolished for the square, which will have duplicates of the older-style buildings.

There is something peculiar about these newer buildings compared with their older Tibetan counterparts. They have a similar thickness of walls, similar ornate windows and coloured beams, similar doorways – what is the difference? It takes me a while to work out why these new buildings have no soul. They are perpendicular. The old buildings in Lhasa are bevelled – their thick walls set on an inward slope. At first sight, these buildings had immediately reminded me of the imperial Inca city of Cuzco in Peru, where the bevelled slope of the buildings ensured that they were earthquake-proof. Like those of Cuzco, the old buildings in Lhasa used stone and wood, but no nails. I much later found evidence of this sloping architecture, in a most surprising source – Luigi Barzini's *From Peking to Paris*:

> Some ruins of ancient Egypt give an instance of that pyramidal slant, which endows walls with a stability capable of enduring for thousands of years, and which has a marvellous effect in perspective, giving to the eye the illusion of an immensity, as if the decreasing upwards was due to some prodigious height. When through photography Lhasa was revealed to us, and we found that type of building repeated there, we were surprised by the extraordinary biblical severity of the Forbidden City, which preserved for us living architectural forms of ancient civilisations. These forms had not reached it from India with its religion, nor from China with its political sovereigns, but must have been transmitted to it by the west of Asia twenty or thirty centuries ago.

Barzini was writing in 1908, and the photographs of Lhasa he was referring to no doubt came from the British invasion of Tibet in

1904. Chinese buildings now dominate Lhasa, with whole slabs of the city being concrete boxes, or ponderous Soviet-style hotels or government offices. The final outrage, for the Tibetans, is that the construction of the square near the Jokhang was being done in the name of 'celebration'.

According to the Chinese, September 1985 would be the 20th anniversary of their creation – the Tibetan Autonomous Region. Around Lhasa, 43 works are supposedly in progress, having been started in 1983 – schools, sports facilities, a new tourist hotel, a theatre – to make Lhasa a showcase for visiting journalists when the 'celebrations' take place. In India, the community in exile is up in arms: what do the Tibetans have to celebrate? Thirty-five years of incarceration, destruction, killing, torture, denunciation; thirty-five years of seeing masses of Chinese pour in to snigger at the Tibetan for being a barbarian, to eat his food, to take away his livelihood, abolish his religion, destroy his monasteries, re-write his history – and, worst of all, try to break his spirit.

The Potala, which offers such promise from the outside, is a total disappointment on the inside. It has none of the lively atmosphere of Barkhor Bazaar; it has the immediate chill of a building no longer in use, or used for quite a different purpose – a museum. Very few of the rooms are open – most have heavy padlocks. As I wander through the maze of shrines, frescoes, and Buddhist images – dimly lit by yak-butter lamps – I cannot not help but think how gloomy and oppressive it all appears. That, in part, was the original intent of the architects and builders – to construct a palace where the God-King, the Dalai Lama, could dwell apart from his subjects, and free himself from any contamination from them. It's not quite clear if the reverse also applied – were the Dalai Lama's subjects free from contamination by him? Apparently, the most sought-after curative pills in old Tibet were made from the excreta of the God-King.

Although the Dalai Lama carried the status of the highest incarnation in the land, there used to be hundreds of other Living Buddhas throughout Tibet. Such positions used to carry great privilege and power, so there was probably considerable pulling of strings and legs to get official recognition. Some reincarnations were so outrageous that debate ensued on whether the choice could be justified. Such a reincarnation was the 6th Dalai Lama, who took over as a grown boy, and not (as custom demanded) as an infant. The reason for this is that the 5th Dalai Lama had requested that the Regent conceal his death, and complete the final building-stages of the Potala. Upon the death of the Great Fifth, in 1682, a monk resembling the deceased was found, and the Tibetans were told that the 5th was meditating – a situation that lasted for a decade.

The 6th Dalai Lama, taking over as a grown boy, never agreed to a vow of celibacy; later he devoted himself entirely to women, wine and poetry. No woman was said to have been safe from the indulgences of this playboy. His subjects rationalised this high contact by claiming the Living Buddha had two bodies – one which stayed in the Potala and meditated, the other which got drunk in the town. At the age of 23, the 6th Dalai Lama was kidnapped by the Mongols, and disappeared in Litang. Latsang Khan, the Mongol chieftan, selected a 25-year-old monk, rumoured to be his natural son, as the 7th Dalai Lama. This choice caused an uprising among the Tibetans.

The Dalai Lamas from the 8th to the 12th all died young, and in mysterious circumstances – their salt-dried bodies, placed in mausoleums with stupendous amounts of gold-plating and precious stones, lie in the Potala. One can only assume that religious fervour motivated the builders of such tombs and shrines, and the palace itself. The Potala is remarkable in that it was painstakingly constructed without mechanical means, without the use of the wheel, and without the use of nails or a steel frame. The walls and the foundations were strengthened by pouring in molten copper. How the Tibetans could bypass the wheel, bypass the iron age, and throw up such a skyscraper remains an enigma.

The skyscraper itself created a transport problem. The Potala had no plumbing, electricity or heating, so there was – in previous times – a constant stream of porters with water for tea, yak-butter for the prayer-lamps, and firewood for the fireplaces. The Dalai Lama was portered in and out of the palace in a palanquin; high lamas were piggybacked up to the entrance of the Potala by porters.

The Tibetans turned the Potala into a tomb, prison and bureaucratic headquarters – isolated from reality; and then the Chinese turned that into a museum, dislocated from its context. Tourism has since turned *that* into a photographic landmark. It has a very strange feel to it. I race through the building, feeling stifled, groping for fresh air.

At Snowland Hotel, waves of travellers come and go. They arrive from distant parts, form impromptu groups to board hired buses, and then a whole section of the hotel vanishes down the road to Kathmandu. The last rented bus took Knut, the wild Norwegian who wanted to hike into Everest; the Yellow Lady – a Dutch woman who dressed entirely in the colour yellow (she had a yellow backpack); Britta, the Swedish woman who spoke Tibetan and dressed Tibetan-style; and Jim, a black American who had a huge suitcase full of tins, and was bound for some obscure monastery.

Tibet has only been open to freelance travellers for eight short months. There are, as yet, no guidebooks in existence for this new travel in Tibet – everyone relies on the traveller network. The opening has caught travellers by surprise – hearing the news in China, they have jumped on a plane to Lhasa – they have no proper clothing, no idea where they're going, no idea what they're looking at – and does it matter anyway? This is Tibet! The rooftop of the world! Closed for centuries!

Those who have done a route instruct those who haven't, so that dinner conversation revolves around who's been where, and why, and how they avoided Chinese authorities. Boasts are made about reaching obscure monasteries. Exotic names are bandied around – Kailas, Lhatse, Gyirong, Tsedang, Batang. Nobody has any accurate maps – the last British topographic surveys of Tibet were done before World War II. Route-maps are sketched on the backs of envelopes; good maps are copied and transmitted down the line – back to Kathmandu or Peking.

Much in demand, in the information line, are the services of an Englishman staying at Snowland Hotel – Bradley Rowe. Bradley has been running around Tibet for the past six months, filling up his passport with Chinese visas, being pursued by PSB, doing treks at the height of winter. His encyclopedic knowledge of the highways and byways is so accurate that he can quote, off the top of his head, exact kilometre stones along the routes, and what temple, shrine or ruin can be found there. I get Bradley to add some of this precious data to skeleton maps I've made up. He sketches, in some detail, a map for getting to the north side of Everest.

Bradley is at work on a five-year writing project: a pilgrim's guide to the holy sites of Central Asia. Such guides have long existed in the Tibetan and Sanskrit languages, but with time and destruction, much has changed. Bradley has a special obsession about the stones which make up most of the shrines along pilgrim-routes. In the course of trying to document every monastery in Tibet – destroyed or not – he has left the locals with a rather peculiar legacy – his British sense of humour. He makes a special point of teaching them something downright disgusting to say – in English – when greeting a foreigner. Leave-taking, Bradley also instructs them, is to be done in the following manner: flap the arms like a chicken attempting a take-off, and shout: 'GOOD-A-BYE-BYE'.

June 5th. We got up before daybreak, grabbed some biscuits and cycled off to the north of Lhasa, toward Sera Monastery. From a distance we could see the large slab of rock that others had de-scribed to us – the sky burial site. A smoky fire was burning on the rock, indicating that the ceremony would take place that day. When we got there on the bikes, a dozen *domdens*, or body-breakers, were gathering round the fire, drinking tea and *chang*, and warming their hands.

Behind them were four bodies, flung face down like rag-dolls and tied by the head to a central point on the rock. They were naked, with a cloth covering the lower portions. The *domdens* paused to urinate on the rock and smoke cigarettes. They passed around a bottle of white spirits. The man from the body-truck came over to warn us that no photos should be taken. You wouldn't, after all, want photos taken if that was your mother over there, would you? The *domdens* were dressed in filthy white coats and leggings – they all seemed in good spirits, laughing and joking, and they seemed to accept the knot of foreigners (now grown to seven or so), despite the bad feelings created by other incidents with westerners – mostly to do with photography at the site.

Shortly after the sun struck the rock, at eight o'clock, the burial squad – five of them – mounted the rock and set to work. Three of them hacked away at the bodies with knives and machetes, and the other two ground bones with mallets, and mixed them with *tsampa*. Two hawks zoomed low over the rock on a reconnaissance mission; on the hilltop beyond, vultures were lined up, knowing the timing well.

There was a horrid fascination in watching the sky burial – seeing the human body cut up like a side of beef. For the Tibetans, once the soul was gone, the body was merely an empty vessel – and they had no qualms about treating it as such. One of the body-breakers had severed and skinned a head – well, by now, it was roughly hacked to a skull. The whole rock was traced with blood, flesh, pulp, intestines and bones. The skull. He placed it down, then picked up a large stone. Up went the stone over his head and – crack! – down it came with a sickening smash that made my whole body wince. The brains had been mashed up, ready for the vultures.

All of a sudden two of the body-breakers came tearing off the rock, aiming straight for us, brandishing their machetes. Oh God, what had we done? There was no point in running – my legs were all weak and wobbly from watching that skull being crushed. And besides, they were moving too fast. They were yelling furiously – before I could understand what was happening, they were past us – heading ...toward a Landcruiser that had pulled up. So absorbed had I been in the horrific cut-up, I hadn't noticed the Landcruiser. It was full of Overseas Chinese. Now we saw what the problem was – one of the Landcruiser passengers had flourished a camera – a strict taboo. The Overseas Chinese swiftly jumped back into the Landcruiser and closed the windows. The two body-breakers were picking up hefty rocks and heaving them at the Landcruiser. This got the Chinese driver's back up – how would he explain these dings to his work-unit chief? So he attempted to get out and argue with the body-breakers. They both went for him with their machetes. The driver scrambled back into the car and roared off.

The body-breakers, apparently satisfied, returned to their grisly work on the rock. Finally, about an hour and a half after they'd started, the body-breakers' cutting and mashing was done. They mixed the human pulp with *tsampa* and moved off the rock. This was the signal for the vultures. The sky turned black – filled with massive wingspans – and soon the rock was a frenzy of activity, a seething mass of birds. Having eaten their fill, the vultures waddled off uphill – too heavy to take off after their feast.

I'd quite lost my appetite on a return to Lhasa. By the afternoon I still hadn't eaten anything. Just when my hunger was returning, I strayed into the yak-meat section of the Barkhor Bazaar. Here, yellowed yak-carcasses were laid over tables, and vendors were cutting them into various pieces. Strewn around were the bloody hides, and stray dogs rummaged around in them, searching for bits of meat. Severed yak-heads and hoofs lay on the ground; the dogs, at least a dozen of them, had the run of the place, with vendors feeding them scraps. So here the yaks are fed to the dogs, and out at Sera, the humans are fed to the birds. The scraps, yak or human, were doled out with the same casual disregard among the butchers. That is what had horrified me out at Sera – the casualness of the body-breakers. It was a macabre double – first the sky burial, then the yak-meat butchers – I'd had my fill of gory scenes. I ran back to the hotel and spent the rest of the day with my nose in a book.

That evening I accompanied John for his Tibetan lesson. We went off through the alleys behind the Jokhang, to a second floor apartment. A man in his forties answered the door. He had a glazed look in his eyes that seemed to be directed right past me, like a blind man. Tenzing was his name. His English was quite good – he'd been educated in India, I found out. Rich Tibetans in the pre-Chinese era used to send their children to India for an education.

'What's the word for foreigner?' I asked.

'*Inji*,' he said. *Inji*, he went on to explain, was a Tibetan corruption of the word 'English' – and it came from the 1904 British invasion of Tibet. Since then the term had been extended to all foreigners.

'And what do you call the Chinese?'

'Oh, we don't call them foreigners – they'd be insulted. Tibet is Chinese,' he said, with a certain amount of conviction.

I glanced around the room – low wooden tables, ornate chests of drawers, and a television set. The television set was Tenzing's biggest worry in life. The aerial would have to be repositioned – the reception was not good. There were intermittent problems with the power-supply. But he had solved one problem – he'd managed to get a Japanese set.

'The Chinese-made sets are bad,' he informed me. 'After two or three months, there is no colour.' Five years before, there had barely been a TV set in Lhasa – now there was a small forest of antennae in downtown Lhasa. TVs were the new family shrines, occupying pride of place in the living-room.

I was determined to draw Tenzing out on what had happened to him. So when John's lesson was over, I seized the opportunity. Tenzing had no hesitation in recounting the past, but he spoke with a zombie-like gaze, staring straight ahead.

'Nine years after Liberation, the Dalai Lama fled to India. That was in 1959, and the Chinese conducted house-to-house searches for weapons. In those days we all carried guns – richer families had more guns. The guns were for hunting. Our family had many guns – American, Czechoslovakian. So they arrested me and took me off to prison. We worked twelve hours a day on a hydro-electric project, and at night we were forced to study the thoughts of Chairman Mao. I was freed in 1980. Others – my brothers – went to Gansu Province, and never came back. Maybe they are still alive. I don't think so.'

And he went back to pouring his tea, as though 21 years in prison and the loss of his entire family was of no consequence. He bore no grudge against the Chinese – in fact he used their terminology – referring to 1950 as 'Liberation'.

*　　*　　*

THERE ARE THREE KINDS of T-shirt on sale in Lhasa Friendship Store – Yak, Potala, and Everest. As an afterthought, Howard purchases five 'Qomolungma'(Everest) T-shirts – one for each member of the Landcruiser trip. If we get stopped in some outlandish place, we may look like an official tour with these gaudy things on as underclothing. We now have several boxes of supplies – cans, drinks, beer – plus large plastic containers of water, and some fireworks. The Nepalese border expedition is ready.

The passes along the route to Nepal are 4,000 feet higher than Lhasa; a 17,000-foot pass is uncharted territory as far as my bloodstream is concerned. On a whim, I visit the Lhasa Hospital of Traditional Medicine to see if the Tibetans have a herbal remedy for the scourge of altitude sickness. An English-speaking doctor ushers me to the top floor, where ancient medical scroll-paintings are on display.

The main diagnosis in traditional Tibetan medicine is done by reading the pulse, to determine which 'humour flow' (bile, wind or phlegm) has been blocked, or is excessive. With deep concentration, a practitioner digs his thumb into my pulse at regular intervals – for about five minutes. Then he writes out a prescription. This is filled in the ground-floor dispensary. I eagerly open the paper wrappers: the contents look suspiciously like rabbit droppings. The medical logic, at any rate, is sound enough: in the event of altitude sickness, one set of pellets is for stabilising the stomach; another set for combating migraines; and a third set for stalling heart-attacks.

Robert is working hard on negotiations for a Landcruiser with the Chinese work-unit involved. We figure that with a Landcruiser we can stop where we want, do what we want, go where we want; though it is far more expensive than a bus to the border, it also allows us to see far more. The itinerary is sorted out. The work-unit boss insists on payment in FECs, which means we can't use blackmarket money. The cost is 350 yuan each. For that price, I insist on throwing Rongbuk into the itinerary. Rongbuk is the ruined monastery near the north base of Everest. From my reading, I know there is a road – a rough one – right through to Everest base-camp on the north side. It was made for Chinese mountaineering attempts on Everest – and it is negotiable by four-wheel-drive vehicle.

Rongbuk throws a spanner in the works – the driver doesn't want to go there. Rongbuk isn't open to foreigners, says his boss. Finally, we reach a stand-off – Rongbuk will be written into the itinerary, and if the road is in good shape when we get there, the driver will take us for a day-trip. 'Good shape' means that there has been no flooding in the area from swollen rivers.

For all his hard work at negotiating, Robert will not be coming along. He wants to stay longer in Lhasa, and he has plans to explore Samye to the east, then go through Qinghai Province to the north-east.

As Robert will not be coming, I have to resuscitate my fragmented knowledge of Chinese to deal with the driver. I get Robert to write down the junctions along our route in Chinese characters

– Gyantse, Shigatse, Sakya, Lhatse, Shegar, Tingri West, Rongbuk, Nyalam, and the final stop of Zhangmu – the border-town. The rest is a matter of being able to pronounce a few phrases – *ting!* (stop!), *women yao zai jelli jusu* (we want to stop here for the night), *mei-wenti* (no problem), *manman zou!* (take it easy!), *kuh-ye* (okay), *che fan* (let's eat), *xiuxi* (siesta), and various words for timing (hours, afternoon, morning).

I'm still mumbling this phrasing to myself and practising the pronunciation with Robert as we load up the Landcruiser at the ungodly hour of 5.30 a.m. Our 'Everest squad' consists of two Americans, Howard and Scott; two Canadians, Sylvia and David; plus myself. I linked up with this ready-made group over dinner at the Banak Shol Hotel. For such a small group there is excellent medical back-up: David is a doctor; Sylvia is a physiotherapist. Howard is also a professional – an engineer – and Scott dabbles in computers. Only Sylvia and myself want to cross into Nepal – the others want to do a return trip to the border. We're still not sure that the crossing into Nepal is possible, since the Friendship Bridge over the Bhote Kosi River – at the border – has been washed away by flooding. Other travellers seem to have made it through, so there has to be a way of crossing the river.

Never much of one on goodbyes, I shake hands with Robert, quickly get into the Landcruiser – and we're off. In ten minutes, we leave Lhasa – and Robert – behind. I check my watch: June 10th, exactly two months since Robert and I met in Hong Kong. Hong Kong seems light years away from the Tibetan Plateau. And yet here, thousands of miles to the west of Hong Kong, the same time-zone still operates, as Tibet runs on Peking time. In practice it is necessary to step back a few centuries to get the right bearings: the Landcruiser is our very own time-machine.

Even with my monosyllabic Chinese, I become linguistic leader of the Landcruiser, and thus the key negotiator. This is because everybody else's pronunciation, with the exception of Sylvia's, is way off. David doesn't even try to speak Chinese – he throws English at the driver as if he were a fluent English speaker. This is one convenient solution to the language problem, but it doesn't get any results from the driver. Being the lazy language-learner I am, I soon give up on forming whole sentences, and stick to twisting simple statements with theatrical hand-gestures. *'Kuh-ye'* (the

Chinese for 'okay'), for example, can be stretched to ten meanings – okay! (yes!); okay? (is it all right, do you agree? – eyebrows raised in anticipation); okay (with nodding of the head – I agree, let's go); okay (wave of hand – it's enough food, no more please); and then *'bu kuh-ye!'* (not okay, forget it, get lost – hands slicing the air in an emphatic 'no' gesture).

I have plenty of occasion to use my repertoire of hand-gestures and monosyllables. As the Landcruiser groans up the first pass out of Lhasa, our driver nods off at the wheel. I am sitting in the front, in the role of The Great Translator, so I'm the first to notice this attack of narcolepsy. Just before, I'd been admiring the huge drop out the right-hand side of the Landcruiser – now I am in a panic. The driver is 'fishing' – head bobbing up and down, going lower and lower, till a sudden jerk sends him bolt upright again – and wide awake. In this case, it is my elbow. In his ribs. Damnation! What is the Chinese for 'watch out!'? The cliff, you fool! Going over – you know? By the time I find the right phrase in the phrasebook we'll all be dead.

'*Bu kuh-ye!*' I shout (definitely not okay).

'What's happening there?' asks Howard.

'Driver's nodding off at the wheel.'

'What?!'

'We'll have to watch him then.'

'Take over the driving you mean . . . '

'We could tell him that.'

'Look – he's doing it again!'

'Jesus – keep him awake!'

Fierce debate rages among us as to what to do about the driver; four-letter words fly around describing what to do *with* the driver. More digs are delivered to the driver's ribs. I rehearse a vital discovery in my phrasebook – *Xinglai!* (Wake up!). It is eventually decided that the passenger in the front will keep an eye on the driver – we will rotate for the front seat posting.

First stop: Khamba La, a pass of 15,800 feet. The crest offers splendid views over a lake of a deep glacial blue – Yamdrok Tso. Beyond it, floating out of the horizon, lie the snowcapped peaks of the Himalayas, forming Tibet's southern border with Bhutan. We get out to pay our respects to the prayer-flags fluttering gracefully on a rock-cairn at the crest. Tibetans leave ceremonial scarves or other items here, or burn juniper – in order to guarantee safe passage.

Back on board the Landcruiser, we regret not having left a substantial offering: the driver, fully awake, and with a maniacal gleam in his eye, goes tearing down the other side of the pass. My limited Chinese has no effect on him; our combined screams have no effect on him – he is in another dimension. All of this adds to the air of frantic abandon as we whip round a hairpin bend, narrowly missing an oncoming truck. The descent has all the makings of a first-class horror-movie – blind corners, no barriers, sheer drops, loose gravel . . .

Mutiny is engraved on our faces by the time we reach level ground. The driver looks around sheepishly and grins. We are all very serious. We are ready to tie the driver up, stash him in the back of the Landcruiser, and drive the thing ourselves – all the way up Everest if need be.

The driver is short, thin, and has a surplus of front teeth. When he speaks, which is not very often, he is all teeth. When he eats, which is quite frequently, he is all teeth and chopsticks – a rice-eating machine, with blurred hands engaged in a rapid shovelling motion from rice-bowl to mouth. I can't remember the driver's name. I wrote it down somewhere but lost the piece of paper. The driver comes up with his own nickname. His ambition is to run us through to the Nepalese border as fast as possible and make it back to Lhasa, where things are more civilised. To this end, he is trying to propel us through the itinerary, moaning '*Zo! Zo!*' (Let's go! Move it!) if we stop for a picnic or photos. So we christen him 'Zoe', and he calls me 'Miker'. *Dzö*, I later discover, is the study of metaphysics in the Geluk school of Tibetan Buddhism; without the umlaut, a *dzo* is a mongrel cross between a cow and a yak. Zoe fitted in somewhere between the metaphysics and the mongrel cross.

One thought dominates my mind as Zoe bounces across the desert: *this road is not too bad*. Far better than I imagined. Far better than the road from Chengdu to Lhasa. What is the difference? Very few potholes. No rivers or streams crossing the road to gouge it up. And, most significant of all, little or no rainfall. The road from Chengdu to Lhasa passes through a monsoonal rain-forest zone. Here, it is high-altitude desert – the road is baked hard by the sun. It is ideal terrain for a mountain-bike.

Soon I am voicing my thoughts out loud. Scott, coincidentally, has been thinking along the same lines. Is it feasible? Has it been done? Chinese cyclists have done trips through Tibet, but no westerner, to our knowledge, has attempted such a journey. On the spur of the moment I issue Scott a challenge: to come back next year and do the Lhasa to Kathmandu route by bicycle. He looks at me, trying to work out if I am serious or not. I am deadly serious. We shake on it. This leg of the trip has swiftly turned into a reconnaissance: I start to jot down mileages, locations of passes, access locations to running water. Lhasa to Gyantse, 160 miles, two passes; Gyantse to Shigatse 60 miles, flat terrain...

By the Tibetan count, only thirteen major religious sites in Tibet survived severe Chinese vandalism. The exact number of monasteries in old Tibet is debatable since even a small building with a single shrine could qualify. A conservative estimate places the number at two thousand monasteries and buildings of religious significance. Among the 'survivors' of the Chinese occupation are the Potala and the Jokhang in Lhasa. In the first couple of days in the Landcruiser, we visited two more sites: the Chorten and Dzong (Fort), at Gyantse; and the vast Tashilhunpo Temple at Shigatse. The third great monastery (still intact) along our route lies at Sakya, a hundred miles across the desert from Shigatse.

The only time Zoe smiles is when he sees a bed. We roll into Sakya in the late afternoon; there is a stand-off with the manager of a run-down hotel. The place is filthy; the out-houses are disgusting; the rooms reek of yak-butter. We are eventually given a room with – it can't be true – windows! How such mundane things can send us into ecstasy. Remember windows? I test the windows. Glass. I have to sit down and think for a moment. Did Tibetans use glass in the making of monasteries? Did they use it in the Potala? No, I reasoned, they didn't – they used oiled paper instead of glass, and as further protection against the wind and cold, they used wooden shutters. They didn't have the means to make glass themselves, and it would have been difficult to import.

I go to put my bag on a bed and bump into a yak-skull suspended from the ceiling. This, I later discover, is a spirit-trap, used to protect the building against demons. Zoe is out like a light – soundly snoring away. David has gone for a walk around the town – even if it is nightfall. Sylvia is searching for food. I join Howard and Scott, the pyromaniacs, in setting up a launching-pad in the rear courtyard. They've brought Chinese fireworks in from Lhasa. They are unable to predict which direction the rockets will travel, which sends amazed onlookers diving for cover.

'Yabadoo!' shouts a Tibetan, as the first of the rockets fishtails along the ground. The crowd is delighted. They give us big grins, and thumbs-up signals. This is the most action that night-time Sakya has seen in ages. The town is devoid of electricity. Up go more rockets. Rockets are launched across the courtyard. The crowd is delirious.

'YABADOO!' shout the Tibetans.

'Got any idea what Yabadoo means?' asks Howard.

'No, but it's infectious.'

'These guys are madmen – they don't even try to get out of the way of the rockets!'

'Holy Christ, Howard – point that bottle somewhere else will you?'

Howard has lost control of the bottle he uses as a his launching-pad; the rocket goes straight into the compound, causing a chaotic stampede.

BOOM! goes the rocket, with a spray of stars.

'YABADOO!' shout the Tibetans.

'YABADOO!' we yell back.

The hamlet of Sakya is split in two by a river: to the north is a hilly section where there once stood a huge monastery, built in tiers. This structure was smashed to rubble by the Chinese; some parts of the walls remain and are used for corralling yaks and donkeys. South of the river, rising out of a valley floor, is Sakya Monastery, which, by contrast, does not appear to have been touched.

Sakya Monastery looks, at first sight, like a fortress. It lies behind massive reddish walls, with corner-turrets and watch-towers. The Mongolian-style monastery-walls dwarf the other structures in Sakya – low, squat housing with roofs festooned with yak-dung fuel or brushwood. In the narrow alleys of this sleepy town are donkeys and snot-nosed children. The place is small – perhaps five thousand residents – but then, towns are scarce in Tibet. The majority of Tibetans are herders or farmers; for centuries, there were no large towns on the plateau – any settlements grew around the monasteries. Thus a pilgrim's destination would not be the name of a town, but that of a monastery: for him they were synonymous. Navigation was done by monasteries.

Shortly after his coronation, the last Abbot of Sakya fled in 1959 to India, at the age of fourteen. There, at Dehra Dun, he established a new base to continue the teachings of the Sakya sect. In this sect, the 'throneholder' is hereditary: the post alternates between two families, unlike the reincarnation postings of the Geluk sect. The abbots are also permitted to marry and to drink intoxicating beverages.

And I wonder, as I stroll around the main hall of Sakya Monastery, how the monks operate in the absence of their rightful leader. A sutra-chanting session is taking place, with the monks seated cross-legged on faded cushions in the lofty central hall. Shafts of sunlight filter through the roof to illuminate this age-old scene. There are massive tree-trunk pillars in the hall, and my eye travels up them in search of a ceiling – up, up, up, until I connect with a row of fierce gargoyles at the top, staring back at me. The gompa, at least, has not suffered any damage. It is a repository for hundreds of statues, artefacts, scriptures, and precious items – attesting to the fact that Sakya was the base of a sect that ruled Tibet seven centuries ago.

Bribery doesn't work in Sakya Gompa. There is a sign in English saying 'No Photos Allowed'. Howard and I entered the monastery with our cameras dangling round our necks, hoping to be able to sneak a shot. Two monks have been assigned to our case – they follow us round to make sure we don't break the rules.

'Wow – I'd love to get a picture of that,' whispers Howard, pointing at a group of statues.

'Which one?'

'The one with the thunderbolt up his ass, and the frog in his left hand.'

'You'll need your flash-gun for that.'

'Got any spare DLs?' asks Howard.

'What?'

'DLs – Dalai Lama pictures.'

'Oh – yes, I think so.'

'Then try one on the monks.'

I dig out a black and white xerox of the Dalai Lama that I got in

Chengdu. The two monks are unimpressed – they've seen much better. They point disdainfully to a statue not far away. Propped against the base of the statue are large glossy colour pictures of the Dalai Lama.

Then I realise that my grasp of Tibetan is non-existent. But I know one word. I point to the colour pictures, and give a thumbs-up signal.

'*Yabadoo!*' I say.

The monks break into beatific smiles.

'*Yabadoo!*' they say, returning the thumbs-up.

The next day, a run through high desert terrain takes us over a 17,200-foot pass, Gyatso La, which is strongly buffeted by winds. The ascent to the pass is gradual, with no terrifying cliff-edges – which is fortunate since Zoe has lapsed back into falling asleep at the wheel. We stop at the prayer-flags at the top for photos; Scott tests the altitude by trying to sprint – he doesn't get far.

Close to this area we stray across a large caravan of donkeys, bearing blankets and woven goods – a scene out of mediaeval times. The Landcruiser obviously represents a scene out of the science-fiction future for the Tibetans. Curious women, drunken men, snot-faced kids, and mangy horses and donkeys hem us in, trying to get a good look at the dashboard, the steering-wheel, and the occupants of this odd machine. They shake us down for Dalai Lama pictures; they beg for ballpoint pens; they fondle the doors, windows and headlights; they ply us with *chang*, the potent Tibetan barley-beer...

At Shegar, the hotel demands a ridiculous tariff of 15 yuan for a run-down bed – arguing gets us nowhere. We fulminate over a meagre supper in the dining-room; I fetch out Bradley's sketch-map. Back at the turn-off into Shegar, according to the map, there is a Tibetan truck-stop hotel, at two yuan per night. We push a reluctant Zoe back into the Landcruiser. He can't believe it – where are we going? Where will we sleep?

It is only five miles back to the crossroads. There we find the truck-stop hotel, right near a Chinese checkpoint. There are dorm-type rooms – comfortable enough, plenty of blankets, no argument on prices. Zoe is looking quite miserable. I remember I still have my travelling Chinese chess-set with me. Perhaps he plays. I dig it out; his eyes light up. He is awake! We play three games – predictably, he wins them all. In the process, we establish a new record for Zoe's bed-time. It is past 10 p.m. by the time the third game ends. And tomorrow we have to be up at the crack of dawn to make a run for Everest.

★　　★　　★

WE REACH THE TOP OF THE PASS indicated on Bradley's sketch-map at about 8 a.m. This must be Pang La. And there, before us, is the whole Himalayan range – previously hidden from our view. It stretches, left and right, for a considerable distance, but not having any other accurate data, we can't make out what is what for mountain-names. We even have to hazard a guess as to which one is Everest.

Ting! Ting! This seems like a fine place for breakfast, so we set to work with cans of tomatoes, pineapple, pork pieces, and the canned fruit staple – mandarin orange segments. Zoe is shivering under the blanket we've stolen from the Tibetan truck-stop. He is squatting on the ground under the blanket, and all that can be seen from a profile is a pair of chopsticks shovelling food into a hole in the brown blanket.

We know we're on the right track now – we have gained the first pass. Further down the road our confidence falters. We lose sight of the Himalayan giants after Pang La; we reach a village, and the road disappears into . . . a waist-deep river. The river flows vigorously over boulders. Have we come the wrong way? Zoe pulls up; we all get out; Howard and David go upstream to look for a possible fording spot; Sylvia and Scott go downstream; I head back to the village to ask where there might be a crossing; Zoe stays where he is. My inquiries at the village yield nothing. The others fail to find a shallow crossing. The river charges across smooth stones and boulders, sometimes branching into several tributaries – with islands of sand and gravel in the middle. It is the same upstream; the same downstream. We rack our brains for over an hour for a way to cross.

'I can't see a way across unless we try wading ourselves,' says David. 'That way we can find out how shallow it is.'

'What if the Landcruiser gets stuck in the middle?'

'Yeah – what if the water gets into the engine?'

'Wait a minute,' says Howard. 'Hold it right there. I've got an idea. We forgot to ask Zoe.'

'Ah, what does he know?'

'A lot more than we think. I'll bet he's done the route before, but he's not letting on.'

'Yeah – he doesn't want to risk the Landcruiser out there, so he let us stop him. He's trying to sabotage the trip.'

'That's what I'm trying to say – it was *us* who told him to stop. If we let him go on, he probably could've done it in his sleep. He knows what that Landcruiser can do.'

'It's worth a try. *Zo!* Let's go!'

We all look at each other. Howard is right... Without a word, we all pile back into the Landcruiser, and signal to Zoe.

'ZO! ZO!! ZZZOOO!!' we all shout at the top of our lungs, urging him forward like a horse on a shaky bridge. Zoe fires up the engine, off goes the Landcruiser, water up past the wheels, straight into the river. 'ZO!! ZZZOO!!!' everybody screams. The driver swirls through the boulders; the Landcruiser hits the bank at a steep angle; Zoe rapidly shifts gears; we mount the other bank; a round of applause breaks out – we have made it! On the other side tread-marks appear again – this has got to be the route.

We bump up and down, banging our heads on the roof. My brain feels like it's been put through a concrete mixer. This stony track is testing the limits of Zoe's four-wheel-drive vehicle, and testing the limits of our personal suspension systems. Then – magic – a stupendous view unfolds as we round a corner. Straight ahead is the peak of Everest – icy white, framed by a deep blue sky. It is glorious. It is awesome. It fills the whole valley ahead. We are in luck, too, as the mountain is not hidden in cloud. There is nothing to stop us now – we will make it to the base.

As the Landcruiser twists and turns round the roads, bumps and grinds over the stones and potholes, Everest seems to balloon out, framed closer and closer – until it looks like we can reach out and touch it. There is something quite unnerving about this whole idea of driving up to the north face of Everest, as if it were no more than a Sunday excursion. Would the view have been more rewarding if we'd hiked in, exhausted, down to our last bottles of water, our last mouthfuls of food? My sense of adventure tells me this would have been the legitimate way to do it – but I am definitely in no mood for anything of the sort. I am worn down from two months on the road, and ill-equipped for hiking. But there is another factor – I've had my fill of adventure – and do not want to overdo it. Something inside me says 'home'. I'm on the home stretch, taking it easy.

But back to the destination: Rongbuk Gompa. Rongbuk Gompa! It comes into view, smashed to smithereens; a small, broken jumble of stone buildings. Silent witness to the destruction is Everest itself, or *herself*, as the Tibetans might think. The wind whistles through the ruins. The sight of the smashed buildings and the spectacular setting has a tremendous emotional impact on us all. Some kind of holocaust has swept through this monastery, leaving not a single wall in place.

At first it appears that the ruins are deserted, but a couple of Tibetans emerge to investigate the Landcruiser and its strange occupants. We pick a grassy knoll to lay out a picnic. As picnic spots go, this has to be the world's finest – the ruins of the world's highest monastery, backed by the world's highest mountain. Some naked kids come out of the ruins, bodies blackened by the harsh sun, and cheeks windburned. An old lady, wearing expedition-issue goggles atop her forehead, zeroes in on our empty tin cans. Even here, in the remote upper reaches of the world, can-pickers thrive! Others beg for Dalai Lama pictures. Howard makes the mistake of handing one out: this brings *everyone* to the picnic-site. They are all praying and giving us thumbs-up signals.

I had read bits and pieces about Rongbuk: indeed it was these tantalising morsels that had brought me this way. Rongbuk figured significantly in the early British expedition attempts on Everest. For the Tibetans, who were not the least bit interested in mountain-climbing, Everest – and Rongbuk – meant something quite different.

The last Abbot of Rongbuk fled over the Himalayas into Nepal in the aftermath of the 1959 uprising against the Chinese. In the 1960s he established Thubten Chuling, a large monastery on the south side of Everest, near Junbesi. The object of worship, one assumes, remains the same: *Jolmo Lungma*, Goddess Mother of the World – Mount Everest.

Pilgrims used to travel hundreds – even thousands – of miles to pay their respects to the sacred mountain; scores of lamas and pilgrims were engaged in meditation in a cluster of buildings at

Rongbuk. Others, in order to meditate or escape the cycle of rein-carnation, had sealed themselves up in caves around the valley, subsisting on water and barley passed through a slit in the cell-wall. They could be there for a month, a year – or a lifetime. If an animal were to be eaten, it had to be killed and quartered outside the valley: there was a strict ban on hunting or slaughter in the Rongbuk area. The result was that the wild animals had no fear, and were quite tame.

The British Everest expeditions of the 1920s had to feign that they were on a religious pilgrimage in order to gain the foothills. They found several hundred lamas in residence at Rongbuk; the monks and nuns were separated, with a nunnery further down the valley. After a catastrophic attempt on the summit in 1922, during which seven porters died in an avalanche, the monks forecast that the demons of Everest would cast down any man who dared to tread the slopes. In a fresco that appeared in the monastery, the man being cast down was European. In 1924, Andrew Irvine and George Mallory disappeared high up on the north face of Everest, triggering mountaineering's greatest debate: did they gain the summit or not?

After this disaster, there was a nine-year ban placed by the Tibetans on expedition attempts. In 1933 the British expedition attempts resumed. In 1934 an unofficial solo attempt took place. A British ex-army officer, Maurice Wilson, announced that he was going to crash-land a Tiger Moth on the slopes of the mountain, and hike up from there to plant a Union Jack on the summit. He got financial backing, learned how to fly, and – incredible but true – he flew all the way to India, where his plane was promptly seized by the Indian Government. Spurred on by his megaloma-niac brand of divine faith, Wilson found his way through Tibet disguised as a deaf and dumb monk. At Rongbuk he got on famously with the head lama. Wilson apparently believed that the earlier British expeditions had cut an ice stairway straight up the mountain – he thought he would simply climb this staircase, and pray his way to the top. He had little equipment, no warm cloth-ing, and no mountaineering experience. Another British expedi-tion of 1935 found his frozen body at around 22,000 feet.

The full story of Rongbuk Gompa is not known. In the early 1970s, by some accounts, the villagers were told by the Chinese that the monastery was oppressing them, so they were incited to smash it. The wooden parts were carted off or used for firewood; since Rongbuk is above the treeline, such building materials are precious commodities. A large *stupa* was split in two and ransacked of its treasures. And now, as we had found, a handful of monks and nuns were restoring the buildings. The *stupa* was held upright by guy-wires; frescoes were being repainted; structures that had been razed were slowly being rebuilt.

Scott and Sylvia, intent on a romantic interlude of some kind, had disappeared into the ruins of Rongbuk. They did not respond to our shouting – or perhaps the message got blown away by the gale-force winds. We had a few hours of daylight, and wanted to go further toward Everest. I had found the track leading off in that direction; Howard and David worked on a reluctant Zoe, telling him that Everest basecamp was on the itinerary. Zoe moaned and pointed at the petrol gauge. It was too far, he maintained. We would have none of it. Eventually, Zoe agreed to going some of the way. Scott and Sylvia were still missing. We got into the Landcruiser. Zoe headed off toward basecamp.

A short distance later, Zoe cut the engine. He would not budge from here. We couldn't twist his arm any further.

'*Meiyou!*' he insisted, pointing at the petrol gauge.

We would have to walk. We piled out, told him to wait. It was 3 p.m. Slowly we chalked up the mile or so to the end of the road. The big E loomed up; we were now at the glacial debris end of things.

There was no doubt that we'd arrived at the basecamp – it was a rubbish dump of sorts, with discarded medical stuff in six European languages. I picked up an empty packet:

SPICE 'N EASY INDIAN MIX FOR TANDOORI CHICKEN
 JUST ADD CHICKEN AND NATURAL YOGHURT!
     BUY ONE, GET ONE FREE!

'Let's start climbing,' suggested David. It sounded like a splendidly mad idea, somehow almost logical.

'Where to?'

'The first glaciers,' he replied. We could see them, hanging dramatically above – and appearing tangibly close. The task ahead seemed to demand more in the way of equipment, so David took an old towel out of his daypack and wound it around his head. He looked like Yasser Arafat. Howard put on the silk balaclava I'd lent him, giving him the bank-robber look, and as for me, I had a woollen hat – and an umbrella. We marched off up a gully of loose rock.

I picked my way crab-fashion across a section of scree, loosening bits and pieces in the process and causing minor avalanches. I stopped, got my breath back, scrambled on again. By this time – which seemed like an eternity – I was feeling *most* peculiar. My pulse-rate had shot up so high that I thought my heart was going to pop right out of my rib-cage. I took out my water-bottle, swallowed a little – but the water got stuck in my throat, blocking it and making me even shorter of breath. David and Howard were now hidden in a fold of the gully, and a vague panic set in. I was alone with the big E – and a gale-force wind. I tried to take stock of this drastic change in the tide. From the position I'd stopped in, there was a view of the valley up in the direction of Rongbuk. In the distance there seemed to be a tremendous dust-storm in progress. It was hard to tell how far off it was, or indeed if it was headed in my direction – but the thought caused my knees to buckle under me. My small daypack felt like a ton. I looked around for Everest. It had disappeared – it was enveloped in clouds. Suddenly I brought up my lunch – which consisted largely of canned tomatoes – a ghoulish red.

Howard and David were standing over me. They weren't in the greatest shape either. They each took an arm, and evacuated me off the slope – by which time I had recovered enough to be able to stagger back to the Landcruiser unassisted. Thus ended my glorious career on Everest – an advance of exactly one hill in the foothills.

Sylvia and Scott were furious that they hadn't been included in the basecamp ride. Tempers simmered down after a while when it was explained that Everest had clouded over anyway, so there had been nothing to see. Back in Rongbuk, during our absence, it had snowed.

Everyone spent a very uncomfortable evening stuffed in the seats of the Landcruiser. I barely got a wink of sleep, failing to find an uncramped position, and being jammed into the gearstick. It was freezing. Zoe had a blanket that we'd stolen from the last hotel, but he shivered through the night nonetheless. At one point, I swear, he woke up and started crying. How had he let these foreigners bring him to such a bleak, frozen place? David still wore a towel wrapped round his head, insisting that it wasn't really that cold anyway; Scott used a pair of woollen socks for gloves; Sylvia used Scott as a blanket; Howard had borrowed some gear off me. We were not exactly prepared.

The next day, when my pulse-rate returned to acceptable levels, I got an inkling as to why we'd got no further on Everest. All of us had come down with headaches – which indicated that the area was certainly much higher than we'd figured on. It was above the tree-line – possibly over 17,000 feet – which meant we'd have to spend at least three days acclimatising before attempting anything as foolish as we had. Walking around Rongbuk itself became a major effort. Oblivious, we all downed cans of beer. A thawed-out Zoe demanded that we depart. He was shivering, and he'd run out of rice. Running out of rice was a serious matter.

'*Miker! Zo! Zo-o-o-o-o!*' he wailed, like a sick cat ...

He was wrapped in his brown blanket, and his teeth were chattering. I gave him several cans of food, which he immediately dug his chopsticks into. He wolfed down a jar of pears in a matter of seconds. We were in no particular hurry. Excuses were found to prolong our stay. David put on a sick-man act, saying he couldn't be moved just yet. Scott and Sylvia disappeared into the ruins of Rongbuk. Howard was out chasing yaks in a field in the distance. He wanted to get the perfect yak-shot: yak in the foreground, Everest in the background. I went scouting through the back of Rongbuk, to climb a ridge.

I arrived at the top of the ridge gasping for air, and heart pounding. From this vantage-point there was a magnificent view of Rongbuk below, Everest beyond, and a slew of peaks forming the west side of the valley. A terrific blast of wind came through, almost knocking me off my perch. It had been very gusty all morning. What a godforsaken place it was, this Rongbuk area and Everest basecamp. It was barren, deserted, and because of the shape of the valley, there was a ferocious wind-tunnel through the place. I didn't envy mountain-climbers one bit – they could have the 70 mile-per-hour winds, and the frostbite.

Something clicked here. An article I'd read, about a group-tour to Everest basecamp. The tour members had paid astronomical amounts of money for the privilege of visiting the north side of

Everest. Why did they pay $10,000 each to sit in a wind-tunnel and eat food out of cans? One of the tour members had been so terrified, according to the article, that he never even came out of his tent. He spent the whole time in his sleeping-bag.

A seven-hour drive from Rongbuk put us in Tingri West, where Zoe booked us into the local army barracks for the night – for lack of any other place to stay. As the sun went down, the snowpeaks of the Himalayas were bathed in a warm, pinkish glow. In the distance, to the east, I could make out the north face of Everest. There was no doubt in my mind now about which peak it was.

*   *   *

THERE WERE A COUPLE of nomad-tents parked on the plains of Tingri. In the morning, out of curiosity, I ventured over to one tent, and received a surprisingly hearty welcome. There was Chinese brick-tea on the boil in a blackened pot: my hosts heaved some yak-butter and *tsampa* into it, forming a brownish goo that had the consistency and strength of putty. Both the tea and the *tsampa* were thrust upon me, and, not wanting to offend, I accepted. I was, in fact, much amused by this rough-house tea-ceremony. The family had brought out their very best silver goblets from a chest at the rear of the tent in my honour. The Tibetans must be among the world's premier tea-drinkers, but they do not dwell on polite foreplay before pouring the tea. In Japan, some schools of thought maintain that ten years is required to become a tea-master; it can take a year just to learn how to sit comfortably in a tea-room.

The nomads and myself had this much in common for language – we could swap notes on our clothing and equipment. The lady of the house, the stunningly beautiful Bemba, showed off her jewellery with the aplomb of a Parisian model – and with far less pretension. She modelled conch-shell armbands, silver belt-clasps, ornate earrings. I, in turn, did a demonstration of the incredible beeping digital watch, and removed one sneaker for closer structural analysis. This smelly item was passed around the tent in great admiration.

Not to be outdone, the master of the tent dragged out a musket that must've been at least six feet long. It was so long it could not be hand-held – it had to be mounted on a tripod made of antelope horns. I wondered what he used it for – it looked big enough to bring down an elephant. After boisterous attempts at drawing and redrawing beasts on pieces of paper, I narrowed the target down to rabbits, or hares.

Once, on the plains of Tingri West, there had been abundant wildlife – the British Everest expeditions of the 1920s had remarked upon the huge herds of wild gazelles, antelopes, donkeys and yaks that grazed the area. Such herds were protected by the Buddhist compassion toward all life – human, animal or insect – and the animals were quite easy to get near since they had no fear of man. With the coming of the Chinese, and increased access to the area, wide-scale hunting took place. Herdsmen moved their livestock into the once-remote areas where wildlife had flourished. Now there was not a single wild beast to be seen on the plains of Tingri.

Sylvia and Scott found me some time later, and they, too, got caught up in the magic of the tent. They settled down to be served tea from a blackened pot. About half an hour later Zoe drove the Landcruiser almost right into the tent. Zoe could not imagine walking anywhere – he simply *drove* everywhere. This action did not endear him to the monks (several times Zoe had driven straight into monasteries, over-riding our protests), or the locals. This intrusion of modern technology put a hole in the person to person relations with the nomads. It was time to go.

From Tingri West the road climbed up to a high pass, with expansive views in all directions. It seemed like the right place for lunch, so we set to work on the remainder of our canned food, and washed this down with some beer. Beer and mandarin slices – what a combination. The beer was a definite mistake – at this altitude it doesn't take much to get tipsy. Zoe got back into the Landcruiser, beaming from ear to ear, and pointed downwards. An hour later, heads banged against the roof several times, dust in the nostrils, and knuckles white from trying to hang on, we began to get the idea. We were dropping off the plateau, down through a dozen different zones of vegetation, through a cleft in the mighty Himalayas – to the border-town of Zhangmu. Once again, Zoe demonstrated his Hitchcock-like mastery of the roller-coaster descent – cornering near precipitous drops at high speed. Sylvia was driving us all to distraction with her talk about the lobster and apple pie in Kathmandu.

I knew, as I made that descent, that I would be back in Lhasa. On a mountain-bike. I thought about the whole route I'd covered. When I came down to it, the bike trip through China – from Shanghai to Xian – had been a battle with officialdom. The challenge had been to see how far I could get without being caught, but after that wore off, the actual cycling wasn't that difficult – except the last section through the mountains nearing Xian. The mountains presented a physical challenge – they also had the least traffic, and the best scenery. Then there was the thrill of coasting down off the top of a hill – dodging potholes, hoping the brakes worked. But we had the wrong bicycles for that kind of terrain – gears were called for.

The Lhasa to Kathmandu highway is open to travellers. On the Xian-Chengdu route, or the Chengdu-Lhasa route, there was a good chance of being stopped by officials if on a bicycle. Chengdu-Lhasa, in any case, was a marathon – because of the length and the sorry road condition. Lhasa to Kathmandu was a good highway – it had all the challenge a cyclist could hope for, concentrated in 600 miles of terrain. Best of all, it rarely rained on this route. In the back of my mind I was stitching together the route...

The talk of lobster and apple pie in Kathmandu got the better of Scott. He decided to carry on to Kathmandu, and make it back to Hong Kong from there. He made his decision as the Landcruiser dropped down the final switchbacks toward the Chinese border-town of Zhangmu. At the customs post in Zhangmu, three of us – Sylvia, Scott and myself – said goodbye to David, Howard, Zoe and the Landcruiser. They would be back in Lhasa within three days. Poor old Zoe – neither David nor Howard was going to attempt to speak any Chinese with him.

After passing through customs and passport checks on the Chinese side, we headed down for the Friendship Bridge, which was supposed to be six miles away. A truck stuffed full of sheep-skins picked us up – we piled in the back. The smell was dreadful; the skins were damp and fluffy; it was humid, sticky and hot in the back of the truck. We all smelled like dead sheep by the time we got down to the real border – the Bhote Kosi River. There was no bridge – it had been washed away, as reported. Instead, there was a small crossing composed of logs and rope, balanced over a precarious selection of rocks. This we negotiated, to be greeted by sturdy Nepalese porters on the other side, keen to carry our packs the few miles to the customs check in Tatopani. Scott picked up a Nepalese visa along the way, at Kodari. By nightfall we reached Tatopani, and got a room in a rickety lodge. From here, it would be a matter of half a day by truck into Kathmandu.

There were shops and restaurants in Tatopani – so no point to carrying food around anymore. I emptied out my pack, found some stale biscuits, chewing-gum, and a silver can – devoid of a label. A mystery can – what could it be? Pork and egg rolls? Or perhaps some tomatoes? Or peas? Or peach halves? I got out my Swiss army-knife and feverishly hacked away at it.

I should have known . . . it was a can of sickly-sweet mandarin slices. In disgust, I hurled the can out the window, into the jungle.

OVER the TOP

བལ་ཡུལ་ཉེ་ཕྲང་ཁྱིམ་

CTU-LXA (CHENGDU-LHASA); Boeing 707: a hundred and forty tons of aircraft (payload of 150 passengers, 40 tons of cargo) soaring along at 550 mph; CAAC flight 4401, departing March 26, 1986 at 0700, and now cruising at 35,000 feet over the snowcaps of eastern Tibet. For the life of me, I'll never understand aeroplanes. And if you put a tribesman from eastern Tibet in my seat, he wouldn't believe it either. As far as he's concerned, it's the Year of the Fire-Tiger, which is not an auspicious year for the return of the Dalai Lama. Somewhere down there are caravans of yaks and donkeys, following ancient trade-routes; somewhere down there is a pilgrim prostrating all the way to Lhasa. By caravan from Chengdu to Lhasa used to take at least five months; by truck it takes up to two weeks; by plane – two hours.

Flying over this piece of the Himalayas during World War II, ferrying supplies from India to China, American pilots frequently reported sightings of immense peaks – higher than Everest, they claimed. Some sightings were hoaxes, and others . . . well, looking out the window . . . There are jagged peaks – thousands of them – a frozen fantasy of rock, ice, and snow – sculpted by gale-force winds; the bases of the mountains are carved up by wild rivers.

In Tibetan legend there is a kingdom called Shambhala, ringed by high peaks and hidden from the sight of mortals by heavy mists. In Shambhala the sacred Buddhist teachings are kept, preserved for a time when the world has fallen into chaos and ignorance; in the glittering palace of Kalapa, there is no sickness, poverty, crime or hunger. The Tibetan legend was reworked by James Hilton in his 1933 story about Shangri-La – he got his main characters to the site by crash-landing a plane. This, coincidentally, is how the first airplane reached Tibet. Five American airmen – flying over the Himalayas during World War II – got blown off course at night, started running out of fuel, and circled Lhasa, believing it to be an Indian town. With no radio response from the town – and obviously no airstrip – they parachuted out of the plane. The startled villagers of Tsedang clothed and fed them; eventually they were escorted to Lhasa – and hustled out of the country, as Tibet wished to maintain its neutrality in the war-theatre.

It has taken us ten days to get this far. I gaze at the snowcaps. Shambhala, Shangri-La, Kalapa; prostrators, pilgrims, caravans, snowcaps – we are travelling backwards in time, forward in fantasy – this is what the plane allows us to do. This is the third plane of the trip: we're getting very sick of trucking mountain-bikes through airports. Chengdu Airport has been the worst so far, with three days lost in simply buying tickets.

Ten days to get this far – a labyrinth of doors, gates and corridors, marked and unmarked. When was it? January? I got a garbled message at work – from Scott Harrison. I phoned him up in California – he had exactly six weeks to get all his gear together and meet me in Hong Kong. By March we fielded three riders ready for the rooftop – we were all in Hong Kong, with a hundred photos of the Dalai Lama hidden in our pockets.

Wait – did I say *three* riders? Yes, it's true – there are three of us. In all fairness to the mystery third rider, I cannot disclose here the nature of our falling-out. Suffice it to say there was a personality clash of the first magnitude in the early stages of the trip – already, by the time we board this plane, tempers are frayed to the point where we know a drastic solution is called for. It's a question of when – and where.

Barren ground appears – we are going lower. Suddenly the plane banks sharply. Passengers grip their seats. A Chinese woman, returning from the toilet, runs at terrific speed down the aisle of the plane, makes a lunge for her seat, overshoots – and slams into Scott, seated beside me. Where is the runway? I am searching for signs of an airport. There are none. There's a lone windsock, and a low building, and that's it. The rest is desert. Lhasa is sixty miles away.

LHASA RECEPTION CENTRE FOR THE UNORGANIZED TOURISTS says the sign at the CAAC baggage pick-up in downtown Lhasa. We have landed – gasping for air, staggering round the streets like drunken astronauts. Here are the characteristics of the biosphere: there is limited oxygen; there are mountains – big ones; there is desert – lots of it; there are monks – living in the shells of monasteries; there are Chinese soldiers – holed up in military barracks.

Lying in a corner of the compound are our bicycles, mummified in plastic and packing tape. If nothing else, we can experience the thrill of riding them around Lhasa. We drag our hockey-bags outside the compound: the altitude has made us weak and lethargic.

Somewhere in Lhasa there is rumoured to be a storage depot for all the British Everest expeditions that passed through in the 1920s and 30s. Some of these expeditions were huge – over two hundred members; the gear was left behind because it was too expensive to cart it out. In the 1940s, Heinrich Harrer found 330 feet of film left behind by an expedition – it was well-preserved by the dry climate, and Harrer used it to document the Tibetan way of life. By the 1980s the expedition gear would be obsolete – imagine setting off for Everest in tweed jackets and studded leather boots, or lugging around a two-man tent that weighed 60 pounds.

Our own selection of camping gear would have appeared miraculous to 1920s expedition members because of its lightness and strength – the tent, the sleeping-bags, the inflatable sleeping-pads, the freeze-dried food, the water-filter – and the selection of Goretex, Velcro and Lycra. We had enough of this stuff to open a camping store.

We each had a Japanese mountain-bike – with thick spokes, aluminium rims, fat tyres, powerful brakes, sealed hubs, and 18-speed gearing for tackling steep terrain. These machines embodied a major design shift: for over a century bikes had evolved to go faster on paved surfaces; in the early 1980s mountain-bikes were made to go slower, but take the punishment – off the road. To combat physical problems, I had an battery of devices – the most important of which was a saddle-pad. This item – which had the consistency of a sirloin steak – promised to absorb vibration, and alleviate a condition known as 'weaver's bottom' (a term from the Industrial Revolution in England, when workers complained of intense posterior pain from 18-hour stretches at the loom).

I was also carrying two dozen packets of chewing-gum: I'd given up smoking in order to tackle the passes. To go up a pass and still smoke would be like putting my foot on the accelerator and the brakes at the same time.

The first serious obstacle to our pilgrimage cropped up within a day of arrival in Lhasa. The bikes were unwrapped at Snowland Hotel, pedals assembled – and then I tried to give the tyres a booster. A dozen strokes of the pump left me totally winded, but had absolutely no effect on the tyres. I borrowed Scott's pump – again no effect. Scott tried his tyres: fifty strokes of the pump yielded a paltry three pounds of pressure.

After wrestling with this problem for close on an hour, we came to the startling conclusion that neither of our pumps was functioning properly. They had a common fault: the rubber plunger didn't fit tightly into the shaft, hence allowing air to escape. We sat on the concrete floor, in a state of deep depression.

'The Schrader valve is the same as the one for trucks. It won't be a problem getting the tyres pumped up around here.'

'Yes, that's fine, but we can't leave Lhasa. It would be a disaster. We'd have no independence.' Scott cursed his pump and threw it across the room.

'Might be able to get a Chinese pump.'

'Then we need one each. If we get separated up a pass, and I'm up top, there's no way I'm going back down to help you fix a flat tyre.'

'Thanks Scott. You're a real friend.'

'Well think about it.'

He was right, of course. We could share tools, but we had to have our own pumps – not only for fixing flats, but for altering tyre pressure. On a paved road, the tyres could be inflated hard; if the road was bad, the tyres could be deflated to act as shock-absorbers. The success of the trip hinged on two lousy pumps.

Scott visited repairman after repairman trying to modify the plunger with a leather piece – which failed. I canvassed Lhasa for a Chinese pump: they were all foot-operated – mammoth pieces made of steel. We gave up: I telephoned Rocky, a friend in a travel agency in Hong Kong, to have two new pumps sent up via a traveller. But what if this took a week or more? We could not depart Lhasa until we had the pumps. We still had 10 days of acclimatisation to go.

Once a day, at Snowland Hotel, a clean-up squad would arrive to sweep the floor and replace the hot water thermoses. The room was a mess of empty yoghurt jars, cups of tea, postcards, batteries, maps – it looked lived-in at any rate. The hotel staff were fascinated by the array of equipment – some of which we handed over for closer inspection. Once I handed over a waterproof shoe covering, made of Goretex and Velcro. The Tibetan woman looked at it puzzled for a while, then slung it round her lower waist – it looked exactly like a codpiece, designed to keep the male appendage warm and dry. Everybody cracked up: the ribald Tibetan sense of humour was contagious.

The annoying thing about baggage is that most of it *is* baggage – bags within bags – stuffsacks, panniers, plastic bags, webbing, straps, buckles... Another third of the equipment was dead-weight – things we had to have, but hoped we never had to use – medical supplies, spare parts, tools. To abandon these was to leave ourselves with no back-ups at all.

Our front panniers were entirely devoted to food and water. The freeze-dried food packages had been packed at sea-level air-pressure; upon arrival in Lhasa they had ballooned out to the point where I wondered if it was possible to be killed by beef-stew shrapnel over a high pass. I stabbed a packet of stew – there was a hiss of air. It didn't matter that the packages were pricked – Tibet's climate would keep the contents frozen and dried – naturally.

Scott was busy churning out postcards – everybody wanted a Lhasa postmark. He was eating dried apricots by the handful – to cut down on weight, presumably by turning them into gas.

'I saw a strange thing in the markets this morning,' he mentioned. 'There was a drunk lady there, shouting, and a whole lot of Tibetans were standing round stoning her – but not too heavily. Not enough to kill her.'

'Just enough to annoy her, eh?' I cut in. 'I'll bet you're not writing that one down on the postcard.'

'No – just the usual crap about forbidden cities and the roof of the world. People don't want to – '

A loud knock on the door. Two breathless young women. In skin-tight shiny jogging-pants, made of Spandex. We'd met them on the airplane coming in from Chengdu. They were Americans on a lightning visit – three days in Lhasa, on a tour. To speed them on their way, the Tibetans had goosed, pinched, kneaded, squeezed, and probed the glowing material on their posteriors for the full length of Barkhor Bazaar. Old men, young women, children – an entire tribe had joined in the fun. Nothing like breaking the ice.

What they now desperately wanted was a change of pants so they could make it back to their hotel across town without being further molested. Well, at least the tourist hotel across town had oxygen tanks so they could get their breath back. We donated some shorts to the cause. Scott went back to his writing chores.

'Did you get that one on the postcard, Scott?'

'You kidding? Nobody would believe me.'

'What about cycling across Tibet?'

'Nobody believes that one's possible either – but I'm going to prove them wrong.'

I'd only known Scott for a short time, but the trip we'd done the previous year cemented a mutual respect. We'd lived through a mad drive across the Tibetan Plateau, through dissident bombings in Kathmandu, through doses of giardia. The strain of the road quickly brings out the real person: travellers meet on equal ground, not defined by jobs, or cars, or apartments – or even clothing. Scott came across as a happy, bouncy person, whose good-natured approach always put him in easy touch with those around him – particularly women. With the Tibetans it was the same: he had a cultural sensitivity – and a winning smile – that got the locals on his side in a matter of minutes.

From Room 4 at Snowland, there was a view over the street: a circus of cobblers, bicycle repairmen, radio repairmen, snack-vendors, pilgrims, sheep, squads of dogs. By midnight, it was down to the dogs – who specialised in making us lose sleep. During the day, not a peep out of them; at night, non-stop barking. Where one dog finished, another took over. Finally, Scott got fed up. He marched off and bought a stack of Chinese fireworks.

The following night, when the dogs started up again, Scott opened the windows and flung out a string of fireworks. The street was alive with explosions; the dogs were scared out of their minds; there was no more barking. What we had here, I told Scott, was a wonderful solution to a potential problem on the road. We had little idea what the dogs were like on the road, or what their reactions would be to bicycles, but instinct told us that there would be close encounters. If we had a supply of fireworks...

Snowland is a courtyard-style hotel: three floors arranged in a wide U-shape, with galleries running along the sides. The galleries function as clothes-lines, and as a kind of courtyard amphitheatre. The ground floor rooms were occupied by members of a Tibetan basketball team: these men seemed to do nothing all day except wander round in their sweatpants. I had yet to see one dribble a basketball.

In the morning, I went out on the second floor gallery. Scott was near the centre of the courtyard, doing his washing at the water-pump. An evil plan was taking shape. When would I get a chance like this again? I went back to the room, selected a bunch of fire-works, strolled back out to the gallery, lit them, and lobbed them into the courtyard below. There was a loud staccato of explosions; Scott shot up in the air like a human cannon as the fireworks exploded at his feet; the shirt he'd been working on went flying into the dirt; a cloud of smoke enveloped the water-pump; all the members of the Tibetan basketball team rushed out of their rooms to catch the action...

Later in the day, Scott got his revenge – with half a bucket of water from the pump.

Lhasa, as the year before, had attracted its quota of eccentrics, mystics and madmen. There were, too, adventurers bent on promoting the names of sponsors to defray their trip costs: for it is always the remote places – the ones that have no multi-national logos – that attract the sponsors. 'Rent-an-explorer' is the name of the game; Tibet had become the magic location.

In a class of their own were the writers – Lhasa was rapidly developing into a travel writers' conference centre. Travel writers seemed to lurk at every corner – each deeply suspicious of the motives of the others. There was Victor Chan, a writer who'd lost girlfriends all over Tibet on various treks. In the spring of 1985 he and a companion rode across the plateau on mountain-bikes: they were booted out by the Chinese, and the bikes were confiscated in Lhasa – which made me uneasy. Also in town were Jeff and Naomi, a North American couple who were preparing to bike down the newly-opened Karakoram Highway into Pakistan. Jeffrey had cycled across the plateau the previous autumn so he was a mine of information on road conditions. He told us he got 27 flats on that trip – from thorns. I immediately went and counted the pieces in my patch-kit: I had enough to fix seven flats.

To pass time while acclimatising, we joined some rented Landcruiser trips with an Englishman researching monasteries around Lhasa for a new Tibet guidebook. This Buddhist scholar – Stephen Batchelor – spoke fluent Tibetan. He came equipped with several hundred Dalai Lama pictures (he said he limited himself to handing out six a day), and 600 yellow strings personally blessed by the Dalai Lama. One monastery – Drigung – proved so elusive that not even our Tibetan driver could find it. It was parked on the top of a mountain, with very steep access. On the way up, we passed donkeys bearing bodies under blankets. Drigung was reputed to have the best sky burial ceremony of all.

We'd been training on the unladen bikes for almost two weeks now, building up our strength at altitude. There came the time when we would have to put on a full load for a practice run. I was dreading this moment because I knew I had far too much equipment. When the bike was finally loaded, I found – to my astonishment – I couldn't lift it.

What to do? We could ditch the freeze-dried food and scrounge what we could off the villagers along the way. Come to think of it, we could throw away all the sleeping gear and just crash in Tibetan villages. All we needed was our supply of colour Dalai Lama pictures – these are a kind of currency in Tibet, easily traded for food and lodgings. But that option made me very uncomfortable – the Tibetans were very poor. Besides, it was the challenge of self-reliance that made this trip interesting.

With the full load in place, we lumbered out to our 'test-site', a steep slope past Sera Monastery. The climb with the full load left me completely winded, wondering if I would be able to tackle the much longer slope up the first pass out of Lhasa. How long that pass was, and what grade it was, we had no idea. And that would only be the first hurdle: there were five passes on the Tibetan side. The mystery pass was the last one – in most sources, no elevation was given for the pass. One tour-pamphlet quoted the startling figure of 5600 metres – or 18,380 feet.

Having reached the crest of the test-site, we turned around, gasping for air, and admired the view. The next test was for the brakes. I lowered my saddle, took a firm grip of the handlebars, braced myself, and shot off down the dirt road. This jackhammer descent was the greatest feeling in the world – the loaded panniers actually made it easier to corner at high speed. Scott came bombing along behind me. Suddenly three yaks to the side of the road bolted. Their handlers were knocked off their feet – the yaks had gone berserk at the sight of the approaching bikes, and were charging up a slope, away from the road. A yak can easily weigh half a ton, so keeping them in line was no easy task: we felt rather guilty about the commotion we'd caused...

Lhasa is changing rapidly. There are more goods, higher prices, more restaurants, more Landcruisers, more sophisticated pick-pockets. There is one more television station – beamed in from Peking by satellite. Lhasa Hotel has opened, under Holiday Inn management. It boasts piped-in oxygen, hot water, and TV; it has a coffee-house serving yak-burgers; it has the only elevator in the whole of Tibet – thus attracting crowds of local sightseers. A group of tourists found themselves trapped inside the thing for ten minutes with no phone or alarm, until skilled Japanese mountaineers prised the doors open.

From the roof of the Jokhang, I can see the long shapes of the prostrators, spread-eagled at the front of the temple; others are burning juniper at a large hearth. From here, the full extent of the new Chinese creation – the square with its Tibetan-style tourist-shops – becomes apparent. Beyond this wasteland of paving looms the Potala.

Directly to my left is the massive Wheel of the Law, at the edge of the temple roof. The Wheel, flanked by two golden gazelles, is a sacred symbol of Buddha's first sermon in India many moons ago. But it is also a symbol of the triumph of superstition over technology – for the wheel was spurned in daily use. There were some exceptions in pre-1950 Tibet: the 13th Dalai Lama had three cars imported in sections over the Himalayas (petrol supplies were limited, however); there were a few wheeled carts; some Nepalese residents in Lhasa had bicycles. But the wheel was largely used in monasteries: from hand-held prayer-wheels – to massive upright ones that spun offerings to the heavens. Heavy loads in old Tibet were dragged about by men, yaks, or donkeys; Tibetans used – and still do – ponies for personal transport, or their own two feet. To introduce wheeled vehicles would require that the narrow caravan trails be expanded into roads – which, it was believed, would scar the surface of the earth, releasing evil spirits.

Ancient Tibetan prophecies forecast that with the wheel came the end: certainly, with the coming of the Chinese, they weren't far off the mark. It was the Chinese who, in the 1950s and 60s, set about building roads for trucks and buses – and army vehicles. From my position on the rooftop, I can trace our routing out of Lhasa, westward. That road-section – to Shigatse – was completed by 1956; but it was not until 1966 that the 'Friendship Highway', financed by the Chinese, fully linked Tibet and Nepal. And although there have been many trucks, buses and Land-cruisers along the route, there can have been very few bicycles.

Actually, my transport consists of three wheels – the third is the Wheel of Fortune: when that spins, it controls the other two. A considerable part of this trip will depend upon pure luck – luck with the weather, with escaping officialdom, with health, luck with the bikes, with the equipment, with the locals . . .

Monday, April 7th. Our first piece of luck is when the pumps arrive from Hong Kong. Daniel, a Swiss traveller, walks in the hotel-door bearing a long package. The telephone-call to Rocky in Hong Kong has been translated into shiny new pumps, delivered within two days. Scott claims the red one; I bag the black one. We are ecstatic – inflating the tyres is effortless. Daniel has just flown in from Chengdu; he is leaving for Kathmandu tomorrow. What is his rush? Scott knows immediately. This is an express delivery – Daniel is a gold smuggler.

The weather report: brought to us by travellers coming from Nepal. High winds – probably headwinds. Snow on the passes; the road is blocked by a snowfall above the border-town of Zhangmu – travellers have had to hike past this section. Whichever way the wind blows, there's no turning back now. Our paperwork is in order: Chinese exit stamp, Nepalese entry visa – these documents give us the right to be on the road to Nepal. The equipment has been modified, packed and repacked, and is ready to go.

*   *   *

ON APRIL TWELFTH, at 8.30 a.m., we roll out of Lhasa, keeping a brisk pace for fear of being stopped. Not much chance that PSB will be around on a Sunday morning, we figure. We quickly gain the blue signpost that designates the road to Gyantse. This time we're not stopping as we might on a training-run: we're going all the way.

Like the best of pilgrims we navigate by Buddhist landmarks: first, the towering Potala; then Drepung Monastery – a ghost-town – pops up on the right, just out of Lhasa, followed in an hour by a large rock-carving of a Buddha by the roadside. By 10.30 a.m. we've reached Droma Lakhang, a small temple devoted largely to lifesize statues of the goddess Tara. We're twelve miles out of Lhasa, and rolling along as fast as we can on the black carpet of road. The theory is that the further we get, the less chance we'll be returned to our starting-point. There is, to our relief, very little traffic – the occasional walking-tractor, and some army trucks.

We make good time, clocking up 30 miles by lunchtime. A motorcyclist pulls over opposite us. 'Hello – coming from Lhasa are you?' A British accent: I have to rub my eyes to get this one in focus. The rider takes off his helmet and introduces himself. His name is Chris Reed.

This cheeky young Briton is riding a 500 cc trailbike; he is riding, too, on a lot of luck – somehow he bluffed his way through the Nepal-Tibet border-post. He is half-way through a round-the-world trip, he tells me; Tibet is an impromptu detour. With his oversized gas-tank and spare containers, he has a range of a thousand miles, and then fuel can be begged from truck-drivers. He has a long way to go – his eventual target, after skirting the Takla-makan and Gobi deserts, is Tianjin. Somehow I doubt he can avoid Chinese authorities for the entire trip. He was stopped in Shigatse: after demanding that he write a confession, PSB let him go. Chris' next obstacle is Lhasa – I draw a map for him, tell him how to slip into Snowland Hotel – and wish him luck with this amazing adventure.

An old acquaintance – the kilometre stone – appears at the road-side. The Chinese have been busy in Tibet.

K-stone 60 – we reach the bridge we'd seen coming in from the airport. There's a sign in Chinese, the second large road-sign we've seen in Tibet, and, for all intents and purposes, probably the only other one in existence. I match the characters off my Chinese map – 80 *gongli* to the right to Nagartse, and 194 *gongli* on the same route to Gyantse; the left fork goes to the airport. Across the bridge, the black macadam welcome mat is brutally ripped from under our tyres – it goes to the left, to the airport. We go to the right, round a corner . . . where I find my old enemy the road-builder. The road-builders have ripped up a lengthy section of road, and are not in the least concerned, or guilty, about what traffic must do. We make detours as best we can through the dusty fields, skirting villages.

K-stone 71 – Scott attacked by dog – he jumps sideways off the bike in an attempt to place the bike between himself and the dog, and almost sprains his ankle in the process. I speed up to try and scare the dog off with my bike; Scott has already done so by lobbing a rock at it.

K-stone 77 – a loud blast sends us diving for cover – behind us, uncomfortably close, a cliffside crumbles across the highway. The road-builders are at it again. We appear to have reached the base of Khamba La, the first pass. We choose a campsite, quickly pitch the tent, and engage in a round of frisbee to entertain the locals who have crowded around to witness the tent-pitching ceremony. Mercifully, we seem to have left the road-builders and their sticks of dynamite behind us now.

A truck comes by – it is heading up the pass. I listen carefully – the engine groans for what seems like a very long time. We're in for some rough weather. I guess I could've found out the exact mileage to the top of the pass – but I didn't dare ask. Some things are better not known. There is one thing we know – we'll have to filter and fill all the water-bottles here at the base. There may not be any running water further up, and with the heavy physical exercise of going up the pass, we can't afford to run out. Yet those extra bottles will burgeon us with extra weight. If we can't even lift the bikes, how the hell are we going to pedal them up the pass?

April 13th. Campsite inundated by goats and curious miniature goat-herders. Kids and their kids, so to speak. Goats a possible menace to the camping equipment – tent in danger of becoming a goat's breakfast. The goat-herders mill around with their slings and pebbles – which serve to keep the goats in line. One tiny goat-herder demonstrates his skill by cracking a sling – and scoring a goat on a distant hillside. The goat in question makes a rapid descent to join its cousins near the tent. I get to practice my Tibetan, which has now advanced to a grand total of five words: the classic 'hello' (*tashi delay*), 'thank you' (*tuduchay*) and 'goodbye' (*kalipay*) trilogy. Then there is the all-purpose thumbs-up signal, accompanied by a vigorous *Yagodu!*, which we have learnt is Tibetan for 'good'. And the common Asian word for tea – which is *'cha'*. Showing a picture of the Dalai Lama or the Potala will take care of any other conversation problems with Tibetans. We've now christened all the camping gear – tent, sleeping-pads, sleeping-bags – and the goats have made sure it's all fully broken in. The sleeping was toasty enough, at any rate.

It takes forever to cook breakfast, pack the tent up, resaddle the bikes, fill up with water and get out of there. Road-blasting continues – we jump back as explosions rock the valley behind us. In a lull, one of the goat-herders whistles for a stray animal and almost deafens me in the process, the little brat. We set out for Khamba La with my left ear still ringing. It is 11 a.m.

Khamba La is very tough going. Each bend promises greater punishment than the last. Aching legs fixed, pumping in a piston-like rhythm, zigzagging up the hills where I can – keeping an eye out for army convoys that edge me off the road and spray clouds of dust. It is no use even thinking about the crest of the pass – all I can do is concentrate on the action of the pedals, try and integrate myself into the machine. *If you can sustain the effort you will make it*, I tell myself.

Kadang! Kadang! My heart is thumping away at reckless speed. *You're going to make it!* I mutter, wheezing along. *You're going to die*, says a voice somewhere in the back of my brain, *Your legs will crumble to dust, your heart will explode, your lungs will collapse. Kadang! Kadang!* The heart beats faster. But I then tell myself, *You're going to do it! You'll get there! You can do it! This is not so bad! Go!* I round the next corner. Another monstrous switchback. *This is bad. This is going to be the toughest thing you've ever done*. Another corner, much worse than the last. *This is really bad, you're going to die on this pass*.

Kadang! Kadang! My heart is beating like a drum. My life glides before me – rows and rows of it, stacked up, on large supermarket shelves – all the ice-cream I've eaten, all the women I've taken out, all the music I've listened to, all the liquor I've drunk, all the exams I've taken, all the jerks who've gotten in my way . . .

After four hours of uphill grind, we stop for a breather: there is a stupendous view back down the valley, and I throw up everything as far back as breakfast. I feel a whole lot better after throwing up, despite a pounding headache. There's no question of me continuing up the pass today. In fact, Scott seems to think it's a question of me making an immediate descent. After all that hard work getting up this far? Not likely. I'm not budging. I don't care if it kills me. But that's the point, says Scott – it could be serious. Besides, we have an agreement. The healthy person is responsible for all decisions, on the basis that the person affected by altitude won't be able to make any rational decisions.

Scott wants to bundle me on the first truck going either way – back down where we just came from, or over the top and down the other side. I refuse point-blank to go back down. This is the first pass – I must conquer it. If I cannot, then all the other passes on the route become immense psychological barriers. I am thus secretly delighted when Scott's attempt to flag down a passing truck fails. We'll have to set up camp right here. The stakes are high now – if I get really sick, it could be serious. *This is it*, I tell myself, *you're completely cracked! You don't care about yourself anymore. The pass is all that counts* . . .

The following morning, the uphill marathon continues – each k-stone becomes a major effort to attain. Slowly, k-stone by k-stone, we battle on – weathered, beaten, fried by the altitude. At most, I can only manage ten minutes of cycling before I have to stop to catch my breath. After several hours of punishing climbs, I sight the prayer-flags at the crest: I push those pedals and sing for all I'm worth.

Sweet victory! My head is clear as a bell, and the view from the 15,800-foot crest is magnificent. Below us is the glacial blue of a large lake. There is no signpost to announce the lake, but what words could do justice to such raw beauty? On the map, it is Yamdrok Tso, the turquoise lake. Myself, Scott and the third rider (still very much in the picture) are ecstatic. We thump each other on the back, shake hands, cry, yell, dance up and down, and go to offer our respects to the spirits of the pass – at the prayer-flags, along with a truckload of Tibetans. They are in a state of euphoria because their beaten-up truck has limped to the top. They seem to think that it is quite normal behaviour for foreign lunatics to prance around – they worship mountains too. Sixty miles down; 565 to go . . .

April 14th; 70 miles from Lhasa, along the shores of Yamdrok Lake. Scott has two major categories for the Tibetan landscape experience: 'brutal' and 'intense'. The pass that we've come up – Khamba La – falls into the 'brutal' category; Yamdrok Lake is 'intense'. Amazing the colours that the lake throws up with the play of sunlight – deep tropical emeralds, subtle blues, browns. And it looks so crystal clear that filtering appears unnecessary. But we know better – we filter the water as needed. The trouble is that the filter has already clogged up. Filling one or two water-bottles is exhausting work: on a full day's load, we need six bottles of water each.

With an illusion of sea-level, and a pleasant breeze, riding along the shores of Yamdrok Tso is a joy, until . . . we strike headwinds. They come up with a dusty vengeance in the afternoon, slowing us to a crawl. We are blinded by blasts of dust – some generated by truck-wheels, some by spontaneous combustion of the elements. If we are to make any progress at all, it will have to be in the mornings. Catch-22: in the early morning, we spend half our time trying to warm up our frozen hands and feet, which don't finally thaw out till around 10 a.m.

April 16th. Last night we pitched our tent on the wrong side of the valley – now the sun shines everywhere except *here*. The water-bottles have frozen up, and so have our hands and feet. Eventually we shake the ice off the fly, roll up the tent, stash it away, and – with teeth chattering – scuttle for the sunny side of the valley, closer to the lake. Here, large white birds are holding a convention – all crowing away. I go to get some water, and fall ankle-deep into some kind of black slush at the lakeside. It is a horrible, smelly black goo that I can't help but think has a nasty connection with the convention of white birds. With half an hour of scraping I have a reasonable facsimile of a shoe again – but the laces will never be the same.

The day can be summed up in one word: headwinds. We spend all day battling them. But there are rewards: the purplish browns of the hills, the deep blues of the sky, the crystal clarity of the lake, and the bright clumps of yellow lichen on the shores. The intensity of these colours is unbelievable, especially at either end of the day when magic new shades appear. Is it the altitude – the thin atmosphere – that gives the landscape such a depth of shading? I have never seen such a blue in the sky, nor such a brown in the hills. The colours glow.

So far we've escaped the dogs. Not so the children. Pulling out of one small village, some kids started to throw stones at Scott. We thought of chasing them, but that would only seem to spur them on, and sadly we departed. The villagers can not have seen too many foreigners – but that doesn't make them any less shy.

April 17th. It has taken me four days to jot this down in my pocket notebook. I keep forgetting to write it down! It is the strange phenomenon of searching for something right under my nose. I spent a whole hour searching for film, which was in the camera-bag hanging off my shoulder. And a similar amount of time looking for my sunglasses. After an hour or so, I realised I was wearing them – the mid-day sun was so strong that it had bleached the landscape, leading me to think I needed the sunglasses. Could this be the effect of altitude? I am not the only one – Scott spent two days searching for his green bandanna. Finally I pointed out that he was wearing it, round his neck.

Last night was a blank. Wind and heavy snow coming through the storm-doors of the tent. Pitched the tent near a wall of rocks – shivered trying to get some food going on the burner. This morning, the wind still wouldn't let up – sent dust along with it. The campsite was in a tundra-like landscape of lichen, rocks and moss. The flat rocks and slate around the place would've been the envy of any landscape gardener. Half an inch of snow on the ground. Not much sleep – tossed and turned all night, with the wind howling outside. Dressed to the maximum this morning, waddled round like a penguin in the Arctic, struggled to pack the tent away. Conquered a headache, and waited for the sun to warm my bones up.

On the sixth day we straggle through to Gyantse. We have averaged only 25 miles a day on the road from Lhasa. This is still faster than horse-travel, and since we have overtaken horseback riders along the road, we don't feel too bad about the miles we've done. A yak-caravan would travel even slower – perhaps eight miles in three hours, or fifteen miles in a day. From Kalimpong in Sikkim to Lhasa used to take up to a full month of horseback travel.

*   *   *

GYANTSE WAS ONCE a bustling caravan stop on the trade-route from Lhasa to India. That route – leading to Sikkim – was closed by the Chinese after they took over in 1950. Gyantse has fallen into obscurity, its role usurped by Lhasa under the Chinese. This situation, however, has left Gyantse intact as a Tibetan architectural entity, which is something quite rare amid all the Chinese destruction and reconstruction. Lhasa itself has little of its original entity left, being now heavily Chinese in architecture, layout, and population. Gyantse has a largely Tibetan population – around 10,000. The buildings are mostly adobe or stone structures; transport in the area is predominantly by horse-cart or donkey-cart. There is a huge fort up one end of town, a walled-in monastery-grounds at the other end, and a ramshackle market-place with older buildings and alley-ways between fort and monastery. Most of the monastery was destroyed during the Cultural Revolution, but a fine Nepalese-style *stupa* remains.

In the late afternoon, we wander up to the monastery. Guarding the entrance to the *Kumbum* – the massive *stupa* – is the same monk-sentry who was there the previous year. He has the same clothing, same chair, same grubby teapot, same overpicked nose – it's as if he hasn't moved for a year. He doesn't recognise us – all foreigners probably look much the same to him. We distinctly remember him, however, as he blackmailed us the year before. We'd arrived in the Landcruiser in the afternoon, when the *Kumbum* was closed. The monk had all the keys to the padlocks within the building. There are nine levels to the *Kumbum* – at each level he had demanded a Dalai Lama picture before he would unlock the next level. Five or six Dalai Lamas later, we had gained the roof. Now, because we arrived at the right time, the *Kumbum* was open – no admission charge – and we could clamber around by ourselves.

Kumbum transliterates to 'pagoda of 100,000 images'. There is a huge amount of artwork and statuary within the rabbit-warren of chapels here. The pagoda is a meditational aid: the pilgrim spirals through the chapels and the narrow staircases to the top canopy, which represents Nirvana – the highest plane of wisdom. On the ground levels are larger-than-life statues of sublime or terrifying deities. These we had seen before, and yet we had missed many details because we didn't have torches on the previous visit.

Higher up, toward the top, are four large chapels containing massive mandalas painted on the walls – circular symbols of the universe. What was the key to their use? To decode one of these cosmic maps must take years of training. I go over the elaborate patterns with my torch.

The floor above the mandala-rooms holds more meditational aids: large faded frescoes of tantric deities and their consorts locked in various couplings. There are no lights, and it is only with the aid of a torch that the images can be made out along narrow passages. In Tantric Buddhism, sexual coupling signifies the bonding of knowledge and insight, joined to eliminate opposites, and thus representing liberation. In former times, such images would've been used in esoteric meditation procedures. Sexual symbolism, in terms of other religions, would appear to be bizarre, but for the Tibetans such symbolism deals with the more subtle levels of the mind – harnessing genetic energy rather than avoiding it.

The first Dalai Lama wrote a treatise on the Kalachakra Tantra in the 15th century, which was roughly the period when Gyantse *Kumbum* was constructed. He detailed a number of initiations required for the strongest followers to gain enlightenment. One of the preliminary initiations required meditation on a mandala, entering the mandala as a child enters the world – the four consorts residing in the mandala bestow a 'water initiation'. As for the higher initiations, the first Dalai Lama elaborates:

> When the blindfold is removed from the disciple's eyes he is told to visualise the spreading lotus of a Knowledge Lady. Fierce passion arises within him, which in turns produces great bliss.

A further level of initiation requires the meditator to:

> ... visualise sitting in union with a Knowledge Lady. The sexual substances come to the tip of his jewel, and the bliss thus induced introduces him to this Fourth Initiation.

From here, the going gets rough, with the meditator having to visualise more difficult tasks, such as union with nine consorts rather than one.

At the top of the *Kumbum* is a small temple-section. Tibetans are murmuring, chanting, leaving gifts at the small altar here. Where is the rooftop? There is a ladder leading up to a trapdoor. The trapdoor is padlocked. We will have to bribe our way up there again.

The monk at the altar scowls – he will not let us up on the rooftop balcony. However, when I produce a picture of the *Kumbum* that I took on the previous trip, his face lights up – he is ecstatic. The trapdoor is opened. We get a glorious panorama of Gyantse town, and the mighty fort.

Another aerial perspective on Gyantse is possible from the top of the fort, which shares the same ridge as the monastery-walls on the east side. Gyantse *Dzong* – the fort – is built tier on tier to the summit of a rocky outcrop; the view from the summit promises to be more spectacular than that from the *Kumbum*.

Our guide to the *dzong* is a bright-eyed middle-aged Tibetan who speaks not a word of English, nor a word of Chinese. However, he is a first-rate mime, and he gets his message across with hand-gestures, a pen, and sheer vivacity. A grasp of the Gregorian calendar is his basis.

I offer my notebook. The first date he writes down is 1015, obviously the initial date of construction of this colossus. He mimes the construction of the fort, then adds dates from the 14th and 15th centuries, pointing to the massive walls of the top-section of the fort. As we approach the main gate, he takes a huge Tibetan key from his pocket, and relieves us of two yuan each.

We saunter through the fort buildings, and come to a chapel with defaced frescoes and damaged statuary. '*Mao-Zedong-Boom-Boom!*' says our guide, giving us the thumbs-down signal. He writes down the year 1966 in my notebook. '*Chenrezig*', he says, pointing at one faded fresco. I shine my torch that way – it is an image with multiple heads, and eyes implanted in the palms of many hands. The Dalai Lama is supposedly a reincarnation of Chenrezig – the Bodhisattva of Compassion. The guide stops in front of a Buddhist statue – the base of it is old, the top new. He writes down 1985 in the notebook – restoration to previous Cultural Revolution damage.

The guide re-enacts wars, battles, destruction – the fort leaps to life. He jumps around showing the blood and guts, the gore, the explosions, the dead – with theatrical expertise. In other parts of the fort there is more Mao-Zedong-Boom-Boom!, and then some Nepali-Boom-Boom! (1793 – Gurkha invasion of Tibet), and by the time we get to the top of the fort, there is British-Boom-Boom!

'*Injilang-Boom-Boom!*' our guide says, throwing up his arms in despair, and pointing at a pile of rubble with a consistency of soggy breakfast cereal. A shell from the 1904 British invasion of Tibet must've landed right there. He shows us fragments of British-made 17 mm shells that had been found in the fort.

Ironically, although the Chinese ran amok in the chapel-section, they left the bulk of the fort alone. The Chinese, so the rumour went, wanted Gyantse Fort left as a monument to the brave resistance of the Tibetan people to the British imperialists. Since Tibet was unquestionably a part of the 'motherland', the thought probably never occurred to the Chinese that they might be guilty of the same thing.

We've now reached the very top look-out turret, with a 360-degree view of Gyantse. In 1954 the town was near-destroyed by flooding. In 1959, local industries were virtually dismantled as artisans and weavers fled for India, or were imprisoned. What remained in the way of buildings – particularly the monastery – was not so lucky as to escape the madness of the Cultural Revolution of the 1960s and 70s. Every two minutes, the guide points at some distant building or object, flaps his arms, and shouts, 'Mao-Zedong-Boom-Boom!' We can clearly see the *Kumbum* from the turret where we are standing. For the first time, the guide gives the thumbs-up gesture – something has been salvaged in this necropolis. I offer the guide a Dalai Lama picture – it is received with a smile, a thumbs-up gesture, and a short prayer. How on earth has this man managed to get a position of tourist-guide here? So critical of the Chinese!

In the dingy teahouse of the Tibetan guesthouse I bump into two Germans and a Dutch woman who are cycling in the opposite direction. Whoosh! They have a tailwind, the lucky bastards. The Dutch woman has a litany of horror-stories to tell – getting caught out on freezing passes without sufficient cold-weather gear; getting sick from the altitude on the push up from Nepal; being refused a place to stay by road-maintenance crews. Close to Gyantse, the two German gentlemen overtook her, and joined her for the ride in. The Germans make cycling in Tibet sound like a picnic in Bavaria. One of them has come all the way from Europe – through Iran, Pakistan, India, Nepal. After this, he says, matter-of-factly, it's off to Japan, then Alaska, all the way down the west coast of the Americas to Tierra del Fuego, zip across to Africa, and then a little jaunt back up Africa to Germany. Ho hum... He yawns loudly.

In the same teahouse, an hour later, I meet Chu-An, a teacher in Gyantse Middle School. Chu-An is one of those amazing specimens who has learnt his English from BBC broadcasts. Since Chu is Chinese, I am curious about the quality of the teaching. Is the Tibetan language being taught in Gyantse? From what I can gather, there are two kinds of schools instituted by the Chinese – one in Chinese medium, the other in Tibetan medium. Those going to the Chinese-medium schools are taught English as a second language; those going to the Tibetan-medium schools are taught Chinese as a second language. Either way, the students have the Chinese language forced on them. Naturally, the facilities and opportunities in the Chinese-medium schools are far superior – this is a subtle method of reducing the Tibetan language to a lowly status, since the student studying in the Tibetan-medium school will have no chance to do any further study after finishing school. During the Cultural Revolution, the study of Tibetan language was banned; it was reinstated in the late 1970s. Most Tibetans are illiterate; only about one Tibetan in five finishes primary school.

Chu manages to field my questions – or dodge them. He is more interested in practicing his English. I can't seem to get him to make any sense on education, so we switch to the subject of family. The usual openers: age and marriage. He is 30, and single.

'In August I will have the marriage,' he confides.

'Where will the wedding take place?'

'What is this 'wedding'?'

'I mean the marriage – where will you marry?'

'Oh, in Shigatse.'

'Your fiancée lives in Shigatse?'

'I live in Gyantse.'

'No, I meant your fiancée.'

'Gyantse? I will stay in Gyantse.'

'But does she live in Shigatse?'

'Who?'

'Your fiancée.'

'Can you explain please?'

'A fiancée is a woman who is going to get married.'

'Ah! So he is my fiancée?'

'No – *she* is your fiancée.'

'Oh I see – yes, my fiancée is in Shigatse, but we will not live in Shigatse. I will live in Gyantse. If I am going to be married, what is the English for the man?'

'Fiancé.'

'But you said *she* was the fiancée.'

'There's only a difference in the spelling – one 'e' different.' I write it down for him, and tell him it comes from French originally. You, the fiancé, I tell him, are in Gyantse, and she, the fiancée, is in Shigatse. We are locked into a linguistic nightmare. I should never have brought up the word 'fiancée'. His sisters, father, mother and fiancée all live in Shigatse. He goes there twice a year to visit.

'Why don't you move to Shigatse?'

'My job is here in Gyantse.'

'Can't you ask for a job in Shigatse?'

'It is not allowed just yet. I must go where the Party wants me to go.'

'And what does your fiancée do?'

'He's a teacher in Shigatse.'

'No, no – you teach in Gyantse – what does *she* do?'

'Ah! The fiancée!'

'Yes, the woman in your life. What is her job?'

'She is a teacher. She teaches middle school in Shigatse.'

'So you are both teachers?'

'Yes, one in Gyantse, the other in Shigatse.'

'And when you marry – how will you see your fiancée?'

'I will have the holidays, and she will have the holidays, maybe two times in a year. Then we will have the visit.'

We now have this conundrum under control. A limerick is taking shape:

> *There was a young man from Gyantse,*
> *Who had a hot fiancée in Shigatse . . .*

April 20th. A fresh snowfall has blanketed Gyantse as we depart a few days later, nuts and bolts all tightened. The fort looms out of the mist like a huge iceberg – a frozen dream-castle. The sun is quick to melt off snowfalls, and soon we're back in the high-altitude desert – the silence, the vastness, the clear blue skies – and I

204

would not have traded saddles with anybody – not for all the tea in the PRC. Any hardships of travel are dwarfed by the incredible sense of escape.

There is very little out here – just us, the odd village, and the telegraph wires. The telegraph wires have been with us most of the route from Lhasa – they are the plateau's lazy concession to the twentieth century. When the British invaded Tibet in 1903, the Tibetans questioned them as to what the telegraph line was. British engineers said it was a device to enable them to find their way back to India when they withdrew, as they had no decent maps.

Traffic is light – the odd truck, an army convoy that sprays dust and diesel fumes, a couple of Tibetan horsemen, a few donkeys, some workers grading the road, some farmers in jingling horse-carts. Otherwise the place looks empty – until, near a village, we make a rest-stop. Suddenly a crowd of biblical proportions materialises – old men, women, goat-herders, sheep, yaks, obnoxious urchins begging for ball-point pens – and all of them intent on an in-depth examination of our persons and our gear. The Tibetans are a very tactile people – in temples and at holy sites they touch all the sacred images, stroke them, rub against them – to accrue merit. Here they pinch and poke at the bikes – test the tyres, feel the gears, marvel at how smooth the saddle is. Then they try and find the engine – refusing to believe that the vehicles can be anything less than motorcycles. The strange mechanism of the derailleur and gear-shifters adds weight to this theory; they are quite convinced that the water-bottles mounted on the frame actually contain gasoline to power the bike. When they're through with all that, they tug at the hair on our faces, or our arms.

The most unlikely of characters shadows us during the afternoon – a Tibetan dressed in a black jacket with gold trim. He has a natty blue cap, and is wearing brand-new Tibetan boots – with bold red, green and black colours. And he is riding a shiny black Chinese bicycle. He overtakes us at a rest-stop, and we pedal after him, if only to demonstrate the superiority of a high-tech 18-speed mountain-bike over a gearless Chinese tank. However, the terrain is dead flat, and the Tibetan phantom keeps pace with us, grinning. No amount of vibration or dust from the road upsets him – he bounds along effortlessly. His legs are more used to the altitude than ours, we reason – this must account for the difference.

After an all-day ride, Tashilhunpo Monastery comes into view. The phantom rider tips his hat, and bounces off into the hills.

*   *   *

SHIGATSE. Paved roads! Fresh mandarin oranges! Boiled eggs! Dried fruit! We help ourselves to all of these, and aim for the hotel to get the bikes out of sight as quickly as possible.

Actually, at the last moment I veer off and head to a new hotel at the market-end of town; the other two riders go to the Tibetan hotel opposite the monastery. Making a sudden appearance here is the mystery third rider, who has thus far been edited out of the story. An irrevocable explosion of tempers has occurred in Gyantse, and I am now determined to go my own way. This split is a very difficult decision: none of us want to interfere with the chances of the others to complete the journey – but for me it won't be at the price of losing my peace of mind any more. I can no longer accept the fact that we're staying together for the sake of the tent, or the stove, or spare parts. So I have retrieved the parts of the tent, which belongs to me; the third rider has the stove. Scott is caught in the crossfire. Since he is on neutral ground, he is in a position of choosing whom he'll ride with – or, if need be, he can ride on alone – he has a bivouac sack as an emergency shelter.

It is a great relief to get myself separated from the other two. It is a big weight off my mind – I've made the right decision.

The hotel near the markets is full; after some insistence, I am shown into the hotel proprietor's room. It has carpeted areas, and ornate chests of drawers, which also serve as table-tops. There is a calendar featuring Tibetan religious deities, a big chiming clock, a row of tea thermoses, and a small altar in a side-room. I am shown a couch – obviously I will be sleeping in the family quarters till a vacancy comes up in the dormitory next door.

Having disposed of bike and bags, I wander out in search of a noodle shop. I recall having eaten some good noodles in the markets on the last visit to Shigatse. The markets have packed up; there is little sign of activity. I stumble into a tent with a circle of people round a blazing crock of food. The cook is making *momos* – Tibetan dumplings with meat in them. I am invited to join the circle; I examine the fuel supply – it is dried yak-dung. The man next to me is feeding the dung into the crock. I am thinking about the stove – if there are stoves like this along the way, then no need for me to worry about one. All I have to do is supply my own cooking vessel and water – I can crash other people's fires. Strange how my behaviour changes when left to my own devices: alone, I am thrust into situations like this – quickly. My hosts are getting me drunk on *chang*, stuffing me with *momos*, and refusing to accept money for any of this. They do, however, require that I sing – doesn't matter what it is, *sing*!

There is a strange energy coming out of Shigatse. The town is dead, in the sense of being a Tibetan town. Only at Tashilhunpo Monastery can a Tibetan presence be felt. The rest of the place is a remarkably ugly collection of concrete blocks and corrugated tin roofing – Chinese-style. It is a drab Chinese administrative and military centre; with a population of 40,000, Shigatse is second only to Lhasa for size.

Tashilhunpo Monastery, founded in the 15th century, is a vast sea of buildings enclosed by high walls. The sheer scale of the place makes the visitor reel backwards in awe. The monastery was one of a handful to escape serious damage under the Chinese. Although the monks were disbanded and abused, the buildings were largely untouched, as Shigatse is the base of the Panchen Lama, the second highest incarnation in Tibetan Buddhism. The Chinese were hoping to promote the Panchen Lama as an alternative to the Dalai Lama. The Panchen Lama, three years younger than the Dalai Lama, fell into Communist hands in 1949, and was brought to Shigatse by the PLA in 1952. With the flight of the Dalai Lama in 1959, the Panchen Lama was groomed as a replacement; in 1960, however, with the seizure of thousands of monks at Tashilhunpo Monastery, the Panchen openly supported the Dalai Lama. In 1964, when asked to denounce the Dalai Lama at a prayer-festival in Lhasa, the Panchen Lama instead praised him. For this aberration he was arrested. He disappeared, and was presumed dead – but miraculously surfaced 14 years later in Peking.

What does a Communist Government do with a province whose major tourist attraction lies in its monasteries and monks? It sets up the Chinese Religious Bureau, of course, to oversee things. Such is the case at Tashilhunpo Monastery: the monks are on Peking's payroll; funds for restoration of the place are approved by the Bureau; initiates are screened by the Bureau. Propagation of religious beliefs is forbidden by Peking – so while on the surface there appears to be religious freedom, in fact this is a form of 'showcase Buddhism' – designed to impress tourists.

In the 1950s, Tashilhunpo Monastery had a population of 4000 monks. Although there are only 700 monks at the monastery now, the place bristles with activity, and the dim interiors – lit by yak-butter lamps – are crowded with pilgrims. The smell of rancid yak-butter permeates everything; there is a film of yak-butter over all the wooden surfaces inside the halls. At the rear of Tashilhunpo Monastery, in the Hall of the Maitreya, there is a framed picture of the Panchen Lama. This picture is the largest of the hundreds found throughout the monastery – perhaps because it sits at the base of the most-revered statue. This is *Champa* – the gold-plated Buddha of the Future – towering three storeys high. Down below, everything is worn smooth from the touch of countless pilgrims – the railings, the stairs, the flagstones, the bronze of the lotus-pedestal. In Tibetan legend, when all human beings have earned deliverance from suffering, *Champa* will return to preside over them. Dozens of pilgrims are muttering mantras; others throw themselves to the ground before the Buddha; others leave gifts of yak-butter, money, bracelets, or *tsampa*; a few pilgrims hurl ceremonial scarves high up toward the Buddha, hoping that they will land in an auspicious place.

Outside, near the gates of the Tashilhunpo, there are pilgrims camped in tents. I wander into one of these – at the request of the Tibetan within. He is dressed in faded orange robes, and a dirty woollen hat. His worldly possessions are scattered around him – thermos flask, cooking pots – and he shows me his prize religious pictures, framed under glass. These include half a dozen photos of the Dalai Lama and the Panchen Lama, a photo of the holy mountain of Kailas, and a photo of the main Buddhist image in the Jokhang Temple. I give him a picture of the Potala to add to the collection.

Scott has made his decision. We will ride together. The third rider is going on ahead, taking the stove and the cooking vessels. I agonise over a solution to this loss. Two panniers full of freeze-dried food is no joke. The packets are examined: most of them only need the addition of hot water to be edible. Those that require long cooking-times are discarded; the fuel-bottles are discarded. We will have to load up on dried fruit, peanuts, and raisins in Shigatse. I find a medium-sized teapot – 555 brand – to heat up water in. We will simply have to use the heating devices of the locals along the route. There are stoves for sale in Shigatse – but they are the size of samovars, and twice as heavy.

While I am scouting around the markets for supplies, I pass a tent that looks familiar. But why? It is stacked to the roof with cylindrical metal containers that are used for carrying water or milk. They are brand-new – stainless steel. I recognise the faces of the vendors – mum, dad, grandma, the kids – the lot that took me in on my first night in Shigatse, and fed me dumplings. What a raving lunatic they must have taken me for! Me, in all innocence thinking it was an after-hours dumpling-shop.

A new arrival in the family overflow room at the hotel: Jean-Paul, the Frenchman. Jean-Paul has a strange air of contentment about him – a smile even though he is alone and not speaking his native language. A small, nervous smile, to be sure, but still a smile. This leads me to believe he is probably a chartered accountant who has snapped. After 30 years on the job, he suddenly gets up one day from his desk, stalks out the door and arranges a ticket on the Trans-Siberian – absconding with the boss's funds, and leaving a nagging wife and kids. It is that kind of smile – he is free.

When I get back to the hotel in the afternoon, Jean-Paul is delirious. He has accomplished something absolutely unprecedented in the ranks of explorers. He has found toilet-paper in Shigatse! It's flat sheets of paper, but toilet-paper nonetheless. The quest – the expedition – took several hours to accomplish. Armed only with a Chinese phrasebook and a good sense of humour, Jean-Paul has succeeded where hundreds of others have failed.

The manager of the hotel interrupts this air of euphoria with a sobering note, written in English:

If you do not have a travel permit you must go to local
public security organ and supply the missing formalities.
Xigaze is not open. If you tour in Xigaze without travel
permit you will act contrary to Chinese laws and regulating
about travel in China.

He wants to see my passport and travel permit. To hell with that. All in good time, I inform him, trying to remain calm. Why me? Why did I get this note? Why not the others staying at the hotel?

Whatever is going on, departure-time has just been speeded up. Tomorrow, I promise the manager, I will report to Public Security. Tomorrow, I promise myself, I will have to leave town...

Jean-Paul, I discover, is a civil servant in France – and is taking a year's leave of absence. He says he'll travel for four months, a spring trip; go back to France in the summer; then head out for another four months in the autumn – probably Mexico and Central America.

I probe for some background.

'I work for ze – how do you call it? – ze Department of Water – it is like a Public Healt section. I make all ze important decisions on ze water in zis town. If I decide zey get water, zey get water. If not, zey don't. It is simple.'

'And why did you take the year off?'

'Zere is too much stress. Everybody he wants water. Zey always ask me for more water. Zere is not enough water for everyone. Zey are all shouting for more water. Finally I am fed up to here – ' Jean-Paul says, drawing a line across his throat with his hand, 'and I must leave ze town for a long time before I go crazy wit ze water.'

The top half of Jean-Paul's pack is all books. It is refreshing to see a 'foreign' set of tourist paraphernalia, guidewise. He carries a prospectus from a travel agency for ideas. NOUVEAU! says the brochure. AU TIBET SUR LES TRACES D'ALEXANDRA DAVID NEEL (21 jours Paris/Peking/ Qinghai/ Tibet/ Nepal/ Delhi/ Paris). There is Nagel's voluminous out-dated guide to China – in French and over 1500 pages – plus a Chinese railway timetable, and a large Chinese-French dictionary. All of these add up to a ton. Wait – there is one thin volume. It is Michel Butor's *La Modification*, written 1970. In 300 pages it tells of one day on a train from Paris to Rome, in which the main character is not I or he, or she, but YOU.

It is 3.30 a.m. This is the wrong end of town – the markets. You awake to a chorus of yapping and barking. Bloody dogs! They hang about at the yak-meat end of the markets. The principal dog does not cease for a full hour, inciting all the others. If only you could lob a bunch of fireworks over there. That would take care of them. Unfortunately, Jean-Paul is soundly snoring next to the windows, and what would happen if the fireworks slipped and landed on his bed? You can't take that risk – he'd have a heart attack.

At 4.30 there's a stirring and a torch at the other end of the room. It's the man from Switzerland, who has awakened to an alarm, and is making a heroic attempt to catch the 5 a.m. bus to Lhasa. You can hear the patter of his footsteps.

Now there seems little chance of your drifting back to sleep. You take stock of your physical condition. Your throat feels like the Sahara after a sandstorm – where is that mug of water you put at the bedside? You pass your tongue over your cracked lips. Lips, tips of fingers, tip of tongue, and tip of nose – all have suffered numbness and damage. Your hands look like they've been washed in acid – severely chapped, nails worn right down, fingers like dry blades of grass. Legs are fine – and so is your stomach. It is important that not all the parts fail at once.

The dogs have started up again. It's five to six. You fumble for clothing – for a match to light the candle. Throwing on the main light wouldn't be polite to the others. Your bladder is bursting. But it's a long way down the ladder to the courtyard, so you check over your gear and oil the bike. You hope you don't leave anything important behind.

It's almost time to wake up the Frenchman. That leaves one other person – the Dutchman – and then you can turn on the lights – which is what you've been waiting for. Still pitch-black outside. You're wondering what the weather's like. Cold? Windy? You step out and go downstairs to the toilet. Weather's not too bad – mild, not too cold.

The dogs have all stopped barking – they do that when everyone wakes up. Uncanny. Damn! The lightswitch doesn't work! Manager must've cut the generator-supply. This will slow everything down. You fumble for a torch. Hard to keep track of all the items in the dark. You move all the bags to the balcony, and try and load them with frozen fingers. You absently check the tyre-pressure with your thumb. The next move is to go downstairs and load.

The bike is ready; there is one final obstacle – the main door. Probably the manager has locked it, and you'll have to wake him up. But no, it's open. It is obstructed by yak-hide sellers, who've slept overnight on top of their wares, waiting for the markets to open. They're squeezed into the door-frame, covered in yak-skins. You manage to get past them.

You're on your way! You ride along the paved street, then turn on a dirt road, past the Public Security Bureau, skirt round a putrid dead dog lying in the road. Closer to the monastery, there are packs of dogs being fed outside by pilgrims. If they turn on you, it will be disastrous. You slow down, keeping a careful eye on the dogs. They do not display too much interest. A truck is visible in the courtyard of the Tibetan hotel at the edge of town. The driver and his assistant are heating up the engine and the radiator with a blow-torch. No anti-freeze in these parts; they have to sleep out on the back of the truck in their sheepskin coats. Now you don't feel so cold. You're on your way . . .

★   ★   ★

ON THE ROAD TO LHATSE, April 23rd; thirty miles from Shigatse; a nap by the roadside. There is a soft tinkle of bells. I open my eyes. A bearded horseman is crouched close by, examining the bikes. *'Inji! Inji!'* he says with a grin. This means 'foreigner' or 'English' – in our case, both. He looks at us with piercing, steely eyes. I offer him some biscuits and cigarettes, and he pours me a cup of *chang*. I down the cup; it is instantly refilled. Neither he nor his horse are going to budge till we drain his *chang*-container. Not satisfied with our progress on the *chang*, he also tries to force Indian snuff upon us. This is a dangerous piece of hospitality, as it has only been three months since I gave up smoking, and the drug still beckons. I watch the horseman put a piece of snuff on his fingernail and snort it up like a line of cocaine.

An indeterminate amount of time later, we stagger off. The horseman is headed toward Shigatse; we are headed toward Lhatse. *'Inji! Inji!'* the horseman shouts. Double bonus – he's not only met his first foreigners, but his first two drunken foreigners.

It is a great day for hospitality – getting hauled off the highway for tea or beer every few miles. *'Tashi Delay!'* is the greeting we frequently get, and the one we shout back. There is one old man who investigates us at a roadside stop. He has a wispy white beard, and a black jacket with silver trim. The old man is looking into my camera-lens. Right into it. It is like flying over Saudi Arabia – I can see every ridge, wrinkle and cracked surface on his face, but I cannot focus on his eyes. I've never had such a willing subject – he is now zeroing in so close that I have to back off, for fear that his oily nose will make contact with the lens and ruin it. But it perplexes me why I can't focus on his eyes – is he moving them too fast from left to right? It's only when I realise I can focus on the left eye but not the right that I get the answer: the man's eyes are slightly inflamed. He is as blind as a bat, which explains why he has to get within an inch of the camera to see what it is.

We have gained about 45 miles from Shigatse when Scott gets very sick. He has stomach troubles. We pull into a road-mainten-ance station to fire up the teapot. Watched by curious dogs and chickens, I get a kerosene stove and start to boil some soup. Scott takes a few mouthfuls, then throws the stuff up. I am wondering if there's a spare bed for him at the road-station tonight, but then more of the crew arrive back – no extra beds. The road-grader rolls in, with horse and cart and a device that planes the road flat. We move off, select a campsite down the road, and pitch the tent. Scott doesn't sleep much during the night.

The next day we bounce over washboard gravel – through a village with unlimited supplies of goats, sheep, yaks and donkeys. These animals clog the highway. The selection of goat horns is quite astounding – every shape and size imaginable. By lunchtime we've only notched up 10 *gongli,* due to a late start, and Scott is too weak to move. It is still 70 *gongli* to Lhatse.

'How are you feeling?'
'My stomach's in an uproar,' moans Scott.
'Can you walk on it?'
'No way.'

He lies down by the roadside. A walking-tractor chugs past, with a Tibetan in a spiffy trench-coat at the wheel. He is planing the road to a smooth finish. Classy road-maintenance crews out here – look like French spies.

'Quick! The fireworks!' yells Scott. The mastiff is getting closer, barking and baring its fangs. Of the half-dozen dogs we've had problems with so far, this one definitely looks the meanest. Trouble is, with the headwinds, I can't light the damn fireworks. Just a minute – there's a spark! A sharp BOOM! echoes across the valley. The explosion has a magic effect – the dog turns tail and shoots up the nearest mountain-side. Bull's-eye. The next half-hour is spent patiently explaining to five burly Tibetans – a road crew – how it was that we indeed didn't shoot their dog, and that those were harmless fireworks purchased in Lhasa (for the purpose of scaring off dogs). To soothe relations, we offer them a Dalai Lama picture. One of the Tibetans takes the picture to his forehead and bows reverently.

Scott is in no condition to cycle. He will have to hitch-hike a ride into Lhatse. The road crew can explain to a passing driver that he is sick.

'You can meet me in Lhatse,' he insists. 'I've got the whole after-noon to get a ride. I'll be okay. Go on ahead.'

'And if you don't get a ride?'

'Then I'll stay with the road crew. They've got a walking-tractor, anyway. And I'll still meet you in Lhatse tomorrow.'

'How do you feel?'

'It's my stomach, not my head, so don't worry about me. I can take care of myself.'

I look at my watch. Two o'clock. Six hours of daylight left – enough time for me to cycle into Lhatse – and lots of time for Scott to get a ride from a passing truck. I wish Scott luck, and cruise off . . .

By 4 p.m. a combination of hills, headwinds and sandy road sec-tions has set me back. It has taken me two hours to cover a paltry six miles. My hopes of getting to Lhatse by nightfall are fading. I round a corner and find a road crew at work. The whole crew downs shovels, and I run the gauntlet of their stares. They must be working from the Lhatse direction – the road is much firmer now, and I manage to chalk up a faster pace. By 5 p.m. I'm still 30 miles short of Lhatse. All I can hope to do now is shave miles off the task ahead tomorrow. Still no sign of Scott – hope to God he's okay. At 5.30 p.m. I gain k-stone 350. I have three more water-bottles in reserve – plus, for instant energy, dried quinces and pears from Shigatse. The wind is starting to cut now – have to put more cloth-ing on – vest, woollen tuque, silk glove-liners, wool gloves.

At 6.30 p.m. Scott comes past in an army truck. The going has been slow, he explains, due to frequent breakdowns. He's not feeling too bad. The army truck is going to Lhatse. The driver offers me a ride too, but I am close to Lhatse now – I want to cycle the stretch. I wave the truck goodbye. Fifteen minutes later, I catch up again – the truck has broken down. The engine splutters to life once more – and Scott and the truck disappear into the distance.

I am alone now – no back-ups at all. It is a strange feeling to be out here by myself. By 8.30 p.m., with light failing, I pass k-stone 360, which leaves 40 *gongli* to Lhatse. I am at the base of Tso La pass. I stop and listen to a truck. It groans up the pass for a good three or four minutes, and then I see it on a ridge high above. The truck appears to go down after this, but there are no prayer-flags in sight.

Just after k-stone 360, the road curves in a U-bend. Is it possible that the headwind I've been battling for the last two hours could turn into a tailwind? The opportunity for getting my revenge on the headwinds is too tempting – even though it has gotten dark, I mount the bike and push on up. A tailwind! I carry on for another hour by the light of a full moon. At 10 p.m. I pick a spot to camp out, using the tent as a bivvy-sack.

At 4 a.m. I wake up with a slight headache. It could turn into a pounding one and stop me moving altogether. I decide to pack up and clear the top of the pass. The moon is out, and I can pick the firmer part of the road by its whiteness. There is no wind now. In five minutes I pass the prayer-flags. I have camped several hundred yards away from them. There is a Chinese concrete marker showing the elevation – 4500 metres. I'm frozen now – have to keep moving. I put one leg down over the road, shift my weight to the crossbar, and cautiously head off down the other side of the pass. At 4.30 a.m. the moon goes behind clouds. It is too dangerous to continue the descent. I pull off to the side of the road and pull out my sleeping-bag again.

At 6.30 a.m. I get up again and wheel the bike down in the darkness. By 7 a.m. I can finally see what I'm doing – and discover that there are nasty thornbushes everywhere. I pray that the tyres are still intact. 7.30: pink clouds. 7.50: finally come into the sun. The road is full of gravel, but I'm closing in on Lhatse.

Six miles short of Lhatse, I sighted Scott. He was sitting in the yard of an army compound to the side of the road. The same officers who'd given him a ride were there, plus a group of others trying out their English. Scott was still in no condition to ride around – we would have to stay at the army base for a few days. Rest and Recreation. The army base had the best supply of hot water in the area – via solar dishes. If Scott was to make a recovery, he'd need good clean water: our own water filter was clogged to the point where it became a major effort to squeeze out a pint of water.

One of the soldiers of 62 Unit drove us crazy with his persistence in practicing English. He tried to read stories to us, got us to correct exercises, made abysmal attempts at idioms, and generally experimented as much as he could. When would another English speaker pass his way? The soldier, Chi, had learnt his English from books. In the process of Chi's pursuit of English, we learnt a lot about life on the base. Chi had been conscripted at 17, and had served two years of his three-year stint in the army. Two years in the middle of the desert in Lhatse. He got a piddling salary of 37 yuan a month, plus room and board, and all the boredom he wanted.

'In the morning we train,' he told us. 'In the afternoon we have politics study, and study of the newspapers; in the evening we are free.' Free obviously meant 'bored'.

'Do you go to Lhatse – to the cinema?' I asked. Incongruously, there was a huge cinema, which had cost billions of yuan to build, right in the middle of Lhatse.

'I have seen all the movies,' said Chi, without interest, 'and Lhatse is a bad place.'

Chi was from the centre of China, from Luoyang in Henan Province. He wanted to study medicine. He was confident he would marry in Luoyang when he was 25.

We needed Chi's help to get hot water, as this week it was his task to supervise the kettles on the solar dishes. These large concave dishes could heat up a huge 555 kettle in 25 minutes, due to the intensity of the sun being reflected at this altitude. 'But you can only do it in the morning,' said Chi. 'In the afternoon, there are clouds.' Small hand-levers enabled the solar dish to be re-angled for the path of the sun as the day wore on. We got Chi to swap kettles, substituting our minuscule 555 on the burner. This was the most successful operation to date – the solar cooker brought the water to a boil from a cold start in less than five minutes. We filled up all our plastic water-bottles, and I had a stab at cooking a packet of scrambled eggs, of which we had a surplus, due to the fact they took a long time to cook.

Chi re-settled the small 555 on the cooker, and I snapped a photograph. Just as I'd done that, I realised the photo could be misconstrued – I'd taken a picture on an army base. Chi looked up and waved at me not to take pictures. It was too late – his superior had seen me, and was entering into a nasty-looking discussion with Chi. I protested I was just taking a picture of my teapot; the army base was a mere backdrop. It was a picture of hot water, I said. Hot water all right – the officer eventually let the subject drop, but it was only due to Chi's intervention on my behalf that the film wasn't taken off me.

To keep the troops amused, and improve public relations, I had dug a frisbee out of my pack. This had dire consequences. The officers had started a round of frisbee near the highway; a crowd of Tibetans – kids, older people – gathered to watch. And then, unbelievably, the soldiers started to stone the on-lookers. I raced over and took the frisbee back; both Scott and myself were furious. We confronted Chi – why did they stone the Tibetans?

'Because they are stupid,' said Chi. 'They don't go to school, and they can't talk Chinese. Never mind.'

'I can't talk Chinese,' interjected Scott. 'Does that mean I'm stupid?'

We hounded Chi for a while, but he shrugged any argument off. For him, and for the other soldiers, the Tibetans were barbarians. Before the Chinese came, they were stupid slaves; now they were 'free', but still stupid.

April 27th – Today we set off for Shegar, past donkeys laden with ceramic pots and firewood, donkey-carts, mist, mountains, and the town of Lhatse. After two days at the army base, Scott's sickness vanished as mysteriously as it arrived. Lhatse is small – a cluster of low buildings on either side of the highway; the town is, however, important enough to have its own traffic-sign. This is a slow-down marker at the outskirts – a marker which the truck-drivers unanimously ignore as they barrel through town at full throttle, spraying innocent by-standers with streams of dust.

K-stone 401 – leaving the town of Lhatse. Despite the strong sun, it is still freezing cold. I have three sets of gloves on, and my hands are still frozen. Two sets of hats – woollen to keep warm, and a cap with a visor to guard against sun-glare. I stand – arrayed in this armour – like a weird warrior ready for another day's battle with the headwinds. In another hour or so, when the day warms up, I should be able to remove some layers of clothing.

K-stone 407 – the turn-off to western Tibet. From here the road divides – to the left toward Kathmandu, and to the right toward the high deserts of Ngari, and the holy peak of Mount Kailas.

K-stone 412 – the climb up Gyatso La pass begins.

K-stone 416 – pull in to a road-maintenance station to fire up some lunch – freeze-dried vegetable pilaf and potatoes.

K-stone 418 – pass some nomads camped out in what appears to be ruins, but on closer inspection, is a bunch of rocks constructed as a wind-break. What an existence – out here in the middle of the desert, with only the howling winds for company. I am thinking about all the things they never have to worry about – dinner parties, car-loans, overdue library books – and then about all the things they have to worry about, like where to get food.

'Wonder what they do for a living,' I say, thinking out loud.

'Computer software,' replies Scott. A kid comes running toward us from the rock-pile. We have been discovered.

K-stone 422 – we are exhausted – caught in a howling gale. The headwinds have defeated us once again, and a bitter cold has sprung up. Now well short of the top of the pass. We'll have to tackle the crest in the morning. We choose an awkward campsite – just off the road, and not fully sheltered – but there is nothing better in the area, and it is almost dark. We struggle to set up the tent, rushing to get all the gear inside before a gust of wind picks up the whole dome and transfers it to Nepal. We climb into the tent like bears preparing to enter a cave for the winter – and probably smelling similar. The winds cannot get us in here – no more sandblasting on the face. There are, however, other overpowering 'winds' *within* the tent. Freeze-dried food, apart from causing dehydration, leads to internal 'combustion' – both of us, I am convinced, have been propelled across the plateau purely on the horsefarts that result from these packages. Wind, wind, and more wind . . .

The wind and dryness have taken their toll – cracks, chips and flakes on the hands, and on the nose, that great barometer of foul weather conditions. The mouth, with its moistening saliva, has escaped damage – but not the throat or the lips. I inflate my sleeping-pad, crawl into the warm cocoon of my sleeping-bag, and dream about being slowly roasted on the beaches of Thailand.

In the morning, the rivulet next to the tent is frozen solid. We've finished all the peanuts, and the wind is still howling. Damn that wind! There is no respite from it. Start off up the pass again, this time actually pushing the bike for short distances to get circulation going in hands and feet. Up here, even the sun doesn't help in warming up. The pass has levelled off somewhat – very gradual uphill now.

K-stone 426 – habitation. A stone dwelling with a wisp of smoke curling up from the roof. Most likely a road crew. Where was the last road-station? K-stone 416. It's uncanny – they're spaced exactly 10 kilometres apart. We are thinking about a teapot invasion, so we can fire up some breakfast – but three large dogs come out, and we rapidly change our minds. There is no time to get out fireworks, or even think – the dogs are right there. I jump off my bike, and place it between me and the dogs. They're going to get some tyre-rubber before they get me. Scott, who is further ahead, decides that he can outdistance them. He shifts himself into top gear and goes flat out for a small rise ahead. One of the dogs runs after him, snapping awfully close to his heels. Scott goes faster; the dog goes faster; they're both racing up the hill. Where does Scott get the energy? He must be off his rocker if he thinks he's faster than the dog. 'Go, Scott, Go!' I yell. He is pedalling like a madman. His legs are a blur... Unbelievably, the dog abandons the chase.

That leaves me. There is a face-off. I am fumbling with the fireworks, cursing the wind. I can't light them. Meanwhile, I have a bicycle pump at the ready, to stall a first-round attack. Holy smokes! One of the fireworks is lit – it almost blows up in my hand. The nearest dog is blasted off the road, and all three of them go whimpering back to the stone dwelling with the wisp of smoke coming from the chimney.

K-stone 432 – the winds are ferocious. Now we seem to be on a tableland of some sort – almost flat. Without warning, we run into prayer-flags. This is it – the top of Gyatso La. It is actually flat ground – a slight rise festooned with prayer-flags. We're so happy to see the prayer-flags that we fling ourselves face-down in front of them, and kiss the ground. A concrete marker gives the elevation – 5220 metres. 5220 metres! That's around 17,200 feet – the highest piece of road I can think of. We are cycling at an elevation three and a quarter miles above sea-level – higher than Mont Blanc, or the Matterhorn. But this pass is only a pimple in the Himalayas – in the distance, rugged snowpeaks loom up – much, much higher than Mont Blanc.

For the next ten miles, it is a gradual descent – the tableland lasts quite a distance. We stop at a cosy-looking road-maintenance station. The courtyard is stacked with brushwood. Goatskins are drying in the sun; basketballs, cut in half, hang from the walls – these are used as feeder-bags for the horses. Yak-dung patties are plastered to the wall, drying out. There is a stove within, fuelled with yak-dung. Hot water is offered to us. We have food cooking up in no time.

'One strawberry or two?' I ask Scott.

'One thanks.'

In the absence of sugar, we have devised a system of sweetening the tea – using freeze-dried strawberries. These shrivelled items expand when dropped into piping hot tea, and though they taste a bit like cardboard, they are sweet enough. Perhaps they even do the same as sugar: my tongue has found, to my great alarm, a cavity where a filling should be. The filling has fallen out. Have I swallowed it? When did this happen? I mean, the road is bad, but . . . I explore the cavity further. It doesn't hurt, so maybe I'll survive.

On the menu today is chicken-flavour noodle casserole, diced carrots, potatoes and soup – a much-needed load of carbohydrates. *Drain well and serve with butter*, teases the packet of freeze-dried carrots. On a soup-packet, the instructions are even worse: *Add, if desired, a small knob of butter, and grated cheese.*

Our host, a pleasant Chinese gentleman with a couple of kids hanging off him, looks on stoically at these cooking rituals. The room we're in is plastered with Chinese posters of generals on horses, or political leaders – in China's case, there's not much difference. These are the standard decorations at road-maintenance stations, although some prefer wallpaper made of old newspapers. Either they're a very patriotic bunch, or the posters have been issued free of charge to every road-worker on this route. There are also badges – including a badge for the 20th 'Anniversary' of the Tibetan Autonomous Region; and there are framed awards of some kind. Not reading Chinese, I can only hazard a guess as to what kind of humble award might be bestowed in these remote parts: perhaps the most yak-dung collected in one shift? the heroic rescue of a bus-load of Tibetans trapped in snowdrifts near Gyatso La pass?

I tell Scott he deserves a special award for outrunning that dog earlier in the day. Scott thought he was far enough ahead to get away from it.

'You know,' says Scott, 'I've been thinking about that all afternoon. We're halfway across Tibet. There can't have been too many bicycles through here. And yet the dogs attack – they must have instincts about bicycles.'

'You mean, if we were to bring an American postman up here, they'd know exactly what to do with him?'

'Get serious. What about the yaks? I mean, they're ten times the size of the dogs, and they're afraid of bikes.'

'They're smelly, stupid draught animals – and besides, they're on drugs.'

Yaks, I contend, do not know that bicycle and man are two different things: all they can see is a mammoth centaur with silver horns hurtling toward them. Dogs on the other hand, will chase anything – not only can they see the man on the bike, but they can distinguish his meaty ankles.

Something catches my eye. It is one of the posters on the wall. Very odd. If I am not mistaken, that is Deng Xiaoping in the poster. What on earth is *he* doing in there? I recognise the poster. It shows the return of Zhou Enlai to Peking after a stint in Moscow, sometime in the 1950s. The photograph has been taken at the airport – he is just stepping off the plane, and is being greeted by Mao Zedong, Liu Shaoqi, and General Zhu De.

There are several versions of the poster. Liu Shaoqi fell out of favour with Mao: he was purged at the beginning of the Cultural Revolution, and died in 1967 – some say 1969. In any case, earlier versions of the poster airbrushed Liu Shaoqi right out of the picture. Posthumously, Liu Shaoqi was restored to favour – and hence was back in the picture. By this time, the viewer is not even sure it is a photograph – is the airplane real? Are the people real? Mao is a man whose stature is so great he was compared to an airplane – in an assassination attempt, he was apparently code-named *B*-52. And there, right in front of me, is *Xiao Pingzi*, or 'little bottle' – the nickname of Deng Xiaoping. He has earned this nickname from his uncanny ability to go under and then bob back to the top again – he has been denounced many times. Is this an updated version of the poster in the reign of Deng? Whatever the case, it is a collector's item.

Shegar, April 30th. This place jogs the memory. The year before, on the previous visit – which lasted a couple of hours – we'd spent all our time arguing about rooms. We had only seen the courtyard of the Chinese hotel. How could we have missed the ruins of a massive monastery and fort behind it? Shegar Dzong and Shining Crystal Monastery – destroyed in the Cultural Revolution – once housed 400 monks, and dominated the village below. Now a handful of monks are restoring some of the buildings at the base. The ruins attested to the daring penchant of Tibetan builders for constructing bastions on impossible mountain-tops, in complete defiance of the laws of gravity and logic. It is a major effort just to climb this peak – how could the original builders have even imagined lugging chunks of stone up there without mechanical aids? This dream-castle must have once looked like a fusion of rock, fort and monastery; now there is barely a single rampart standing upright . . .

Tingri West, by contrast, I recall well – not because of a monastery or ruin, but because of its spectacular backdrop – an unrestricted view of the mighty Himalayas. The most impressive peak seen here – Cho Oyu – is over 26,000 feet. This time, however, Tingri West is memorable not for its views, but for the fact that I finally manage to wash my hair. It has been several weeks since a shower in Lhasa, and my hair is matted with dust and sand to the point where I can't stand it anymore. I go to the local river with a washbasin, douse my hair with freezing cold water, run a towel through it, and race back for the hotel-room.

At Tingri West we make a second bid to find a bike-trail into the back of Everest. The first attempt, near Shegar, failed when it was found that the track – leading over a pass – was far too stony for a mountain-bike. The vibration was so bad that nuts and bolts had to be inspected hourly in case they went missing. At Tingri, it looks much easier – a wide open plain with the peaks of the Himalayas tantalisingly close. This proves to be an optical illusion – the closer we cycle, the further away the peaks become. We've set off early in the morning from Tingri, with enough gear for a couple of days.

An hour out of Tingri, headed for the peak of Cho Oyu, we strike mud and ice, then sand, lichen, loose rocks, hardpacked clay, more mud, loose gravel. Not even a horse-cart can make it through. We have to dismount. This is more like trekking than biking. A village appears – with yaks and cows roaming the streets, and a couple of mangy dogs feasting on a dead goat. The locals escort us over to a small temple, where we manage to cook up some food, an activity closely monitored by the entire populace of the village – their heads and limbs poking through every available window and doorway. The monks roar with laughter when I almost crack my skull exiting a low door.

Struggling across the plains again, we run into severe problems. Scott gets a flat tyre from a thorn; this is promptly fixed. Just as we are about to set off again, a group of Tibetan women, working on an irrigation ditch close by, confront us. They surround us, grab the handlebars of the bikes, and demand money if we want to continue further. Maybe extortion is easier than digging ditches. We pretend not to understand what they want, but some nasty skirmishes follow. We are forced to back off – retreating to a spot a mile back, where we set up tent.

The next day we decide to return to Tingri West, to the guesthouse where we've stashed our spare gear. The rest of the day is spent knocking all the mud off the gears, derailleurs, wheels and brakes in the courtyard of the guesthouse. I wire up my front rack as best I can – it is broken in several places. Two Nepalese traders wander over. They speak some English. They've walked in from Nepal – their yaks are sitting in the courtyard, or roaming around the town.

It is an extraordinary place, the Tibetan guesthouse. The central kitchen is filled with smoke – so much so that it makes your eyes water. Sides of various animals hang from the walls; an old lady with a huge goitre on her neck administers a cooking-crock that turns out *momos* – Tibetan meat dumplings. Half-drunk figures slurp down *chang*. The room adjacent to the kitchen is filled to the ceiling with brushwood. Where does it come from? We haven't seen a tree or a bush for hundreds of miles. Other fuels consist of assorted animal droppings. We join the Nepalese traders for some *chang* and *momos*.

'You know,' reflects Scott, 'my bank-account is never going to recover from this, but I have no regrets. This trip is the best I've been on.'

'The highest trip, you mean.'

ILLUSTRATIONS, TIBET, LEAF 9 – LEAF 16

Back Cover – author with Potala Palace in background, Lhasa.

9 *Top right* – hitting the Tibetan Plateau on the road up from Chengdu. *Mid left* – Fuzzball, the Boss, and driver at pit-stop en route to Lhasa. *Top left* – Landcruiser group on way to Everest, with Zoe in foreground under blanket. *Bottom* – ruins of Rongbuk Monastery, with the north face of Everest.

10 *Top left* – Khampa horseman, Chamdo area. *Top right* – view of new square in front of Jokhang, with Potala Palace in background. *Mid left* – Indian trader in the markets. *Bottom* – Tibetans in foxfur hats trading in Barkhor Bazaar, Lhasa.

11 *Top left* – prostrators and pilgrims outside Jokhang Temple. *Top right* – pilgrim outside his tent, Shigatse. *Mid right* – Khampa tribesman, Lhasa. *Bottom left* – woman in traditional dress, near Shigatse. *Bottom right* – Tibetan with Dalai Lama picture.

12 *Top left* – Scott with new-found friend, Jokhang rooftop. *Top right* – locals examining Scott's bike, near Shigatse. *Middle* – Scott on the crawl up Khamba La pass. *Bottom left* – tea-stop by the roadside, with Tibetan host mixing up *tsampa*. *Bottom right* – travel Tibetan-style – in freezing open back of a truck.

13 *Top right* – Scott with prayer-flags at crest of Khamba La. *Top left* – overview of Gyantse. *Bottom right* – Gyantse Dzong guide showing author shell-fragments from 1904 British attack. *Bottom left* – a road-grader planing the bumps out of his piece of turf. *Mid right* – in Shigatse, with Tashilhunpo Monastery in background.

14 *Top left* – feeling high – Scott at crest of Gyatso La pass. *Top right* – whoops! classified photo – army officer at Lhatse, firing up tea-water on solar cooker. *Middle* – fetching water at Tingri West, with a backdrop of Cho Oyu and the Himalayas. *Bottom left* – author setting up tent in white-out near Tong La. *Bottom right* – Scott toiling up the last section of Tong La pass.

15 *Top* – author at prayer-flags on crest of Tong La. *Mid left* – pushing off from Tong La on the descent to Nepal. *Mid right* – going down! *Bottom left* – a brush-gatherer near Nyalam. *Bottom right* – Suomeishi with yak herd.

16 *Top left* – find the bicycle-rider in this picture! – switchbacks winding down toward Zhangmu. *Top right* – at Chinese border-post. *Mid right* – cruising through Nepal. *Bottom* – journey's end, Durbar Square: for the locals, picture-taking is a serious business.

13

'No, the best. My friends are jealous that I got it together – but I'm glad I did.'

Scott launches into a soliloquy on bank-accounts and motivation. His life was scattered – long hours of work, breaking up with his girlfriend – too many dead-ends. Tibet provided a way out of the doldrums, a rallying point for renewed motivation. But a second trip to Tibet seemed impossible financially – he was still paying off the first trip. After a particularly tedious day at work, he snapped. He threw his job in, booked a plane-ticket, phoned everyone he could think of, and got the money together. And here he is – considerably in debt, totally irresponsible, but feeling just great.

May 4th. The back on this trip has been broken – we're on the home stretch now. There is one last pass – long and high – and then we head for Kathmandu. On leaving Tingri West, we follow the trusty telegraph wires: it is a gorgeous day – clear, cloudless, crisp. The barren mountains are showing off tones and textures that one might never have expected barren mountains to possess: dark green, orange, deep brown.

There is suddenly a lot more greenery injected into the landscape, and flocks of goats and sheep feeding on it; shepherds are living in makeshift shelters adapted from ruins. Projected onto the landscape, in the distance, is a snowcap with a sharp, jagged cone, standing up like a piece of cheese chopped on a block. It has a soft peak as a neighbour.

I am constantly distracted by this changing vista – stopping to admire it, or take photos. Scott, as usual, is further ahead – he likes to maintain a brisk pace. He gets annoyed when I dawdle, but I can see no particular reason for rushing through – the advantage of the bicycle, for me, is that it allows a slower pace. Apart from pacing, things are smooth enough, considering that this is the first time we've cycled together. I can think of lots of other types I don't get along with on the road: the silent sulker, Der Führer, the Tour de France sprinter, the ear-chewing gossip, Hamlet, Don Quixote, the window-rattling snorer, the early morning grump . . .

*　　*　　*

THE LAST PASS on the Tibetan side, Tong La, turns out to be a killer. It is a double pass; having camped near the base, our aim is get over both crests in one day. However, we haven't counted on the length of the first crest – ten miles – nor on a snowstorm near the top of it. A quick decision is made to ride down and camp in the depression between the crests. Snowflakes get stuck in my beard as I whizz along, trying to make good time on the downhill run. With vision obscured by snow-flurries, and face freezing up, it is a very eerie ride – I have to concentrate very hard to make sure I don't rocket right off the edge of the road in this white-out.

By the time we get down the 'dip', we are frozen, tired and hungry. We have to get some hot food into our systems. There's a road-maintenance station – we knock on the door. A man answers the door with a stern look on his face – no, he will not let us in to cook food. A little further back we'd seen a nomad-tent with smoke curling out of it; we rush back in the blizzard. Ignoring the usual formalities, we burst right into the tent and shove our teapot on the burner. *'Tashi Delay!'* I shout at the nomad. *'Cha!'* shouts Scott, pointing at the burner. The burner is fuelled by yak-dung, and sits in the middle of the tent, with the smoke going up through a hole above. The tent is filled with hessian bags – the filing-system of the humble nomad.

One very startled nomad gazes in wonder as we pour powders and potions into our mugs, and spit snowflakes all over the place. We consume three whole packets of freeze-dried food, and with hands and feet thawed out, we're ready to make a dash for it to set up tent. We bid the speechless nomad goodbye. *'Tuduchay!'* says Scott, putting his palms together, and touching them to his forehead. *'Kalipay!'* I add, waving my hand. As an afterthought, Scott adds a thumbs-up signal, with a *'Yagodu!'* as he backs out the flap of the tent, into the pelting snow. We have now exhausted our total command of the Tibetan language and our repertoire of hand-gestures. The man actually manages a smile. He is toothless. As I go to shake the snow off my bike outside the tent, something catches my eye. It is another eye. Wait – hundreds of eyes! In a stone-walled pen next to the nomad's tent are hundreds of silent, frozen sheep, all huddled together for warmth. They are huddled together so tightly that they form a landscape of their own. In our rush to get into the tent, we didn't even notice them. The status of our host is altered from nomad to shepherd – not so transient.

We hop on our bikes again, ready to tackle a slight rise in the road ahead. The toothless shepherd – still speechless – follows us into the blizzard. He stands there with his mouth wide open as we tackle a hill. It is rare enough to see a bicycle round these parts – but to see one going *up* a pass – that is a once-in-a-lifetime experience.

The two mastiffs were upon me so fast I didn't even have time to dismount – one ripped my left ankle to shreds, the other bloodied the right calf. Dazed, I kicked at them, scrambled to dismount, and reached for the bicycle pump. Crack! I scored a hit squarely on the skull of the dog in the lead. It whimpered, causing the other one, which had been barking wildly, to change its tone. Suddenly it turned around, baring its razor-sharp fangs – it leapt forward and . . .

It's a good thing I can only remember my dreams when sleep is interrupted, as it is this morning. What is it that wakes me up? Scott is shifting the bulk of the snow off the dome of the tent. That dog – I know where it comes from. It was the one chained up near the road-maintenance building we passed yesterday.

'Pretty heavy snowfall,' announces Scott, unzipping the front vestibule of the tent. *Heavy snowfall. Dog attack.* Where am I? What am I doing here? My sluggish brain is trying to piece these things together. A bicycle wheel comes into view, covered in snow. Now I remember.

After a breakfast of soup and potato-flakes, we set off early for the second crest. The climb is slow and tortuous, raked by winds, desolate. There is no end to it; it taxes the last ounces of strength and will-power – why is this horrendous obstacle thrown up when my energy is at its lowest ebb? I imagine myself to be operating a giant winch with my legs – pulling myself up the mountain step by step. And if the winch should snap? If I should stop pedalling?

A cyclist is coming down the pass toward me. Not Chinese. Not Tibetan. Must be a westerner. It is Brian, from New Zealand. He has a Swiss altimeter. It reads 4900 metres. Brian says he measured the top of the pass – it was almost 5200 metres, or 17,100 feet. We have 300 metres of elevation-gain to go. At least the end is in sight.

Brian has had an action-packed trip. He shared a taxi from

Kathmandu to the Tibetan border with two kayakers, who were off to try and run the length of the Brahmaputra River from its source near Mount Kailas. Strapped to the roof of the taxi were two plastic whitewater boats, weighing about 40 pounds each, and Brian's mountain-bike. The kayakers had made it through customs, and Brian had last seen them load the kayaks into a truck full of Tibetans headed westward. This place is crawling with crazy dreamers! Brian was bitten by a dog in Nyalam – not sure if it was rabid or not – he shows us the wound.

Atop the second crest of Tong La, we linger at the last set of prayer-flags, surrounded by snowpeaks in all directions. From this point on, we are through with those rotten headwinds; through with the major climbs at altitude. We stand here as conquerors. But it is not Tong La that I have conquered, nor Tibet, nor this highway – it is myself – my own fears: fear of altitude, fear of getting sick, fear of the cold, fear of having an accident, fear of a dog-attack, fear of having my bike stolen, fear of being stopped by the Chinese, fear of mechanical failure, fear of damaging my knees, and . . . fear of facing my own limits . . . The mind magnifies these fears – making them far greater than they actually are.

Tong La is a moment of victory, a moment of quiet power. There is, away from the cluster of prayer-flags, a simple rock-cairn with a *khata* – a ceremonial scarf – fluttering from it. The strength of the cairn lies in its simplicity. I have to leave something here – my own offering to the spirits of the pass for a safe passage. I take out a silk scarf I bought long ago in Shanghai, and tie it on the cairn to be buffeted by the winds.

We take our souvenirs in photographs. Somehow this is a moment of great sadness too – because once we leave this pass, we know we'll be dropping off the plateau. Down, down, down – right down into Nepal, through the Himalayas. I dig out some extra clothing – for the run to Nyalam I will need the maximum downhill gear. That means three pairs of socks, three sets of gloves, rainpants, a scarf, parka, woollen hat, sun-visor, and a balaclava. The cold can even cut through this array of armour.

A Landcruiser pulls up. Some familiar faces from Snowland Hotel. But there is something most peculiar about those faces. They are all overdressed – down jackets, woollen tuques, gloves, scarves – more clothing than us. Why? It takes a few seconds to work out why we can see them so clearly – there is no windscreen.

'Been a hell of a ride so far,' says Paul.

'What happened?'

'A stone flew up and smashed the windscreen. But that was *nothing*.'

'The driver's a maniac,' says Janet. 'He almost put us over a cliff near Lhasa.'

'Tell them about the sheep.'

'Oh yeah. The sheep. So he comes ploughing down off a mountainside and hits a flock of sheep on the road. Killed one on the spot. Injured sheep everywhere. The herders charged him 20 yuan for the dead sheep.'

'You've been keeping yourselves amused then?'

'Keeping ourselves alive more like it. How's the biking?'

'It's been tough, but all downhill from here.'

'We've got some extra food here if you want it. We won't need it – getting to the border pretty soon.' Paul fetches some boiled eggs, biscuits, and a few cans. We pocket the booty. The Landcruiser takes off, with its frozen passengers muffled in scarves.

We are on the brink of the greatest downhill drop in the world – a drop of some 15,000 feet. Scott lets out a couple of yelps of triumph as he gets started on the descent. Yee-ha! *Going down!* Kathmandu here we come!

This is our reward: no more rotten headwinds. No more high-altitude climbing. We start off at a suicidal speed down toward the town of Nyalam. The edge of the road holds ice, snow, mud and slush – too bad if the bike hits that stuff at high speed. *Going down*. The exhilaration of pure speed! We notch up 15 miles in less than an hour. It is only another ten or so miles to Nyalam. As we thunder along, yaks by the wayside stampede at our approach; their masters struggle to control them.

*   *   *

NYALAM IS AN OLD TRADING-TOWN. At first sight, it appears to be totally Chinese, with an army-barracks, small tin restaurant-shacks, truck-stop hotel, shops, and a post-office disguised as a dormitory. The Chinese section lines the highway through town. On the slopes above this section, hidden from view, is the old Tibetan sector – composed of stone structures with ornate beams of wood and overhanging balconies.

T I B

T

Lhatse

Tso La

Gyatso La

Sakya

Shishapangma
26,295'

Tingri W.

Shegar

Jong La

Pang La

H

Nyalam

Rongbuk

M

Everest
29,028'

Cho Oyu
26,750'

A

L

A

KATHMANDU

Zhangmu

Kodari

Makalu
27,825'

Dolalghat

Kangchenjunga
28,168'

Dhulikhel

NEPAL

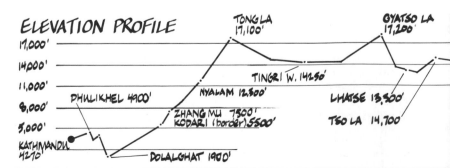

ELEVATION PROFILE

TONG LA
17,100'

GYATSO LA
17,200'

17,000'

14,000'

TINGRI W. 14,250'

11,000'

PHULIKHEL 4900'

NYALAM 12,300'

LHATSE 13,300'

8,000'

ZHANG MU 7500'
KODARI (border) 5500'

TSO LA 14,700'

5,000'

KATHMANDU
4270'

DOLALGHAT 1900'

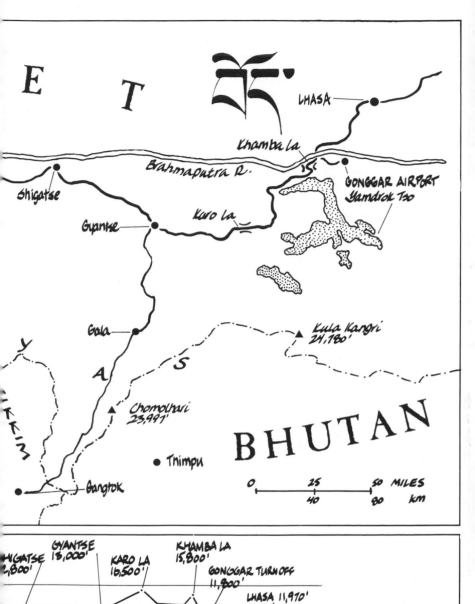

E   T

LHASA

Khamba La

Brahmaputra R.

Shigatse

GONGGAR AIRPORT
Yamdrok Tso

Gyantse

Karo La

Gala

Kula Kangri
24,780'

A   S

Chomolhari
23,997'

BHUTAN

• Thimpu

SIKKIM

Gangtok

0	25	50 MILES
	40	80 km

SHIGATSE
12,800'

GYANTSE
13,000'

KARO LA
16,500'

KHAMBA LA
15,800'

GONGGAR TURN OFF
11,800'

LHASA 11,970'

YAMDROK TSO
14,800'

Lhasa to Kathmandu Route

The first thing to be noticed about Nyalam, assuming an approach off the plateau, is the presence of trees. Nyalam has clusters of trees growing around the Chinese section: I have to touch them to make sure they're real. Lying around town are huge pieces of lumber, most likely brought in from the forested areas to the south. No shortage of fuel here, anyhow. Nepalese faces and Nepalese goods attest to the fact that we were now only 20 miles away from the border. In a Nyalam tea-shack we find a mix of Chinese, Tibetan and Nepali faces – and we get our hellos and goodbyes garbled in three languages. On the shelves are Nepalese biscuits and bottles of perfumed hair-oil from India; on the radio is Indian music. On the way back to the truck-stop hotel, we stuff ourselves with eggs, vegetables, biscuits, and apricots – the latter item being a rarity that comes in glass jars.

The truck-stop hotel is miserable. The rooms look like prison-cells – blackened walls, a bare lightbulb dangling in the middle, rockhard beds, and barred windows. The management comes in the form of a Chinese woman dressed in pink, with thick glasses, and armed with a pair of knitting needles – knitting, of course, a pink sweater. Miss Pink, as we christen her, is immovable. She cannot be swayed over anything. First she doesn't want us to take the bikes into our room. We skate past her on this one. Then she tries to put two truck-drivers into the already overcrowded room, even though the rest of the prison-cells are practically empty. There isn't enough room for us, the bikes, and the truck-drivers. After a round of protest, we have to pay for all four beds in the room, an extortionate rate to guarantee a secure place for the bikes. Miss Pink refuses to give us a hot water thermos. Eventually, we find out from a Tibetan woman, stationed in another office, that a 20-yuan deposit is required on the thermos.

May 7th. A change of pace was called for – a final fling before departing Tibet. I had the perfect excursion in mind – a trek to Mount Shishapangma, the 14th highest peak in the world, standing just over 26,000 feet. This colossus was, as far as I knew, about 25 miles out from Nyalam, and I reasoned that it should be possible to rent a yak to carry supplies once under way.

The first problem was storage of the bikes. Miss Pink didn't want to know about it – if we wanted to leave the bikes, we'd have to leave them in a room and pay for the room. She walked off in a huff, knitting faster than ever. We tried the other end of town – the friendlier teahouse. The man there was agreeable to leaving the bikes in his brother's room, but that probably meant five thousand people would traipse by to look at them. In desperation, we returned to the hotel and found . . . the Tibetan woman who'd helped us before with the hot water thermos. No problem, she said, follow me – we shoved them on a woodpile in a shed, locked them, and exited – to run straight into Miss Pink. We side-stepped her, and raced off to get our hiking gear before anyone could alter the arrangements. Miss Pink was having a furious argument with the Tibetan woman.

Conversion of bags from panniers to backpack-type equipment was a dismal failure. The bags, held together by webbing, hung poorly and made for aching muscles. The tent had to be carried underarm; the freeze-dried food dug into my back; my camera banged away at my ribs. We plodded along a river-bank with crystal-clear water, green grass, meadows – and great walls of snowpeaks.

About an hour and a half of walking brought us to a small encampment spread around some ruined buildings. A cluster of yak-herders had pitched their tents in the shells of the buildings. One came over to talk to us. Suomeishi was his name.

Suomeishi was small and wiry. He had the kind of battered, leathery face that resulted from a lifetime of exposure to the harsh elements in the mountains of Tibet. His pants were far too big for him, and were held above his waist by a long, thin belt. He helped carry our bags over to a large canvas tent. There was a fire-crock going in the middle of the tent; his wife was spinning wool and making tea; dogs snapped at our feet. We sat down on a thick and comfortable yak-hide 'couch'. A pet goat started chewing on Scott's shirt.

We were presented to Suomeishi's wife, Soundoma – a stocky, high-cheeked woman with a big grin. She scooped out some black tea from the huge pot on the boiler. There were wooden pails of yak-milk in the tent, but they were more interested in putting huge dollops of yak-butter in their tea.

I took out my teapot, and we used the fire-crock for heating up some soup. Suomeishi picked up a goat-leg and casually started to hack pieces off it with a large Nepalese knife. Some pieces he ate raw – others he put aside on a plate – possibly for sandwiches?

233

Then they both started eating *tsampa* – raw *tsampa* – not even adding water to it. They offered Scott some – then me. I already had my soup in a cup, and made a wonderful discovery. *Tsampa* is a tasteless flour – it can be used for thickening soup.

'The *tsampa* cookbook!' I exclaimed, taken by the idea.

'What's that?' asked Scott.

'It'd be a national best-seller – 101 ways to cook *tsampa*.'

'Tibetans can't read.'

'Do it with pictures.'

'You mean, like throw it over your left shoulder?'

'Yes – or knead it into the shape of a hamburger.'

'*Tsampa*-burgers.'

'Sprinkle it on your cornflakes.'

'Make a porridge from it.'

'Use it to plaster your walls.'

'Coat it with chocolate.'

'*Tsampa*-bars.'

'*Tsampa* with cheese.'

This banter actually improved the appetite, except that the word 'cheese' should never have been mentioned. The word 'cheese' could throw me – and my stomach – into a depression lasting several hours. It amazed me that our hosts were not the least bit interested in our foodstuffs. Suomeishi took one look at the greenish soup offered, declined, and went back to his *tsampa*. Still, *tsampa* has a lot to recommend it – it's cheap, sustaining, filling, and easy to digest.

To keep our hosts amused, I produced some pictures I had with me – of the Potala, the Jokhang, Everest, and one of Canada. Soundoma spent a good ten minutes examining each picture before passing it on to Suomeishi. I used a combination of a Tibetan phrasebook and my blank notebook to get our message across – we wanted to rent one of Suomeishi's yaks. One yak, we figured, could carry all our gear, leaving us free to amble along. I drew a yak-head, and wrote a price of six yuan on it – the cost for Suomeishi plus the yak for each day of the trip. Suomeishi wrote down twelve yuan, and many cups of tea later, we agreed to nine yuan, which came to 36 yuan for a four-day rental. The deal was sealed with a handshake. Suomeishi also agreed to bring along a big bag of yak-dung as fuel for our teapot. There was a huge mound of the stuff right outside the tent, and it was the fuel

Soundoma was using to ply us with tea.

Suomeishi indicated that we could pitch our tent in a corner of his walled-off enclosure. Where could we get water? He took us out of his tent to a small creek nearby. One of his guard-dogs had just had a litter of puppies, and we were returning from a water-filling sortie at the creek when it made for Scott. Scott hit it with a water-bottle on the snout, and I smacked it with a full bike-pannier – Suomeishi got into the fray and pulled the dog off. He assured us that the dog would be tied up at night.

We pitched the tent in the enclosure in record speed – to impress Suomeishi. He was indeed impressed. But he was more impressed by a band-aid that I'd shoved on a small cut on my hand. He thrust his own hand forward. For starters, there were six fingers on that hand – there were two little fingers. The problem was the third finger, however, which had swollen – probably sprained or dislocated. Scott patched up the bruised fingernail as best he could, and we improvised a splint for the whole finger with a piece of wood sealed with tape. We told him not to move the finger for a week or so.

About half an hour before nightfall, Suomeishi took us out to patrol his domain – boulders, thornbushes, rocks, snowpeaks, grass . . . and yaks. Where we'd previously seen only a dozen yaks around, there were now over a hundred of them coming down from all parts of the valley, bells tinkling. They were being corralled for the night. Whistling and shouting got them into several stone-walled enclosures where they would bed down. A large proportion of them had calves – the herd was growing. A few of the yaks were diverted to a special enclosure – these were tied up, ready for milking.

We went back to our tent, congratulating ourselves on how fortunate we'd been to find Suomeishi, and a what a fantastic trek lay ahead of us. We both still had enormous appetites, and cracked open more biscuits. Half the food – the sweets, the biscuits, the bread – was gone. The same bitch that had earlier tried to attack Scott came back, barking at the tent, disturbed by the crunch of the biscuits perhaps. Suomeishi hadn't tied her up as promised. I opened the front vestibule and threw out the largest firework I could find.

In the morning there was a huge yak waiting for us. We transferred gear to a duffel bag, and to several woollen bags supplied by Suomeishi. These lozenge-shaped packs were tied to the yak, which by now looked rather apprehensive. This was not what the yak planned to do that day. The yak looked at me, then at Scott, with a murderous shift in its eyes. We were all excited about having our very own yak, but the feeling was by no means mutual. Suomeishi and Soundoma posed for photos next to the yak, with Scott. We were ready to roll.

There was a minor glitch – Suomeishi handed us the rope that was attached to the yak's nose. Was he serious? No, he couldn't be. Yes, he was – the deal was for the yak only, no guide. We protested, cursed, jumped up and down, swore, demanded – but it seemed all our negotiating from the previous night had been a waste of time. What were we going to do with a headstrong yak? What if it decided to wander off with all our gear on it? What if it decided it wasn't going any further, and refused to budge? What if it decided it didn't want to be saddled up in the morning? Yaks, we knew, had filthy tempers. It would've been foolhardy to think we could handle such an animal without experience. I pointed to the yak-dung heap outside Suomeishi's tent – what about that part of the deal? Why hadn't he loaded up the fuel as promised? Suomeishi pointed up the valley, indicating there was plenty of fuel to be found up that way, so now he'd decided there was no need to take any along. We unloaded the yak and shouldered our gear. He obviously wouldn't change his mind about coming along, and nine yuan a day just for the yak was too expensive.

As we trudged off, there was a tremendous commotion nearby, and clouds of dust: all the dogs in the neighbourhood had ganged up on Suomeishi's unruly dog, and were ripping it to shreds. This was exactly what we feel like doing to Suomeishi; but in lieu of that, we cheered the other dogs on. Our hearts weren't in the excursion any more.

We camped out another night further along the trail. This was easily the best campsite we'd staked out – by a river, on a grassy knoll, with breath-taking mountain backdrops. The final straw was when the water-filter decided to clog up: I threw it away, and we headed back for Nyalam.

The 555 teapot, rest its soul, had acquired a high gloss black finish from the campfires and other indignities it had endured. We donated it to some incoming French backpackers in Nyalam, along with a supply of freeze-dried food, some Chinese money, maps, and other odds and ends that we had no further use for.

★   ★   ★

GOING DOWN! May tenth: mobile again – two wheels eating up the dirt. We are just below the snowline at Nyalam, and the road coils off the plateau, coils through a cleft in the mighty Himalayas, coils out toward Nepal. *Going down!* Top levels: dry desert. Mid-levels: foliage appearing – dipping down to the treeline again. Road getting worse – due to rain. *You're losing Tibet.* The sun catching the snowpeaks in the brilliant light. *You've lost the snowline.* The darkened switchbacks – increased shade – with wild rockfalls in the path – down, down. *You're losing it.*

It takes a while to sink in: we have conquered the highway. We've done it! All downhill from here. Nothing seems impossible now. I will take on all roads – desert, snowpeak, jungle – from here to Bombay and back again. Weaving along sidestreets, running red lights, wheeling on, wheeling through, racing the finned traffic, swerving to avoid Brahmin bulls, flying, riding up on the bars, wheeling on, wheeling through – all roads from here to Bombay and back again.

Trees! A gushing river, one hour down from Nyalam. *Going down* – getting greener – bushes, flowers, shrubs. *You're losing Tibet, you're losing it.* Moister now, browner, greener. Life coming back to the mouth and nostrils – moist now, keener. Can smell those flowers. The sound of birds and insects. *Going down!* There are sheer drops off the cliffing at the edge of the road. *You've lost it; you've lost Tibet.* Bamboo, yellow and purple flowers. Now you're sweating. Sweating? Not in Tibet. Too dry, too high, too cold back there above the snowline. Here – below the treeline – ferns, grass, vines, willow-trees, butterflies – it's as if you've come out of a state of sensory deprivation – all these are novelties, marvels. Sounds sharper, colours sharper, senses no longer dulled. Getting hotter now – have to take off some layers of clothing. *Going down* – the lower levels – and the border-town of Zhangmu comes into view.

The town of Zhangmu is arrayed along a series of sharp switch-backs which snake down toward the gushing Bhote Kosi River. Although the Chinese passport and customs check is at the base of the town of Zhangmu, the actual border is another seven miles of winding road away – at the Friendship Bridge, which spans the Bhote Kosi. The bridge has been fully reconstructed – we get to ride across the border this time. In the centre of the bridge is a red line. Once we cross that, we're in Nepal.

At Kodari, a portly Nepalese passport officer greets us. He is wearing a smart army uniform, and sits on a chair out on the verandah of a small hut. This hut is the passport control office. The customs post is further down the road, at Tatopani.

'You're the only foreigners to come through today,' the passport officer says. 'Here in Kodari, it's very quiet.'

'How quiet?'

'I used to work at Kathmandu Airport, so it's *very* quiet.' The passport officer shifts his beer-gut around, gives our documents a cursory glance, stamps them for entry, and returns them. He sits there nursing his beer-gut, content that he's done something of use that day.

'Please, do you mind if I ask a question?' The passport officer directs this query to Scott.

'Go ahead,' says Scott.

'Well, how is the *fucking* in Tibet?'

That one throws Scott right out. He peers at the officer to see if he is joking or not. He isn't. He's heard all kinds of strange rumours about the action in Lhasa these days. He sits there, Buddha-like, in a trance – waiting for Scott's reply.

'Heart attacks,' mumbles Scott finally.

'I beg your pardon?'

'The altitude – too high for that kind of thing,' says Scott.

'Ah, I see!' says the officer. 'Can't get it up eh?'

'More like running out of steam halfway through.'

'What is this *running out of steam*?'

'Can't keep it up – too much for the heart.'

'Ah, I see! The heart is overworking!'

'You've got it.'

Traffic increases after the customs check-post at Tatopani. Most likely the traffic can't be bothered dealing with customs, so buses and trucks delivering passengers to the border-zone go no further than Tatopani. Thus far we have been spared a sampling of Nepalese drivers.

Past the customs-post, I am riding down the road, minding my own business when a taxi comes straight for me. He's not just driving along the road – he's out to *get me*. I swerve off the road into a ditch. Scott does likewise; the taxi-driver hits his horn.

I let loose a string of four-letter words. The taxi-driver has disappeared in a cloud of dust. God spare us. How will we survive the next couple of days into Kathmandu? And we haven't even sampled the tempers of the dogs and children of Nepal yet. I'd heard from cyclists who'd tackled India that the traffic there was damn dangerous, since drivers had no respect for cyclists, and didn't care if they knocked them down. Is it the same thing in Nepal?

Several more close calls with the Nepalese motoring public have me really worried. It is less than 70 miles from here into Kathmandu, but there is a good chance of being killed if the drivers continue to act like this.

Around the bend, a fully-loaded bus careens along the side of the road: I am looking head-on at the radiator grill – decorated with bright colours. It is a miracle the bus doesn't hit me. I slam on the brakes and go sailing off the handlebars into the side of the road. The bus carries on at full speed, with an earsplitting blast of the horn. The passengers piled on the roof of the bus shout. Scott arrives, out of breath.

'Are you okay?'

'I think so.' I get up, dust myself off, rub a bruised leg.

'I've got it figured out,' says Scott.

'Got what figured out?'

'The drivers.'

'They're fucking madmen – anyone can see that.'

'No they're not. It's partly our mistake.'

'What?! You saw that – the bus came straight for me. Same as the taxi, same as the other drivers.'

'Yes, but think about it – which country are we in?'

'Nepal – so what?'

'In China they drive on the right, and in Nepal . . . '

I stared down the highway. So? Nepal – *so what*?

'They drive on the left.'

It takes a while for that to sink in. We collapse at the side of the road and roar with laughter.

How odd that on a previous visit to Kathmandu, down this very road by truck, the left-hand driving did not really register in my brain. Now that it is a matter of life and death, that left-hand detail becomes very important. As we resume pedalling, I start to tally up the countries in Asia where they drive on the left. Japan, Thailand, and – as part of the former left-handed British Empire – India, Burma, Malaysia and Hong Kong. This is most of Asia – and in the days of the treaty ports, China had left-hand drive too.

Switching to the correct side of the road, we cruise off. The road is in good nick – very smooth dirt. A mirage on the horizon: can it be? Yes, it is an attempt at a paved road. Gouged up by monsoonal deluges, but tar nonetheless. Civilisation cannot be far off. By nightfall we reach the town of Lamosangu, where we take a room, awkwardly placed at the top of a spiral-type staircase. The adjoining room has loose potatoes and onions strewn all over the floor.

Going down! The following day, unbelievably, the descent continues, down through banana trees, small villages with bandy-legged Nepalis and naked kids, women in saris, crowing chickens, birdcalls, brilliant greens of rice-paddies, water-buffalo lolling around in the mid-day sun.

On the second day, we reach the lowest point – at Dolalghat, elevation 1900 feet. From Tong La, at 17,100 feet, that meant a drop of 15,000 feet off the Tibetan Plateau, over a distance of 90 miles.

Going up: after Dolalghat comes a killer climb of some 3000 feet, spread over a gruelling double pass of at least 15 miles. The pass seems to go on forever – the last big obstacle between ourselves and Kathmandu. There is no altitude to stymie progress, but the noon-day sun has caught me clawing at the gears, sweltering on the long ascent. Surly Nepalese dogs and unruly gangs of children test my patience to the limit by taking advantage of my slow progress up the pass. I stop to take some photographs of the deep rusts and greens of the rice-paddies and hillsides – staggering beauty. Scott has gone on ahead.

Some kids throw stones at me, which puts me in a very bad mood, and destroys any further relations. Their parents make no effort to restrain them. It is of little use if I stop and try to confront the kids – this will only spur them on. All I can do is speed up and lose them. But with the dogs, I have to stop. The master is invariably off to the side of the road, gazing benignly on as the dog attacks. I am in no mood to get a dose of rabies. The 20th dog of the day has a go at me. I dismount, and reach for a rock – a huge one – which I raise above my head. At this point, the master rushes off his perch to restrain the dog. He can tell I mean business.

At 4 p.m. it *pours*. The monsoon is early this year. Rivers of brown muck are on the move down stormdrains and run-offs. No sign of Scott. Must be up ahead somewhere. I dive into a nearby house like the other refugees, but no chance to take the bike in, so I have to unload the panniers and sneak them in as I can. Inside, apart from those sitting out the downpour, are two cows, two goats, and a few chickens. In one corner of this straw-lined hovel is a smoky fireplace. Damnation – my sleeping-bag is soaked. At six o'clock the tap is turned off. The rain has stopped. I decide to make a dash for the next town marked on the map, which is Dhulikhel. I head off up the pass again.

The wooden structures of Dhulikhel finally come into view – and I catch up with Scott. We are both wet, hungry, tired and caked in mud and sweat. We stop at a teahouse; the owner directs us to a place called Dhulikhel Lodge.

Dhulikhel Lodge is filled with an American college group studying 'other cultures', and a sprinkling of westerners who work in Kathmandu. The latter are on a weekend escape. We hurriedly stash the bikes downstairs, run upstairs, distribute our wet clothing and gear over an entire room, change into what we can, and race back to the dining-room. Dinner is being served in Room H, an occasion not to be missed. The American college group – mostly made up of nubile young women – is seated on cushions on the floor. On the low tables is a mouth-watering selection of curry, bread and noodles.

Scott and I settle down at a table with Kirsten and Cathy, two of the college students. It is hard to know which way to look first – at the food, at Kirsten, at Cathy, or at a nearby newspaper. Newspapers! Out of the corner of my eye, I can also see the cover of a *Time* magazine. We haven't a clue about what has happened in the world for the past month.

In between large dollops of curry and healthy portions of noodles, Scott casually says (burp) that we have just dropped in (literally) from Tibet. This is a sensational hit with Kirsten and

Cathy – and with the other college students. They're all planning to head up to Tibet after completing their six-month study stint in Nepal. Scott has the whole of Room H tuned in to his blurb on Tibet. I am tuned into Kirsten's smile. Have we fallen into paradise?

'Is it cold up there?' asks Kirsten.

'Not too bad – cold on the passes,' I answer.

'What about the water – can you drink it?'

'Well, I wouldn't – you can filter it, or use the hot water from thermoses.'

'Do they have dogs there?' (*DO THEY HAVE DOGS THERE?!*)

'Ah, yes, lots of dogs. They're meant to be reincarnations, and they get treated quite well around the monasteries. They're supposed to be monks who didn't quite make the grade and have returned to their old haunts.'

'Are they tied up?'

'No. That's half the problem – could have rabies.'

'What about getting to Lhasa – is the road good?'

'Yes. It's in good shape for a dirt road. It doesn't rain much up there.'

'What was the hardest part of the trip?'

She has me stumped there. I don't really have an answer. Everything was difficult. What was the most difficult? Going up the passes? Dodging officials? Giving up smoking?

'Getting on the first aeroplane,' I blurt out. No, I didn't say that – she doesn't want to hear that. She wants to hear something more heroic. 'Getting the gear together, the maps, the paperwork, the panniers, and slinging it in the first plane,' I add, to try and justify the first statement. 'By then, you've made the commitment – there's no turning back.' This still doesn't sound heroic enough. Time to switch the subject. 'Listen, I was going to pick up the newspaper, but perhaps you could tell me the news instead. We don't know what's happened in the last month.'

'Oh, then you haven't heard about Chernobyl?'

'No – what's that?'

'A city near Leningrad. There was a melt-down, and half of Europe is under clouds of radiation. The Russians didn't realise how bad it was, and they didn't inform anyone for a few days.'

'My God,' I mutter, stunned. I am unable to fathom the extent of this technological disaster. Has half of Europe been erased? Or is it just part of Russia that was erased? How many deaths were there? How much radiation is there? How are they going to dispose of the source of the radiation? The brain is suddenly chilled – the implications are too far-reaching to contemplate.

'There was even a satellite photograph,' continues Kirsten, 'that showed a helicopter hovering in the centre of the radioactivity, trying to put out a graphite fire, and men playing soccer in the background.'

'Nobody can drink the milk – that's contaminated. As far as Sweden,' adds Cathy.

'When did it happen?' asks Scott.

'They're not sure. About two weeks ago. A week after the Tripoli raid.'

'The Tripoli raid?!' Visions of World War III flash through my head. Madman Kaddafi. Madman Reagan.

'Nothing much really – Reagan bombed Libya. The Libyans shot down one of the F111s. It was a reaction to terrorist bombings in Europe, directed at Americans.'

'The French are mad at Reagan,' says Kirsten, 'And the Americans are avoiding Europe altogether this summer. Too much trouble with terrorists, and now with Chernobyl.'

This is like television, this verbal report, delivered by a team of beautiful newsreaders. And now for the editorial:

Americans, hounded in South America, detested in Central America, are now hated in Europe. But let's face it, they've always been hated in Europe anyway. Europeans think they are crass, big-mouthed, loud-mouthed, bad-mannered, brash, and ill-informed. Our suggestion this year is to avoid Europe altogether. It's much too messy with the machine-guns and the nuclear spills. Try Asia instead.

Whatever the case, Kirsten fits none of those stereotypes – and she has a smile that makes me weak in the knees. Cycling through the mountains of Tibet couldn't do as much damage. Scott hands me a cardboard folder. His eyes are wide open. More bad news? No, this is the good news. It is the snack menu from Room H at Dhulikhel Lodge. My eyes almost drop out of my head. *Cheese toast, peanut butter toast, French toast, apple fritters, apple pancakes, banana bread, grilled cheese sandwiches.* Who needs to go to Kathmandu?

In the morning, I get three things I'd been dreaming about: a hot shower, to wash off three weeks of scum; a week-old copy of the *Guardian Weekly*, including extracts from *Le Monde* and the *Washington Post*; and a grilled cheese sandwich – goat's cheese. These mundane things send me into raptures.

Within 24 hours at Dhulikhel Lodge, our combined bill surpasses 500 rupees. We have been through the entire snack menu at least twice. Can't keep my eyes off that menu. 'Cheese toast, please,' I call out to the kitchen-hand. 'Make that two,' echoes Scott. What does the kitchen staff think of us? While we are setting a new record for cheese toast consumption, we get a briefing on local diseases. This sobering run-down is delivered by an Australian nurse, who works in Kathmandu.

'Because of the rains and the humidity,' she says, 'it's a prime time for hepatitis. You can also get worms, dysentery or giardia, but spinal meningitis is not in season at the moment. You are taking malaria pills, aren't you?'

Disease of the week: hepatitis. Have to watch the water. Damn this early monsoon – it's not supposed to arrive until June. This disease roundup dampens my appetite for a full five minutes. The kitchen-hand walks past. 'French toast, please,' I call out. 'Make that two,' says Scott.

Many grilled cheeses later, we waddle off through the maze of alleys in Dhulikhel, to a small view-temple, Baghvita. Below the temple women are gathered at a water-pump, washing their hair. A pig saunters past and gobbles up a piece of human excrement nearby. So much for the plumbing and sanitation system.

From the top of the temple, it looks like a level – or downhill – run from here in the direction of Kathmandu. This comes as a relief because in every other compass-point there are undulating hills. Dhulikhel marks the top of the awful pass that we toiled up in the rain. On the skyline, way above the rice-terracing, is a magnificent string of Himalayan peaks. Why does it look so impressive, breaking the clouds, so *high*? Now I begin to understand. We are standing at around 5000 feet; the Himalayan peaks stand at 25,000 feet, so there is a 20,000-foot difference. In Tibet, on the north side, the observer would be already at an elevation of 15,000 feet, so there would only be an 10,000-foot difference. We retrace our steps back to our sanctuary, Dhulikhel Lodge, past the goats, the women washing their hair at the water-pumps, the mud, the muck, the pigs, the chickens, and the intricate Newari woodwork of the tiny shops and teahouses.

*   *   *

MAY THIRTEENTH: WE ARE CYCLING through the bazaars of Asan Tole in old Kathmandu. The trading crossroads of the empires of India, China and Tibet in former times, Asan Tole is a jumble of ancient alley-ways lined with rickety buildings and temples, patrolled by docile Brahmin bulls, and filled with the smells of curry, incense, and mangoes. This country *smells* different. The eye is baffled by the signs flashing past, by the explosion of stimuli and choices: hustlers, porters, touts, taxi-drivers, Gurkhas with fixed bayonets, beggars, Tibetan refugees, sadhus, Buddhist shrines, SWEDISH MASSAGE, PARADISE GUEST-HOUSE, *ROLEX*, TENZING TREKKING CO., *TOYOTA*, UNICEF, *Coca-Cola*, 'number one hash', 'hashish oil?', 'change money?', MASSAGE YOGA, BICYCLE ON HIRE, SHORT TREK – 3 DAYS, THE THIRD EYE, *THE POTALA HOTEL*, LHASA RESTAURANT, *ROOF OF THE WORLD INN*, LE BISTRO, THE OLD VIENNA, KG OVERLAND BUS CONCERN, fresh oranges, ice-cream, white *stupas*, women in saris, motorcycles, blue jeans, rock music, *TIBET GUESTHOUSE*, PUMPERNICKEL BAKERY.

Forty years before, Kathmandu was a remote corner of the world – mediaeval, inaccessible, and forbidden to foreigners. Now tourism is Nepal's chief income-earner after foreign aid; the art of fleecing tourists is the next best thing to pocketing foreign aid funds. About 200,000 tourists pass through Kathmandu Valley each year, a rather astounding figure given that the population of Kathmandu itself is only 300,000. And how long would it take to fill Lhasa with signs for trekking outfits, guesthouses and restaurants?

I have mixed feelings about arrival in Kathmandu – ecstatic that I've made it; depressed that the trip is over. In any case, we have already celebrated our arrival by feasting in Dhulikhel. And as I plunge into the motorised madness of the bazaars of Kathmandu, I feel a need to transport myself mentally to the unpolluted majesty of central Tibet – that sense of quiet, brooding landscape; of destroyed monasteries; and of a people who have remained remarkably cheerful for what they have weathered.

245

Even more challenging than getting through Tibet without a flat tyre will be getting through a week in Kathmandu without blowing out my intestines. The place is a breeding ground for diseases – things they never tell you in the posters and tour-literature. *Welcome to Nepal – land of the corrupt one-party system! We have everything – we have mountains that will knock the wind out of you, food that will damage your intestines permanently, and hashish that will make you forget what intestines are anyway. Our corrupt bureaucrats and greedy officials welcome you! Our rabid dogs and fierce mosquitoes await you! Welcome!*

Scott and I have turned into professional eaters – only interested in the insides of restaurants. Alcohol – the celebratory kind – lubricates full course dinners. Whatever the risk to the intestines, there is no stopping the shovelling in of steaks, chocolates, strawberries, croissants, lasagna, apple pie, pizza, tacos... We are, to some degree, rewarding ourselves for a mission completed.

We are sitting in the Pumpernickel Bakery garden one morning, watching the flies doing an autopsy on the jam, when in walks... a face that I can't place. I've seen him before; he knows my name – but I can't place him.

It is David, the doctor who was with us on the Landcruiser trip through Tibet the previous year. It has been almost a year, and he is still wearing the same stupid green shirt. I am just about to laugh at him when he informs me that I am wearing the same stupid brown shirt I wore a year ago. He is right – it is my favourite travel shirt, a tough one with button-down top pockets. Scott, as it happens, is wearing the same stupid brown and grey shirt he wore the year before. David has been wandering around Asia since we last saw him – China, Indonesia, India – obviously at a slow pace. I am trying to calculate the chances of three people, who'd taken the same trip a year ago, meeting in the same restaurant in Kathmandu, still wearing the same silly shirts –

There is more to this story, but I'm going to break it off now because, after two attempts, I can't find a suitable ending. The truth is that there is no ending – the last journey is a preparation for the next one. And the next journey will be bigger, better, more challenging – and crazier – than the last one.

POSTSCRIPT

On June 18, 1987, the United States House of Representatives passed an amendment condemning China's human rights violations in Tibet. The bill tied the sale of arms to China with the human rights issue. On September 21, the Dalai Lama presented a five-point peace plan for Tibet to the US Congressional Human Rights Caucus. The plan called for the abandonment of large-scale transfer of Chinese settlers into Tibet, for respect for the fundamental rights of Tibetans, and for restoration and protection of Tibet's natural environment.

Three days after the Dalai Lama's address, Chinese authorities publicly executed two Tibetan prisoners in Lhasa. On September 27, a group of Tibetan monks and lay people assembled near the Jokhang Temple for a silent procession in memory of those executed. The procession snowballed into a series of spontaneous demonstrations over the next ten days as thousands of Tibetans took to the streets of Lhasa demanding independence. At least fifteen people – nine of them Tibetan and the rest Chinese police – were killed in the rioting; many more Tibetans were imprisoned. On October 6, the US Senate voted unanimously to accept a resolution condemning China's human rights record in Tibet, and supporting the Dalai Lama's peace plan.

Immediately following the rioting, Tibet was unofficially sealed off to foreign news-reporters and individual travellers – since they were thought to be giving support to the Tibetans. Chinese authorities evidently wished to handle the situation without western eyewitnesses. If the doors to Tibet do open again, it seems unlikely that travellers will be allowed the same freedom to roam around as before.

GLOSSARY

Alien Travel Permit – a small cardboard document listing (unusual) places that the traveller wishes to visit, with official approval.

Bund – Anglo-Indian term for waterfront promenade in Shanghai.

CAAC – Civil Aviation Administration of China, the national airline – otherwise fondly known as 'China Airlines Always Cancels'.

Cadre – a term usually applied to all workers in the Chinese bureaucratic system. There are several dozen ranks of cadres, with each rank accorded its own privileges. Those on the upper echelons are entitled to soft-class on the trains, to a chauffeur-driven car, and to foreign goods – amongst other perks.

CCP – Chinese Communist Party.

Chang – Tibetan barley-beer.

CITS – China International Travel Service, the official tourist arm, which specialises in parting tourists from their money, and in handing out misleading information.

Cultural Revolution – period of severe dislocation and repression under Mao Zedong. Mao Zedong initiated the movement in 1966; it ended with his death in 1976, and with the arrest of the 'Gang of Four' shortly after.

Daoism – esoteric mix of philosophy and superstition in the ancient tradition founded by Lao Tzu – emphasising a mystical harmony with nature.

Dzong – Tibetan for fort.

FECs – Foreign Exchange Certificates, used by tourists and diplomats in China. FECs are more highly rated than RMB and have developed into a kind of hard currency. This system of currency control – based on a Russian model – was introduced in 1980. FECs come in denominations of 1, 5, 10, 50 and 100 yuan bills.

Fen – Chinese pennies (small bills, or sometimes coins).

Frenchtown – former French Concession in Shanghai.

Friendship Store – store where imported luxury goods and hard-to-get Chinese-made goods are sold to foreigners and privileged Chinese at duty-free rates, using only FECs. Local Chinese are not allowed to purchase these goods – thus leading to blackmarketing.

Gompa – Tibetan for monastery.

Gongli – Chinese for kilometre.

Jokhang – the main temple in Lhasa, and object of pilgrims from all over Tibet.

La – Tibetan term for mountain pass (as in Shangri-La).

Mantou – steamed white bread-rolls, eaten at Chinese breakfast.

One child only – official population policy introduced in 1979, after a baby boom in the 1960s and 70s. In rural areas, wealthy peasants sidestep regulations by paying a thousand yuan fine for having an extra child – a practice referred to by some as 'buying a baby from the government'.

Overseas Chinese – person of Chinese origin or ancestry, now bearing a foreign passport (for example, a Canadian born in Canada to parents of Chinese origin). Overseas Chinese are given lower prices in hotels and on trains than 'big-nosed' foreigners.

PLA – People's Liberation Army, estimated at over 4 million soldiers.

PSB – Public Security Bureau, China's police force (*Gonganjiu*).

RMB – renminbi, or People's Money – the regular currency used by the Chinese; comes in denominations of 1, 2, 5 and 10 yuan bills.

Stupa – a large shrine, shaped like a handbell, said to contain the remains of a Buddhist saint. Tibetan term is *chorten*.

Taichi – slow, ballet-like gymnastics practised at dawn – especially by the older generation – to keep fit.

Tantric Buddhism – esoteric form of Buddhism, most often associated with Tibet, which emphasises radical steps for obtaining enlightenment.

Trans-Mongolian – the express train from Moscow to Peking, running weekly via Ulan Bator in Outer Mongolia. The trip takes six days. The Trans-Siberian shares the same line as far as Ulan Ude, where it branches and heads for the Russian port of Vladivostok.

Tsampa – roasted barley-flour, a staple food in Tibet, often eaten mixed with tea or yak-butter.

Work-unit – the all-pervasive school, commune or work-place group (*danwei*) – responsible for distributing coupons for food and goods, and for approving marital, housing and numerous other rights.

Xiuxi – sacred mid-day siesta, guaranteed in the constitution.

Yuan – Chinese dollar (slang – *kwai*), subdivided into 100 fen. The yuan is either in FECs or in RMB. There were fluctuations in the value of the yuan during the period covered in this book (1981-1986), but US\$1 was equivalent to about 2.3 yuan and £1 equalled about 3 yuan. A worker's salary would be roughly RMB 70 yuan a month.

TRAFFIC

Boeing 707 – used on flight from Chengdu to Lhasa. The best planes in the Chinese fleet are used on tourist runs; lesser breeds, such as turbo-prop Ilyushin-18s, are relegated to backwater runs.

Concertina trolley-bus – the rear end of a dead bus is grafted onto a live bus to increase passenger-carrying capacity to absurd proportions.

Diesel train – the most common form of long-distance travel in China. Composed of about a dozen coaches in two classes – hard-class (seats or sleepers) and soft-class. Steam trains are only used on slower runs.

Dongfeng truck – made in Wuhan. *Dongfeng* is Chinese for East Wind.

Flying Pigeon – respected brand of bicycle (*Feige*), made in Tianjin. Unlike the revolutionary names adopted for trucks and trains made in China, bicycles often have animal brand-names such as Flying Eagle, Five Rams, or Golden Lion.

Forever – a brand of bicycle (*Yongjiu*) made in Shanghai. Superior parts, paintwork and extra features make this brand highly-prized.

Handcart – wooden cart with motorcycle wheels, used by peasants for transporting goods. Most are hauled by one or two people; richer versions use donkeys, or are hauled by walking-tractors.

Jiefang truck – made in Changchun, in a Russian-built plant, this is the most common kind of truck seen in China, and the one used by the Chinese army. *Jiefang* is Chinese for Liberation. It is a 6-cylinder, 95hp truck.

Landcruiser – made-in-Japan four-wheel-drive vehicle, ideal for the desert terrain in Tibet.

Phoenix – a brand of bicycle made in Shanghai, and thus highly-valued and prestigious (Chinese name – *Fenghuang*). It comes in several models – including a 60-pound all-steel farmer's model.

Pony – common form of transport in Tibet, probably derived from Mongolian stock. Other pack-animals include donkeys and yaks.

Red Flag Limousine – (*Hongqi*) made in Changchun – a sleek black chauffeured vehicle with two red flags fluttering up front, used by cadres or visiting foreign dignitaries.

Sanlunche – motorised 3-wheel trishaw, used as a poor man's taxi, and called 'little turtle' by the Chinese. They carry two passengers, and weave through traffic at suicidal speeds.

Shanghai Saloon – sleek Shanghai-made vehicles, used as taxis.

Tricycle Carrier – 'semi-trailer class bicycle' – a sturdy construction of a wooden cart at the back and a bicycle section up front. It can carry stupendous loads – up to 400 pounds – and is frequently used as a delivery vehicle.

Trishaw – bicycle-taxi with three wheels and covered back section.

Walking-tractor – a stripped-down version of a tractor – an uncovered engine with a crossbar attached to it for change of direction. It is used for hauling loads of goods or people in rural areas; also used for harvesting.

INDEX OF PEOPLE & PLACES

ACKNOWLEDGEMENTS

My heartfelt thanks go to those whose role is obvious from the text – my fellow-cyclists, and fellow-travellers – in particular Robert Strauss and Scott Harrison.

For help in seeing this book through, special thanks go to Patricia Lamarre, who listened and lent moral support – and ploughed through piles of drafts, muck and print-outs.

My gratitude goes to Bill Hurst, Ron Blair, Vic Marks and Jack Joyce for suggestions, to Michael Robinson for computer assistance, to Rajan Gill for lively repartee, and to Jacki Ritchie, who drew maps.